365 SCIENCE AND TECHNOLOGY FACTS

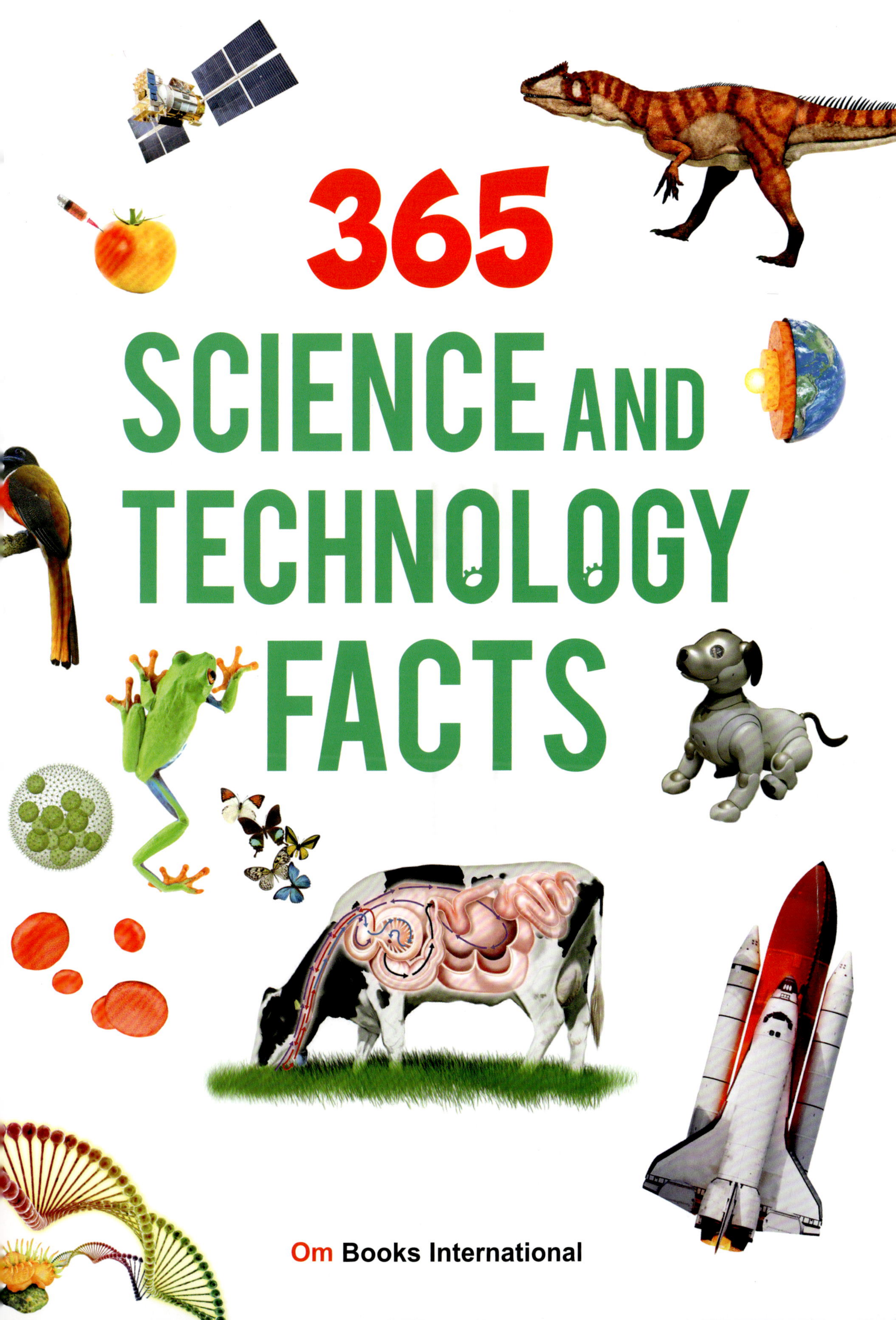

Om Books International

Om Books International

Reprinted in 2025

Corporate & Editorial Office
A-12, Sector 64, Noida 201 301
Uttar Pradesh, India
Phone: +91 120 477 4100
Email: editorial@ombooks.com
Website: www.ombooksinternational.com

Sales Office
107, Ansari Road, Darya Ganj
New Delhi 110 002, India
Phone: +91 11 4000 9000
Email: sales@ombooks.com
Website: www.ombooks.com

ISBN: 978-93-52760-96-1

Printed in China

10 9 8 7 6 5 4

BIOSCIENCES (64-118)

EARTH SCIENCES (91-118)

Contents

PHYSICS (11-36)

CHEMISTRY (37-63)

SPACE (119-146)

TRANSPORT (147-173)

TECHNOLOGY (203-236)

PHYSICS

The 'knowledge of nature', or physics, is a natural science that includes the study of matter, its movement in space and time, energy and force. Its main goal is to understand how the universe behaves. Physics is one of the oldest known fields of study and usually explains all the other sciences. It is ever-evolving, expanding almost every day to cover new technologies and exciting discoveries in the known universe and beyond.

1 We Are as Wee as a Sugar Cube

Even though the human race is large enough to occupy almost half the Earth's surface, it can strangely also fit into the volume of a sugar cube. Before you go crazy wondering how, here's an easy explanation that may help you understand the phenomena.

Each human being is made up of a countless number of atoms. And atoms, as we know are 99.99 per cent empty space. That would almost be equivalent to the space between the Sun and the Earth, which sure is a lot of space! Should all this space be taken out, the entire human race could be compressed enough to fit into one single sugar cube. Mind boggling isn't it?

2 Magnetic Water

Did you know that apart from its life-giving properties, water also embodies certain magnetic properties? In other words, water can act like a magnet.

So, if you rub a comb to a piece of wool and hold it near a tap of running water, you will notice that the water seems to move towards the comb. Water contains several dissolved ions, positive and negative. When you hold a negatively charged comb close to the running water, it repels the negative charge in the water, sending it back up into the tap and all we are left with are positively charged ions. As droplets of water flow down the tap, the positively charged ions in it are attracted to negatively charged ions in the comb, causing the water to get attracted to the comb and swirl by its side.

3 Clumping Cheerios

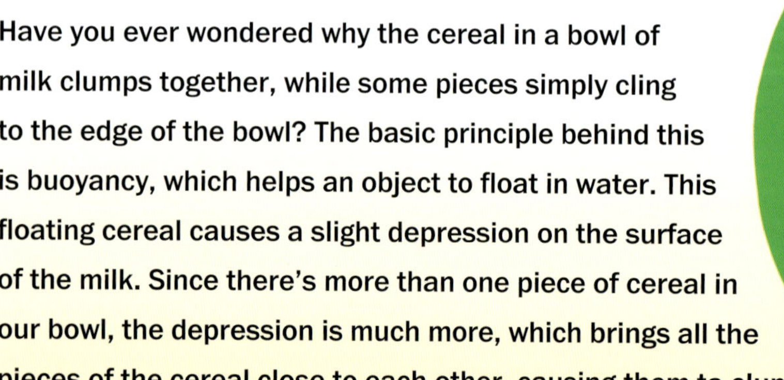

Have you ever wondered why the cereal in a bowl of milk clumps together, while some pieces simply cling to the edge of the bowl? The basic principle behind this is buoyancy, which helps an object to float in water. This floating cereal causes a slight depression on the surface of the milk. Since there's more than one piece of cereal in our bowl, the depression is much more, which brings all the pieces of the cereal close to each other, causing them to clump together. This effect may also be termed as the 'Cheerio Effect'.

The pieces that cling to the sides of the bowl do so due to a phenomenon known as the 'Meniscus Effect'. A meniscus is an upward or downward curve. The meniscus in the bowl of milk is floating upwards and this is what causes the cereal to float upward along the edges of the bowl.

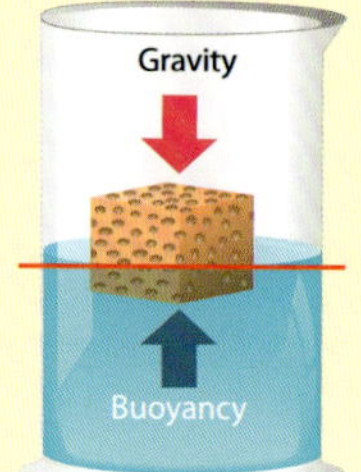

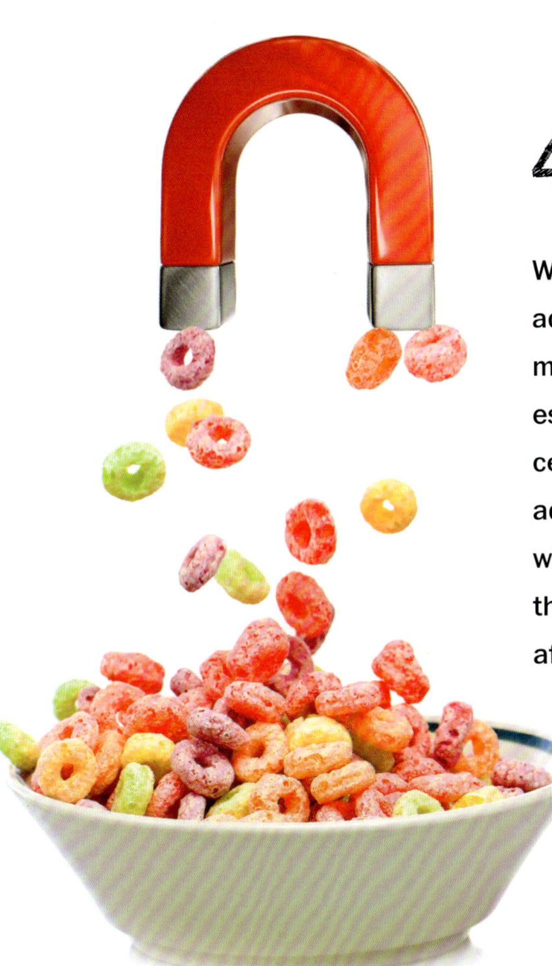

4 Cereal Magic

We are all familiar with the tall claims made by advertisers that certain foods have vitamins and minerals. But sometimes, what they say is true, especially when they say cereal has added iron in it. Most cereal we eat does, in fact, have a certain amount of iron added to it. To do a quick test of this, grind some cereal with water and add this to a bowl. Now drop a piece of the magnet into this bowl and stir. Take out the magnet after five minutes. You will notice tiny specks of iron stuck to the magnet. Sounds like something fun to try, along with your healthy dose of cereal every morning. Now, with food and facts combined, we are sure that breakfast mornings are going to be a lot more interesting!

5 Yell for Coffee!

As weird as this may sound, yelling for eight years, seven months and six days can produce enough heat to brew one cup of coffee. This is because the chemical energy from yelling gets converted to sound energy, which gets converted to vibrations that cause a slight rise in the temperature around us. It is this rise in temperature that would lead the coffee to heat up. So, while yelling for eight long years really doesn't make sense, you could try it when you are feeling cold and do not have something to warm you up.

6 Eggs – They Love a Good Spin

Be it a raw egg or a hard boiled one, eggs totally love a good spin. Sounds funny? Well then, try it yourself.

Take a raw and hard-boiled egg and set both spinning. Both the eggs stop spinning as soon as you try stopping them. However, you will notice the raw egg begins spinning on its own once again. This is because, while the shell has been stopped, the liquid inside the egg still continues to spin.

Now in the case of a hard-boiled egg, set it rotating at super-fast speed, and you will notice that instead of spinning horizontally like it generally does, the egg spins vertically and begins to stand.

7 How to Spot an Old Egg

The shell of an egg is made up of around 7,000 tiny pores that allow the passage of carbon dioxide and oxygen through it. If kept for a long time, bacteria enter the egg through these pores, causing the egg to rot. Apart from this, an egg has two membranes; the outer and the inner membrane. When an egg is freshly laid, it is warm. However, with time it starts cooling. As it cools, the inner membrane contracts, while the outer one doesn't. This causes an air pocket to form between both the membranes. As time passes, more air enters this air pocket. Thus, when you put a relatively fresh egg in water it sinks, while an egg that is old will float due to the amount of air it has in it.

8 Toasted in a Bolt of Lightning

The most exciting part of a thunderstorm is the lightning that it brings in its wake. The whole sky around us lights up, looking like ten thousand sparkling stars. But what is even more exciting is the fact that from now on when the weather guy informs you that a thunderstorm is on its way, a toast party is something you should think about! Why is that?

Believe it or not, just one bolt of lightning can provide enough power to a 1000-watt, double slice toaster for 84,000 long minutes. This large amount of energy is more than sufficient to toast around 100,000 slices of bread in one go. That is more than enough bread for your schoolmates, your dance class friends, your art class friends and the entire neighbourhood! Perfect for a toast party, isn't it?

9 How Rocket-tea!

Believe it or not, but when a teabag is lit from the top, it actually resembles a rocket as it takes off into the air.

This happens because as the teabag is set ablaze, and begins to burn, the air inside expands since it is heated up. This expansion causes the air to lose its density, and be pushed up into the air by the cooler air that surrounds it. This explains why hot air rises, while cooler air remains at the bottom. Well, this also explains why a teabag which is set on fire, resembles a rocket that's just taken off. This is too cool an experiment not to try, but just a word of caution: this could also be too hot an experiment and hence whenever you undertake it, make sure you have an adult around you.

10 The Mpemba Effect

Who doesn't love the crunch of a chilled ice cube in their mouth? We all do! But the next time you are about to freeze those ice cubes, try this: instead of cold water, add some hot water into those ice cube trays. What happens will be hard to believe. The hot water will freeze faster than the cold. Why so?

This phenomenon is known as the 'Mpemba Effect', where due to its heat, the hot water tends to evaporate at a much faster rate than the cold water. Therefore, there is a lesser amount of volume present in the cooler water, causing it to freeze faster.

11 Sinking and Floating

When Neil put up his counter to sell lemonade in summer, his aunt Martha handed him a little lime that she thought he could use. So, Neil decided to slice the lime and add it to his jug of lemonade. But doing so left him confused as ever because while the lemons floated, the lime began to sink. Neil wondered, *why*?

That's when aunt Martha explained to him that a lime has a higher density as compared to a lemon. And this is exactly what causes limes to sink and lemons to float in water. We bet with this information, our lemonade boy Neil will not be as confused anymore.

12 Sunshine and Rainbows

Who doesn't love a rainbow? We all do! Its mesmerising colours, and the way in which it brightens up the sky does not fail to leave all of us awestruck. But how are these beautiful rainbows actually formed? And most importantly, why are they formed? Let us take a look.

Rainbows are the outcome of sunshine and rain or mist, which are present at the same time in our surroundings. Sunlight gets refracted (bent) as it hits the front of the droplet. This happens since light is moving from one medium to another, that is, it is moving from the air to water. On refraction, this beam of sunlight is separated into various colours. It then hits the back of the droplet, which causes it to get reflected and then refracted once again, as it exits the raindrop. This refraction and reflection of sunlight as it enters the droplet at a specific angle causes the droplet to separate the white light of the sun into many different colours, thus forming a rainbow that brightens up the sky.

You can make your own rainbow at home.

All you would need is:
A glass of water
A white sheet
A bright sunny spot

DO IT YOURSELF

Directions:
Go to a sunny spot and hold the paper below the glass of water.

You will notice the sunlight passing through the glass, then refracting and finally forming an array of colours on your sheet of paper.

13 The Sticky-footed Gecko

A gecko is undoubtedly one of the world's most amazing creatures simply because it is a master at defying the force of gravity – something which very few living and non-living things on this planet can do. So, what makes the gecko a master at this?

Geckos have more than a million tiny, hair-like structures on the soles of their feet. The ends of these hair have something called spatulae, which are microscopic. When geckos attach themselves to ceilings, the generally weak van der Waal force (an attraction between atoms and molecules) comes into play. But here each hair on the gecko's sole produces the van der Waal force, which turns out to be strong due to the millions of hair the sole of each foot possesses. This results in an adhesive kind of effect, which causes the gecko to attach its feet to the wall and hold more than 50 times its weight.

Fun Fact

When geckos run, they attach and detach their feet around 15 times in a single second.

14 Static Spiders

Just as hair sticks to a comb, so do tiny insects or any prey stick to a spider's web. You must have guessed it already. They both possess something in common – static electricity.

A spider's web, which is coated with a certain kind of glue that it produces, contains electrostatic properties. The dry air that the web glides in, causes it to become charged. This makes the web reach out and grab all charged particles, whether prey or pollutants. Now you understand why you always find spiders' webs in a room full of dust!

Fun Fact

A spider's web also does a great job at filtering airborne pollutants, including pesticides.

15 Electrifyingly Electric Eels

Have you ever watched 'The Little Mermaid' and wondered what were those sparks that came from the snake-like creatures under the sea? These creatures are Electrophorus electricus, more commonly known as electric eels. And they possess traits that are as interesting as their name. But let us first understand why they are given such an electrifying name. This is because electric eels, which are actually a type of Knifefish, have the ability to generate an enormous electrical charge that can go up to a whopping 600 volts. Now that is literally shocking!

These fish have electric organs that contain about 6,000 cells called electrolytes. These electrolytes act like a powerhouse of batteries that are highly charged. Due to their poor sight, electric eels use low voltage electricity to navigate through the water. They mainly discharge electricity when they sense a prey, or a predator is near.

Fun Fact

Eels are very thick skinned and hence do not generally shock themselves. However, where wounded, the eels can stun themselves.

However, rarely have there been human deaths due to electricity generated from these eels, and hence electric eels are not a threat to human beings. But then again, no one likes the idea of getting shocks while under water, do they? So, unless you plan to go swimming anywhere in South America, where these eels are found in plenty, you may go swimming without any fear!

16 Puff the Hot Air Balloon

A hot air balloon is made up of three parts: an envelope, a burner and a basket. The basic principle on which the hot air balloon works is that warm air rises since warm air has much lesser mass per unit of volume, and it is lighter than cool air. This gives an upthrust to the ballon.

Therefore, the actual balloon which is also referred to as the envelope has to be large enough to trap a huge amount of hot air with which it is filled to lift it off the ground. A burner with propane gas is used to heat up the air in the envelope in order to lift the balloon off the ground and into the air.

Once the balloon has been lifted off the ground, then starts the role of the burner. It propels hot air upwards into the envelope in order to let the balloon float in air and rise higher. The burner must be kept fired at regular intervals to ensure that the balloon stays stably afloat.

What is amazing is that although the envelope is open from the bottom, hot air does not escape from it as hot air has a tendency to move upwards.

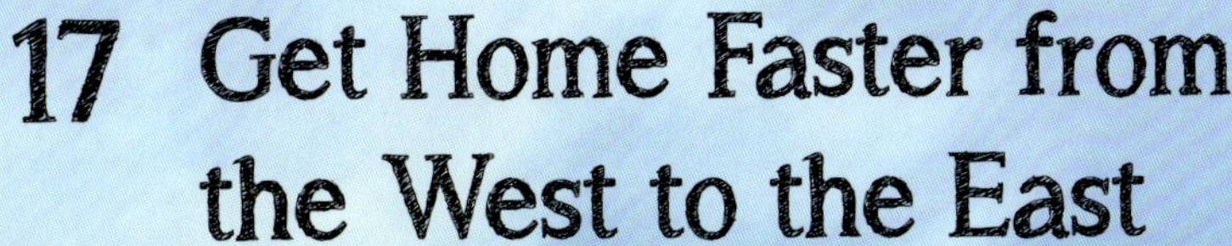

17 Get Home Faster from the West to the East

If you ever fly from the west to the east in the Northern Hemisphere, you will notice that the time taken is much less than if you fly from east to west.

This is because of an atmospheric phenomenon known as, 'jet stream', a high-altitude global wind above the earth that blows from the west to the east. Thus, when planes are in constant motion, this added push from the jet stream makes them fly even faster when they are flying west to east. Interesting, isn't it?

18 A Tough 'Tea' Time up There

Bet you couldn't refuse a nice hot cuppa tea when the weather outside is cold.

Well then, can you imagine how much a mountaineer would wish for a nice warm cup of tea, up in the freezing mountains? Sadly, this is something that only remains a wish. This is because, as we scale higher altitudes, the air pressure decreases, and liquid water becomes easier to boil, thus leading to rapid evaporation.

So, while at sea level the boiling point of water is 100°C, at higher altitudes such as mountains, this reduces to just 72°C, which is certainly not enough to make a decent cup of tea.

19 Shimmery, Sticker-ee Glitter

We have all had those fun art classes at school with art paper, scissors and oodles of glitter on our projects as well as all over us! Anyone who has worked with glitter will agree that glitter sticks to almost anything, especially our skin! Here's one of the reasons why it happens.

The metal coating of glitter is negatively charged and the moisture present in our skin is a polar molecule that is, positively as well as negatively charged. Thus, while working with glitter, its negative charge is attracted and sticks to us due to the polar molecules present in our moisture-filled skin.

20 A Beauty Called Fluorescence

Have you ever come across a light that emits the most beautiful colours? What we are talking about isn't just a normal lamp but a fluorescent lamp. These stunning colours are created by a phenomenon called fluorescence. Fluorescent marker pens, paint, chalks, colours are all things that you love to use because of that special magical glow. The light given out by certain mineral materials after absorbing light energy is called fluorescence. This light is absorbed at one wavelength and then given out instantly at another wavelength.

The best examples of fluorescence are seen when the absorbed radiation is ultraviolet and invisible to us, while the emitted light is visible to the human eye. So, the next time you use a fluorescent highlighter to mark something, you know where that bright glow comes from!

21 Hula Hooping: The Physics Way

A hula hoop sure could be a tad bit difficult to spin around oneself, without it falling. However, understanding the physics behind it could make things easier the next time you attempt hooping. While you move inside a hoop, you create something called 'torque' force which arises due to twisting in an outward direction.

The stronger this force, the higher the chances of the hoop continuing to spin uninterrupted. Another force at play here is that of friction between your clothes and the hoop. This friction causes the hoop to stay put on your body, while it is being pulled down by gravity. Now that you know the science behind hula hooping, we bet you'd do a much better job at it the next time!

22 The Masters of Mass

Ever tried hugging a tree? It truly is one of the best feelings in the whole wide world. But sometimes trees are so big, that it almost becomes impossible to wrap our arms even half way around them. So, where is it that they acquire all this mass from?

While the general concept is that trees get their mass from soil, the real source of the tree's mass is 'carbon'. Yes, the same carbon dioxide that we humans let out into the atmosphere is taken in by trees during the process of photosynthesis, to make up their mass.

23 The Funny Little Rubber Band

While most things expand on heating, a rubber band will act exactly in the opposite fashion. Sounds funny, right? Have you ever heard of something contracting when heated? Let's take a look at what causes the rubber band to behave in this way.

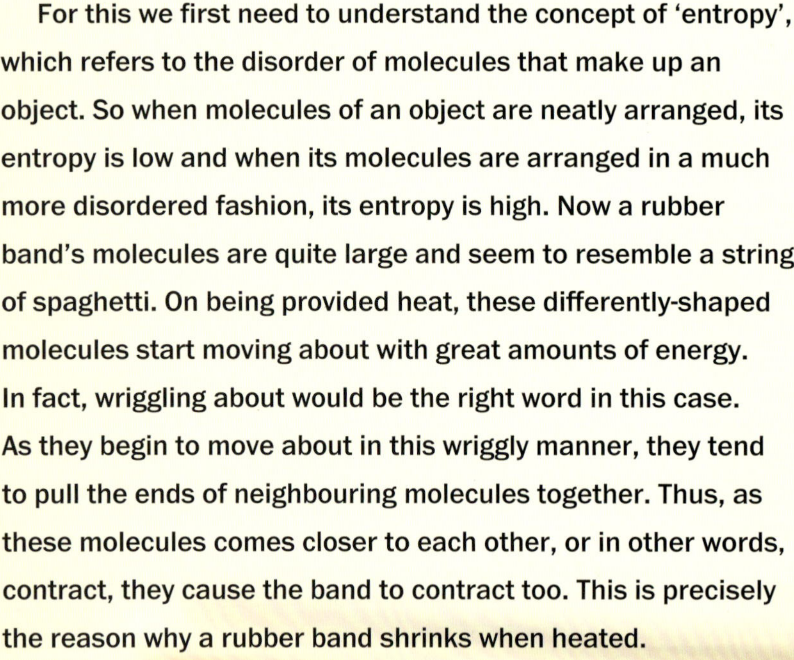

For this we first need to understand the concept of 'entropy', which refers to the disorder of molecules that make up an object. So when molecules of an object are neatly arranged, its entropy is low and when its molecules are arranged in a much more disordered fashion, its entropy is high. Now a rubber band's molecules are quite large and seem to resemble a string of spaghetti. On being provided heat, these differently-shaped molecules start moving about with great amounts of energy. In fact, wriggling about would be the right word in this case. As they begin to move about in this wriggly manner, they tend to pull the ends of neighbouring molecules together. Thus, as these molecules comes closer to each other, or in other words, contract, they cause the band to contract too. This is precisely the reason why a rubber band shrinks when heated.

24 The Flying Frisbee

We've all played with a frisbee at some point. With just a flick you can send this air powered toy to long distances. Ever wondered how?

There are two contributing factors to a frisbee that spins long and free in the air. The first is a phenomenon called, 'gyroscopic force', where a spinning object remains stable as it spins in the air. The second factor is the structure of the frisbee. If you've noticed, a frisbee has a curved surface, a wider central portion, and it tapers towards the edges. The structure of the frisbee causes it to move faster, since air moves rapidly over a curved surface, as compared to a flatter one.

Fun Fact

Walter Frederick Morrison founded the frisbee and sold the rights to Wham-O toy company in 1957.

25 The Physics of Cup Phones

Have you ever played with two plastic cups or tins tied together with a thin string? If yes, you'll know that you can use this toy like a telephone!

So, here's what happens. Vibrating molecules are produced when we speak, which in turn make other molecules in the air around us vibrate, causing sound to be produced. However, since the molecules in air are spread out, the vibrations caused by our speech tend to fizzle out if the receiver is far away. Using a phone made of cups and strings helps because a string is much denser than the air around us. The phone captures the vibrations produced when we speak, and it travels distances.

Fun Fact

Before the very famous, 'hello' that everyone uses as a greeting on the telephone, 'ahoy', was the originally used greeting.

26 A Minute as Good as a Year

On days that are sweltering, most of us wonder, *How much heat can the sun produce*? It already is as hot as a furnace and the heat only seems to rise. If you thought the sun produced heat only to match a furnace and more, then here's an interesting fact you ought to know: The sun produces much more than that. As a matter of fact, enough solar energy reaches the earth just within a single hour's time to make up for the entire world's energy demands for one whole year!

27 The Eiffel Is Growing!

Located in Champ de Mars in Paris, France, the Eiffel tower is undeniably one of the most beautiful monuments in the whole world. Apart from its beauty, what leaves visitors speechless is its height. The gigantic Eiffel Tower stands all of 320 metres tall, that is, a whopping 1050 feet. Huge, isn't it?

Now, if you thought at 320 metres the Eiffel Tower was immensely tall, this is what you should know as well. In summer, owing to the hot sun, the Eiffel Tower undergoes thermal expansion. This means the tower increases in height by about 6 inches until the sun sets for the day. Interesting, isn't it?

28 No Birds in Space, Please

So, this one's especially for all you bird and animal lovers. If you ever plan to become an astronaut, you must forget about taking your pet birds into space. Why's that? That is because birds need gravity in order to swallow. When birds swallow, they tilt their heads backwards, thus allowing gravity to let the food and water run down their throats. However, since there is no gravity in space, you can well be assured that your little birdy would not be able to swallow anything.

29 A Walk Around the World

While technically, walking around the earth even once would be a tough feat, five being an impractical number, an average human being walks around 7,500 steps a day. Given that number, and 80 years of an average human life span, you walk around 216,262,500 steps in your entire lifetime. That makes it about 110,000 miles, which is equivalent to five whole rounds of the equator!

While that might seem like a lot, it is the average most human beings in their life span do actually walk. As surprising as it is, the fact is that if we live until 80, we sure would have taken five rounds of our globe!

30 Slippery Socks and Friction

Ever tried sliding across your floor? For those who have, you would have surely noticed, that while you can slide in your socks, you are unable to do so in your shoes. Now, why is that?

Not only are the bottom of our shoes rough, but they are also made of rubber, most often. When this rough, rubbery bottom rubs against the floor, it produces something called friction, a force that works in the direction opposite to the direction in which one object moves over another, thus creating resistance. Why is it that you can slide in your socks so easily? Simply because the amount of friction produced depends on the material of the two surfaces moving against each other.

31 Levitating Frogs

Frogs, like everything else are made up of atoms. Atoms have loads of electrons that circle around a central nucleus.

However, when these atoms are exposed to a magnetic field, they tend to develop a magnetic field of their own.

But, everything is made up of atoms, so why is this true specially in the case of frogs? This is because frogs have a high-water content within them and water as a substance is a very good diamagnetic material. So, from now on whenever you see a levitating frog, rest assured that it doesn't have any secret yogic powers but is simply exposed to a magnetic field.

32 Doubly Bubbly Fun

Blowing bubbles can be the most fun game you have ever played. Those large amazing bubbles, each competing with the other to grow bigger and bigger, while nervousness takes over us in the hope that the bubble shouldn't burst. What a burst of exhilaration!

But have you noticed that blowing bubbles with plain water is almost next to impossible? The reason for this is that in a jug filled with water (from which we are to make our bubbles), there is a high amount of surface tension. In simpler terms, water molecules from the jug are attracted and drawn towards each other. While there is water in the jug, the molecules at the surface of the jug are drawn towards the molecules below as there is nothing above the surface, but air, that the water molecules could get attracted to.

Now, adding a little bit of detergent to this jug causes the distance between the water molecules to increase as the molecules of detergent come in the way. This reduces the force of attraction between water molecules. In other words, the surface tension of the water reduces, giving rise to some of the most colourful shapes in the form of bubbles! Blowing bubbles has always been fun. But now that you are aware of the science behind it, we bet it is now going to be doubly bubbly fun!

33 Did You Hear that Boom?

Ever heard that noise produced by the aircraft and other flying objects?

We bet it sounded like a loud bang or a giant clap of thunder. And you must have had a million questions in your head like: What is that booming sound? How did it occur? What caused that massive sound? Along with fear, your mind is filled with so many questions. So, we've decided to unravel the mystery of the big boom for you.

Here it is: The rumble you hear from planes is known as a sonic boom! But what exactly is a sonic boom? A sonic boom is a shock wave produced by an aircraft or any other object flying, moving at a supersonic speed as it passes and reaches the listener. This now makes us wonder, what does supersonic speed mean? Supersonic speed is the speed which is equal to or greater than/above the speed of sound. As the aircraft moves forward, it creates many wave fronts in the air. These overlap with each other and cause a large build-up of pressure. This pressure is then pushed in front of the aircraft, letting out a huge shock wave. This reaches the listener in the form of a sudden loud noise. And that is exactly what a sonic boom is.

So, the next time you see an aircraft and you hear that big bang, be assured that it is not the earth giving way, but merely a sonic boom and go back to watching movies and playing games, knowing that you are safe!

34 The Enigmatic Aurorae

Deriving its name from the Roman Goddess of Dawn, the Aurora is a truly enigmatic phenomenon that leaves its viewers speechless. But, what is it that causes these beauties to light up the sky?

Solar winds which contain ionised gas are drawn into Earth's magnetic pole fields. As they move rapidly towards Earth, they collide with the nitrogen and oxygen atoms in our atmosphere, leading to a burst of energy that are called the aurora lights. The auroras occurring in the Southern Hemisphere are known as Aurora Australis, while those occurring in the Northern Hemisphere are called Aurora Borealis.

35 Space Can Make You Taller

Always dreamed of becoming taller? Well, then you must make a trip to space! Studies have shown that astronauts who lived in space for some amount of time actually grew taller by around three inches. This could be attributed to the fact that since there is no gravitational pull in space, the spine becomes relaxed and hence expands. However, this is just a temporary phenomenon and our height gets back to normal once we are back on planet earth.

36 The Balancing Act

Let's try a very simple experiment at home today. And that would be finding the centre of mass of any stick. So how do you do it? All you need to do is to balance the stick between your thumb and the fingers, which are placed at the extreme ends of the stick, respectively. Next, gently move your fingers from the outside to the centre of the cane.

What actually happens here is one of your fingers on which the cane is placed is actually closer to the centre of the stick's mass. This is why the friction force of the finger that's closer is greater and the finger that's further away moves faster. As the further finger comes closer to the centre, the situation reverses and the finger that's closer begins to slide faster.

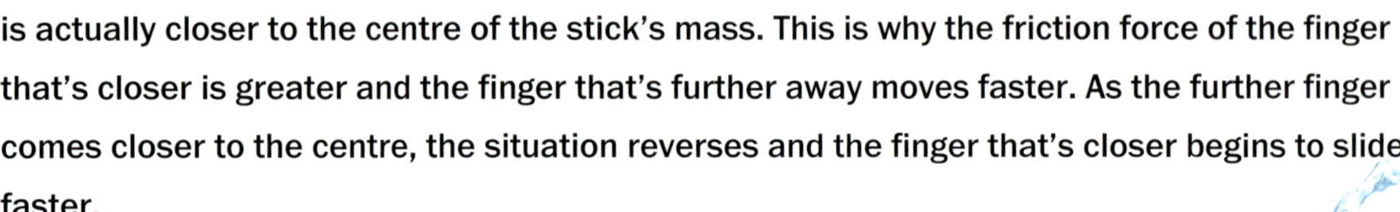

37 A Burst of Water

Those of you who have lived in cold countries, may have sometime or the other observed a pipe burst when the weather was extremely cold. So why does this happen really?

Molecules of a liquid tend to slow down when the liquid gets cooler. As the molecules slow down, they draw closer to each other, thus increasing the density of the liquid.

In the case of water, the density goes on increasing until about 3.98°C, and once the temperature goes below that, something strange happens, water starts expanding again. It is precisely this expansion that causes water pipes to sometimes burst in extremely cold climatic conditions.

38 Gravity, Mass and Inertia

We know that our Earth has a strong gravitational force and that most objects are influenced by its pull. Well then, imagine yourself standing on top of the tallest building in the world with two balls in your hand: a bowling ball and a basketball. Now you drop both of these. Which one do you think will hit the ground first?

The answer is, both will hit the ground together. You are probably thinking, *How is that possible?* Well, although the force of gravity on the bowling ball is greater, since it has more mass, it also has a lot more inertia (resistance to acceleration), and therefore requires more force to accelerate. On the other hand, even though there is less gravitational force on the basketball, due to the lesser amount of mass it contains, the amount of force required to accelerate is much less since it has lesser inertia as compared to the bowling ball. And that is why, both the balls end up hitting the ground at the same time.

39 Immortal Diamonds

While diamonds are indeed highly priced, it's also very true that each of us is in awe of those glittery, shimmery rocks that don't fail to catch the eye. And their strength matches their beauty too. To put it more simply, nothing can destroy a diamond. Well actually, that would be over exaggerating. Let us put it this way, nothing can destroy a diamond, except heat!

Yes, the only thing that can destroy diamonds is heat. And by destroy, we mean completely getting rid of them. While crushing a diamond will only cause it to break into pieces, the pieces of the stone still remain. But heat is something that can totally wipe them out. Heat a diamond to over 700°C in open air, and whoop, it vanishes into thin air. Basically, what happens here is it reacts with the oxygen in its surroundings and gets converted to carbon dioxide. So, while this is a sure shot way to completely wipe out a piece of diamond from the face of the earth, we aren't sure that is something anyone would like to do to such a stunning piece of jewel.

Thus, even though a diamond is almost immortal, heat is the only force that prevents it from being so. Very rarely does one find such a stunning combination of strength and beauty. No wonder a diamond is one of the most exquisite and expensive things on this earth, and may we also add, 'a girl's best friend'!

40 The Brazil Nut Effect

Every time you buy a box of nuts, you will notice that the biggest nut is always on the top. Why is this?

Also known as the Brazil Nut Effect, this relates to a phenomenon known as 'kinetic sieving'. According to this phenomenon, when a box or container that contains objects of different sizes is shaken, voids are created below, and smaller objects tend to fall into that space and fill it, thus causing the larger objects to rise to the top. In this case, the same phenomenon occurs with the large nuts, making them sit atop a can of nuts. So the next time you buy a box of nuts, you should easily be able to tell which nut sits on top.

41 A Hot Chocolate Soprano

Did you know that when a spoon is tapped on the bottom of a mug of freshly made hot chocolate (with the mug held in your hand), the pitch of the tone produced is constantly rising? Yes, that's absolutely true. This is also known as the, 'hot chocolate effect'. But what is it that is actually happening here?

When you stir cocoa powder into a cup of hot milk, air bubbles are formed in the milk. Sound travels faster in liquids than it does in air, thus causing the air bubble to reduce its speed. The pitch of the tone we hear when a spoon is tapped at the bottom of the mug is directly proportional to the speed of sound. Thus, when the air bubbles clear, the pitch of the sound heard increases.

42 Floating in the Dead Sea

If relaxing in water without moving even a limb is what you would love to do someday, then the Dead Sea is some place you must visit. While in other water bodies floating becomes a task, in the Dead Sea, floating is not any tougher than eating a piece of cake. This is because the Dead Sea is highly saline. In other words, it has a high salt content. While water is dense by nature anyway, the high salinity in the Dead Sea causes its waters to become much denser than water that isn't so saline. Thus, anybody or anything that makes an attempt to plunge into the Dead Sea, is naturally pushed up to its surface, causing them to stay afloat.

43 Why Ships Float

Have you tried dropping a steel bolt in a bucket of water? No? Ok, so here is what happens. The moment the bolt hits the surface of the water, it begins to sink. Well then, in that case how do steel ships that are far larger than a little bolt, stay afloat in the sea?

This depends on the density of the object in the water. Should the density of the object be more than that of the water, the object is bound to sink. However, should the density of the object be lesser than the water, the object will stay afloat. In the case of a ship, the density of the vessel is lesser than the density of the water, while the opposite is true in the case of the bolt. Now you know the secret to the sinking bolt and the floating ship.

CHEMISTRY

The branch of science that looks at what matter is made of, how it is put together, what it can do and how it reacts is called CHEMISTRY. It is also often called a 'central science', because it links all the other sciences like physics, geology and biology.

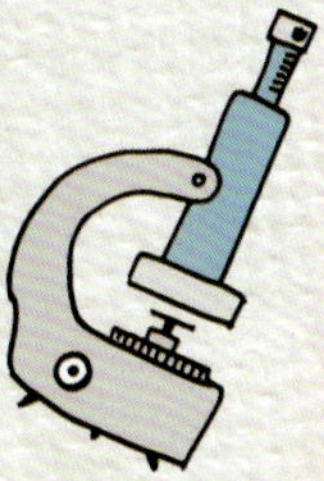

44 Jean-Digo!

Today we have jeans in a number of colours. However, the 'blue' denim, will always remain a classic. Did you know what causes the blue colour of jeans? The answer is indigo dye! Thanks to a German chemist Alfred Von Baeyer, indigo dye was chemically synthesised and invented. In fact, he won a Nobel Prize for this in 1905.

Indigo also occurs as a natural dye. Indigo plants are harvested in order to extract the dye. When you add sodium hydroxide and sodium hydrosulphite to indigo, it reduces to its colourless form. Then it is applied to the cotton denim fabric causing the dye to adhere to the fabric, while fading little by little over time. Upon drying, the dye comes in contact with oxygen in the air and once again changes its colour to blue.

45 Oh-nions, They Make Me Cry

Hate chopping onions? Well, considering they make us cry, who doesn't? Let's look at why we cry while chopping onions.

Onions produce a compound called S-oxide, a chemical irritant. This stimulates the tear glands in the eyes, called lachrymal glands. When S-oxide is released into the air, it comes in contact with the eyes to produce tears. When we cut an onion, the enzyme called 'L factor synthase', gets into the air. It continues to act on certain amino acid-containing compounds that are present in the onion, and converts them into sulfenic acid, further converting them to S-oxide, which causes our eyes to water.

46 Fiery Peppers

Why do you feel a burning sensation in your mouth and in your system when you consume chilli peppers? This is because they contain compounds called capsaicin and capsaicinoids. The partially purified form of capsaicin known as Capsicol causes a burning sensation when it comes in contact with our mucous membranes. It also causes increased secretion of the gastric juices present in the stomach.

The painful sensation felt by us is associated with capsaicin and its chemical interaction with sensory neurons. After binding to specific neurons in the brain, it gives rise to sensations similar to that of excessive heat, which explains the feeling of spiciness. Hence, it can be considered a rather irritant compound.

47 The Goodness of Honey

Honey is a sweet and sticky, yellowish-brown substance made by bees as they suck on the nectar of plants. The nectar present in the flowers is a mixture of water and sugars. Enzymes secreted by the bees, called invertase, break down the carbohydrate disaccharide (double sugar) sucrose into monosaccharide sugars (simple sugar) namely, fructose and glucose. The liquid yield is stored in the beehive. From here, much of the water content evaporates, leaving only about 18 per cent water, and the sticky texture we know of. The hives are stripped off their honey and packaged into bottles for us to use.

Honey contains vitamin B, potassium, flavonoids, riboflavin and folic acid amongst other useful contents.

Fun Fact

There are three types of bees that live in a hive – a queen, workers and drones.

48 Why Is Food so Colourful?

Much of what we eat would not be appealing if it was not coloured. Natural dyes have been utilised to colour food for ages. The most common are carotenoids, chlorophyll, anthocyanin and turmeric. Carotenoids, the pigments found in sweet potatoes and pumpkins, are generally added to colour dairy products such as cheese and margarine. They add a red, yellow and orange colour to food. Anthocyanins, which provide deep blue and purple colours to grapes, are used as natural dyes in brightly coloured soft drinks. Furthermore, mint and lime-flavoured foods like candy and ice cream, are sometimes coloured using chlorophyll. Turmeric is another natural food colour that is used, and you can mainly find it in mustard sauces and other such yellow foods.

49 How Lipstick Sticks

Lipstick is usually an important part of every make-up kit. Some lipsticks wipe off easily, while others last long. Ever wondered, what makes it retain its colour when applied? It all depends on what goes into lipsticks!

In the prehistoric period, lipsticks were made from natural sources like fruit and plant juices. In fact, the first ones to make them were Mesopotamian women. They would grind precious gems to dust and decorate their lips. Then the women from Indus Valley Civilisation too started using lipsticks regularly.

Today, however, most lipsticks are made from a solid waxy substance (like beeswax, ozokerite and candelilla) that does not dissolve easily; these are mixed with oil to retain spreadability and softness. Sometimes, lipsticks also contain various oils and fats such as olive oil, mineral oil, cocoa butter, lanolin and petrolatum. Other chemicals like titanium oxide create brightness, fatty acid esters give the stickiness and alcohol prevents the wax from melting. Pigment or a colouring material added in, reacts with proteins on your skin and gives the lipstick its colour and durability.

50 A Jelly Called Vaseline

In 1859, Robert Chesebrough, began his studies on a substance called 'rod wax', an unrefined form of petroleum jelly, as he was curious to know about its healing properties. The Vaseline petroleum jelly, in its present form, was obtained through the chemical process of refinement, purification and distillation. Originally called 'wonder jelly', petroleum jelly comprises natural waxes and mineral oils, making an effective and intensive moisturiser. Therefore, when we speak about petroleum jelly, we're commonly referring to Vaseline petroleum jelly, the actual brainchild of Chesebrough. Vaseline jelly is a triple-filtered substance, which contains no impurities, and is known for its wonderful ability to protect and lubricate the skin. It has also been given various other names, including petrolatum, white petrolatum, soft paraffin/paraffin wax and multi-hydrocarbon.

51 Diamonds Are Forever

We've all thought of the beauty and price of diamonds. And yes, we love them! But have we ever wondered where the word diamond came from? It comes from the Greek word, which means 'unbreakable'. Diamond is one of the most well-known allotropes/forms of carbon.

Here is the history of some of the world's finest ones. The 'Koh-i-Noor' diamond, once considered the largest diamond in the world, was found in India. It is now a part of the British Crown Jewels in the Tower of London. The rather famous 'Hope Diamond', which carries a weight of 45.52 carat, appears blue owing to the presence of boron in its crystal structure. It has been known to carry a curse. The 'Tiffany Yellow Diamond' was first discovered in the Kimberly Mine in South Africa. It was a whopping 287.42 carat, when first isolated!

But how are diamonds formed? It takes billions of years to form naturally occurring diamonds under the effect of intense pressure and heat. They are often brought to the Earth's surface by deep volcanic eruptions.

Diamond is the hardest natural material known and is used most often for industrial cutting and polishing tools. It is also the best known thermal conductor found among naturally occurring substances.

Fun Fact

Diamonds are found deep inside Earth almost 90 to 120 miles below its surface.

52 Light a Match!

Matches are really useful things – they are especially helpful when there is a power failure and you need to light a candle. Do you know what makes a matchstick catch fire? Matches need a special surface to be struck on to ignite! This surface contains phosphorus and the head of the match contains potassium chlorate, which speeds up the process. The friction between the two causes the spark that 'lights' the match. The fire moves slowly along the wood stick, which is often coated with paraffin to slow down the burn. That is why you can carry the burning match a short distance away, to light a lamp or candle without singeing your fingers!

Fun Fact

The earliest known matches were found in China. These were wood sticks soaked in sulphur.

53 The Phlogiston Effect

Ever wondered what fire is all about? In the eighteenth century, before the discovery of oxygen, phlogiston, a colourless, odourless, and weightless substance was believed to be released during the process of burning. A classic example was that of wood, which was said to be a combination of phlogiston and wood ashes. The residue, or ash, that was left behind was known as the dephlogisticated air.

In the 1800s, Georg Ernst Stahl, who applied the name phlogiston to the substance from a Greek word meaning 'burned' said that phlogiston was an immaterial 'principle', rather than an actual substance. He also hypothesised that phlogiston was lost in the atmosphere during the corrosion or combustion of certain metals in air (rusting of iron). With advancements in the field of chemistry, it was thought of as a true substance. Some considered hydrogen to be pure phlogiston as it was a flammable gas. By 1800, the Phlogiston theory was derecognised and was replaced by the Oxygen theory.

54 Discovering Fireworks

A dark night that's lit with fireworks is truly a treat to the eye, isn't it? Words would be insufficient to describe this beauty! God bless the person who invented fireworks! But wait a second, who actually invented fireworks?

It was the Chinese who discovered that a combination of sulphur charcoal and potassium nitrate burnt quickly and produced a big flash. Excited by this, they filled the mixture into bamboo shoots and threw them into the fire. The green bamboo shoots exploded creating a huge sound. And there you go, fireworks were born. In order to make coloured firecrackers, chemists had to determine compounds which gave out their characteristic colours.

A magnesium and aluminium alloy 'magnalium' is responsible for the blue fireworks. Certain metal chlorides also produce colour, like strontium creates the colour red, while barium creates green.

55 Good Bugs Indeed!

Think before you savour a bowl of strawberry yogurt. You're probably eating bugs! However, these are the good ones, so don't worry! An extract from a type of insect name 'cochineal' is purposely added to these foods by the manufacturers, as it is supposed to add a deep-red colour. What's this dye or pigment called? It's called carminic acid. It has also been used in a variety of cosmetic products which need a red colour. The dye does not contaminate the food and is considered non-toxic and safe to consume and ingest. In very rare instances, it is possible that someone could develop allergies or hypersensitivity reactions to this compound.

Fun Fact

Centuries ago, the Aztecs used this insect to dye fabrics to a deep red colour.

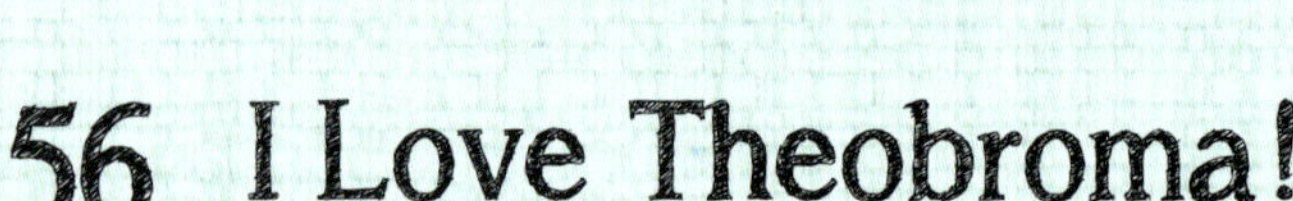

56 I Love Theobroma!

We all love chocolate, don't we? It's not just yummy, but also makes us feel good. In short, chocolate works wonders. And why is that so? Simply because chocolate consists of theobromine, which is a chemical compound and a bitter alkaloid just like caffeine, bringing about similar effects on the human body. Theobromine acts as a smooth muscle stimulant and a relaxant. It has a molecular formula $C_7H_8N_4O_2$. This compound has been found in other natural food sources such as the leaves of the tea plant and kola nuts. In 1841, Alexander Voskresensky discovered theobromine in cacao beans, while Emil Fischer synthesised it in 1882. As a result of this, its name has been derived from the cacao tree genus Theobroma. Commercially, it is also used as a therapeutic agent in certain disorders such as high blood pressure.

57 Let's Bake Some Cake

Baking, one of the most interesting hobbies common to people, is based on the rather complex interactions and chemical reactions of one ingredient with another ingredient. Have you ever thought about the chemistry of baking? This involves flour, yeast, fat, sugar and baking soda/ powder. And each of these ingredients has a different function and purpose.

Wheat flour contains a protein called gluten, which supports the rising of the cake. Yeast feeds on and hydrolyses starch and sugars, releasing carbon dioxide, alcohol and sugar. This is all carried out through a process called 'fermentation'. The carbon dioxide bubbles give the dough a light, airy texture. The fat helps prevent these bubbles from escaping too soon, as well as weakens the complex gluten network, making it softer. This further causes the dough to expand or rise.

Sugar is a natural source of food for yeast. And finally, baking soda, which is chemically sodium bicarbonate, releases sodium carbonate, a strong base, which has to be neutralised. Hence, baking powder is used. This is baking soda with acid added to it, in order to neutralise the base and increase carbon dioxide production.

So now you know the number of chemical reactions that are involved before you get a piece of soft, fluffy cake that melts in the mouth.

58 Sleepless with Caffeine

It's close to bedtime, and you've just had a large cup of coffee. You suddenly feel as refreshed as ever. Why is that so?

The active ingredient of coffee is caffeine, which belongs to a class of chemical compounds known as alkaloids. Caffeine is believed to stimulate receptors in the central nervous system of the brain, boost concentration, enhance alertness, physical performance and increase your thought process. It is also added to consumer products such as colas and energy drinks for the same reason. Now you know why a cup of coffee or a can of energy drink does such a good job of robbing away your precious sleep. Caffeine enters the bloodstream about 10 minutes after its ingestion and remains in the body for up to 12 hours! Hence, excess of it is capable of having some powerful physiological effect on humans.

59 Antacids

Had a large, sumptuous meal? Experiencing acidity and indigestion? Here comes the role of antacids. Most antacid preparations consist of basic compounds as they function to neutralise the acidic gastric juices of the stomach. As a result, the incidence of heartburn and acid refluxes reduces to a great extent. Most commercially available antacids include sodium bicarbonate, magnesium hydroxide and aluminium hydroxide. Magnesium hydroxide, most commonly known as milk of magnesia, is also used as a laxative. However, the most potent antacid is calcium carbonate, as it causes complete neutralisation of gastric acids, thereby proving to be highly effective.

So, the next time you know anyone who has over indulged in a delicious meal and is suffering from a bout of acidity, don't forget that antacids could come to the rescue.

60 Antioxidants, a Saviour!

What if someone said there was a way to make us look, 'forever young'? Wouldn't we all be delighted? Of course, we would! But the truth remains, we all age with time. Why do we age? What causes the process of ageing to take place?

Free radicals are atoms, molecules or ions with unpaired electrons. They actively react with other molecules and are often got from oxygen, nitrogen and sulphur molecules. They produce molecules called Reactive Oxygen Species (ROS), Reactive Nitrogen Species (RNS) and Reactive Sulphur Species (RSS). They are formed by the cells of the body during activities. However, very high amounts of ROS can have damaging effects on cells and attack many molecules present in the body including proteins, lipids, DNA and RNA. This causes something called oxidative stress.

Antioxidants, on the other hand, fight against these reactive species. Hence, they are molecules which counterbalance the free radicals. They gain or lose electrons causing the unpaired state of the radical to be removed. They finally destroy harmful radicals. Foods rich in antioxidants include Vitamin C and Vitamin E and are present in avocado, nuts, and dark chocolate. Other natural sources are fruits, vegetables, spices, grains and herbs such as ginseng, curcuma, rosemary, green tea, grape, ginger and garlic. They contain a variety of antioxidant compounds such as phenolics (phenol and polyphenols), flavonoids and carotenoids.

Fun Fact

Digestion produces free radicals which is why each meal you eat needs to contain antioxidants.

61 Something's Fishy

A trip to the fish market is one trip most of us wouldn't be excited about. Just the thought of the stench of the place makes you feel queasy. But what is it that causes fish to emit this kind of smell?

The smell from the body of a fish is the result of a natural process of decay. As bacteria feed on the flesh of the fish, an oxidation reduction reaction is triggered. The muscle of the fish contains a compound called trimethylamine oxide (TMAO), which breaks down when the body of the fish decomposes. TMAO is further broken down into trimethylamine and dimethylamine. These two amines give out the characteristic fishy smell. By using a mixture of lemon, vinegar or baking soda, the smell of the mixing amines can be considerably reduced and removed. This is because, amines are alkaline based and lemon juice is acidic. Combining an acid and base leads to a neutralising effect. Now we know why lemon is added to fish preparations.

62 Making Fine Wine

Wonder why we often see a bunch of people jumping on a huge barrage of grapes? Making wine, is the answer. So how is wine really made? It's made from grapes.

Grape juice is a combination of water, carbohydrates, trace amounts of organic acids, phenolics which impart flavour and vitamins, minerals and nitrogenous compounds, which are critical to yeast growth for the process of fermentation. The commercial process of winemaking is a complex chemical process, which involves the addition of certain other compounds like sulphur dioxide in order to prevent oxidation. This is done post crushing of grapes. Gentle crushing releases the juices so that other components and enzymes can act on it. The juice is allowed to stand in order to separate the solids. The yeast is then added to feed on the sugar releasing alcohol and carbon dioxide. Ultimately, the unwanted solids and bacteria are removed by a variety of chemical and physical processes. This process is known as, 'purification'. And voila! There we have some fine wine.

63 Once Precious, Aluminium!

At one point of time, more specifically, before the refining process was discovered, aluminium was more expensive than gold!

Aluminium has 13 electrons orbiting around the nucleus. It is a metal popular for its strength and lightweight property. It is nonmagnetic and resists oxidation (rusting). Highly conductive, aluminium is the core material in wiring for electrical transmission networks. Aluminium ore (bauxite) was mined and chemically refined through the Bayer process from which aluminium oxide was obtained. It was further refined through the Hall–Héroult process and the pure metal was obtained by an electrolytic process.

64 POP!

Scribbling on the cast of a friend has always been so much fun! What is it that makes a cast so hard? Also known as POP, Plaster of Paris is manufactured from the mineral gypsum. The chemical core of gypsum is hydrated calcium sulphate. In fact, that's where it gets its strange name from that is, the calcium sulphate hydrates found in large deposits in the Montmartre hill in Paris. When gypsum is heated at very high temperatures of about 150°, it loses water and a white powder is left behind. This is the powder that forms POP. When we add water to POP powder, it readily absorbs the water, hardens and solidifies. POP is used to make casts, moulds and sculptures.

Fun Fact

Gypsum was used in ancient Egypt in the construction of pyramids.

65 The Dangerous 'Fat Boy'

In the late 1940s a team of scientists at the University of California, Berkeley, discovered they had made a new element. They called it Plutonium.

When they studied it further, they found that one form of this element could be used to make an atomic bomb. This worried them and hence they kept it a secret until after World War II, to ensure that it would not be used as a weapon of mass destruction. Sadly, in 1945, plutonium was in the core of an atomic bomb called Fat Boy that was dropped on Nagasaki, in Japan.

Fun Fact

Plutonium should have been the tag of PI, but one scientist from the team wrinkled up his nose and suggested Pu (peeyoo) instead!

66 Let's Ka-boom with Sodium!

Please beware! We're mixing sodium with water. The reaction is spectacular, producing sodium hydroxide, hydrogen and large amounts of heat. The intense heat ignites the hydrogen gas, creating a huge explosion. It has been studied that when water and sodium first combine, the sodium releases electrons, leading to a positively charged state. And don't we all know, likes repel but opposites attract? Hence, all the positive charges repel each other, creating a greater surface area for an even bigger reaction that goes 'ka-boom'!

Phew! That looks highly exciting and intriguing. A word of caution: do not try this without adult supervision!

Fun Fact

Sodium compounds containing natrons were used for preservation of mummies by the ancient Egyptians.

67 The Colour of Life

For life to exist, oxygen is essential. You probably know oxygen best as a gas, which is part of the air you breathe every day. Oxygen is a lot more interesting as a chemical. It has a boiling point of –297.33° Fahrenheit or –182.96° Celsius.

When oxygen is at a lower and colder temperature than that, it turns to liquid. At that stage, its paramagnetic qualities kick in. Its reaction is fascinating as a drop of liquid oxygen can be held suspended between the two poles of a powerful magnet. Best of all, liquid oxygen has a pretty pale blue colour. It happens to be the shade you generally colour the air while painting a scenery!

68 Beware – Liquid Oxygen!

While oxygen is essential for life, doesn't the term, 'liquid oxygen' sound like an irony to breathing? No one can breathe liquid, right? But the liquid oxygen we're speaking of here isn't really used to breathe.

Liquid oxygen is a blue coloured cryogenic liquid. Now you may ask, 'What are cryogenic liquids?' Cryogenic liquids are liquefied gases that have very low boiling points. Liquid oxygen has a boiling point of –297°F (–183°C). Oxygen is primarily used as a gas, but is stored as a liquid. It is generally used as an oxidant for liquid fuels in the propellant systems of aircrafts, missiles and rockets. Contact with or exposure to liquid oxygen can cause cryogenic burns and lead to tissue damage. The low temperature of liquid oxygen and the vapours it releases, can also cause many materials of construction to shatter as they lose their strength and become very brittle.

69 Mercury Rising

What's the first thing that seems intriguing when we look at a clinical thermometer to check whether or not we are running a fever? It's the long, fine amazing silver line in the centre that catches our attention.

What is that silver line actually? The answer is: mercury! Mercury is the only metal which is liquid at room temperature. This leads us to the next question, what keeps it in its liquid state? The electrons that spin around the nucleus of a mercury atom share weak bonds with other mercury atoms at room temperature, keeping the metal in a liquid state. These are called 'cohesive forces'. An important point to note! As pretty as it may look in its shiny, fast-moving liquid form, mercury is not to be touched!

70 What Is 'Oxygenated Water'?

Oxygenated water is nothing but hydrogen peroxide! It is a colourless liquid at room temperature and has a bitter taste. Small amounts of gaseous hydrogen peroxide occur naturally in the air. An unstable compound, it decomposes readily to give oxygen and water with the release of heat. Being a powerful oxidising agent it can also cause spontaneous combustion when it reacts with organic material. However, it is otherwise non-flammable. In higher concentrations, hydrogen peroxide is used for industrial applications such as, a bleach for textiles and paper, a component of rocket fuels, and for producing organic chemicals. When it comes in contact with certain metals, it decomposes violently. Its vapours cause irritation to the eyes and mucous membranes. Hydrogen peroxide is used as a 6 per cent solution for bleaching hair. Some disinfectant solutions for contact lenses contain a 3 per cent hydrogen peroxide. Chlorine free bleaches also contain 6 per cent hydrogen peroxide.

71 The Secret of Acetic Acid

Do you know that you have been consuming an acid in certain of your foods? Don't worry, it's not a corrosive one, like sulphuric acid.

It is, in fact, vinegar, which is primarily acetic acid or ethanoic acid and is obtained by the chemical fermentation of alcohol and its products. Generally used as a condiment and a preservative, for pickling processes, the word vinegar comes from the French word meaning, 'sour wine'. Anciently known as the 'poor man's wine', acetic acid gives vinegar a characteristic sour taste and pungent smell. The pH of vinegar lies in the range of 2 to 3.5. It is typically derived from a sugar-containing source such as malted barley, rice, and cider.

Other interesting varieties of vinegar include coconut vinegar, cane vinegar, fruit vinegar, (made from fruit wines, usually without any additional flavouring), raisin and date vinegar, honey vinegar, flavoured vinegar and herbed vinegar that are flavoured with thyme or oregano. You also have spiced vinegar, which is flavoured with chilli peppers, onions and garlic. Apart from the flavour it adds to your food, vinegar has also been studied for its very interesting role in medicine. It is used medicinally in cardiovascular diseases, skin infections, blood glucose control and is even known to act as an anti-cancer agent.

vinegar

baking soda

Fun Fact

Vinegar also acts as a great stain remover.

72 A Wonder Drug

One of the most sought-after painkillers, Aspirin is a commonly found drug in most first-aid kits.

Chemically, aspirin is acetylsalicylic acid, a derivative of salicylic acid. These are found in plants such as white willow and meadowsweet. Hence the drug has a coined name derived from acetyl and spirea. The Egyptians as well as Hippocrates recommended willow bark and leaves for pain, fever and swelling. Salicilin, a yellow bitter crystal was isolated from willow barks, by a group of German pharmacologists. Swiss pharmacologists isolated a similar substance from meadowsweet. After ten years, French chemists synthesised salicylic acid. The rise and emergence of Aspirin in 1899 caused it to make its way into one of the world's first industrial research laboratories. Although a lot of controversies surrounded it and still do, here's an interesting fact. The 1950 Guinness Book of Records announced it as the world's most popular painkillers.

73 Miraculous Phytochemicals

Plants are known to provide us with food, fuels, fibre, etc. But chemicals? Phytochemicals are chemical compounds derived from plants. Also called secondary biological metabolites, phytochemicals have extensive medicinal uses. They have a wide array of disease-preventing roles, which has led to extensive studies in the light of their properties and biological functions. They have antibacterial, anti-fungal, antioxidant and even anti-cancer properties.

Apart from the human body, phytochemicals also protect plant cells from pathogen-causing diseases, pollution, UV radiation, stress and damage. Additionally, they provide characteristics to the plant such as their aroma and flavour. More than 4,000 phytochemicals have been classified and over 150 have been researched. Now, with all of this given, who wouldn't call phytochemicals miraculous?

74 Borax – It's Everywhere!

Borax is a chemical element that is extremely rare in our solar system. So rare, that the earth's crust contains only 0.001 per cent of it. Borax, however, chemically known as sodium tetraborate, or disodium tetraborate is an important boron compound and mineral. In chemical terms, it is the salt of boric acid. It appears as a white powder consisting of soft, colourless crystals that dissolve easily in water.

Not only is it a component of many detergents but also a part of cosmetics, and enamel glazes. It is used to make buffer solutions in biochemistry, and most notably has anti-fungal properties. It is also used as a flux in metallurgy, neutron capturing shields for radioactive sources, texturing agents in cooking.

Interestingly, borax is utilised as a food additive in some countries but is banned in a few countries as it could be harmful to health. In Indonesia, its role as an additive to foods such as noodles, bakso (meatballs), and steamed rice has been forbidden.

Initially discovered in dry lake beds in Tibet, borax was imported to Arabia through the Silk Road. It first came into common use in the late 19th century, owing to the Pacific Coast Borax Company. Borax occurs naturally in evaporate deposits produced by the repeated evaporation of seasonal lakes. Borax can also be produced synthetically from other boron compounds. Naturally occurring borax is refined by the process of re-crystallisation. With borax in so many daily uses, indeed it is borax everywhere!

75 What's in Sand?

Sand is a mixture of two commonly known elements, silicon and oxygen, more precisely, silicon dioxide or silica. It is also believed that certain types of meteorites called 'aerolites' are primarily and majorly composed of silicon. And have you ever wondered how glass is made? It is produced by a complex chemical process of heating sand at extreme temperatures.

Did you know silicon is actually a metalloid, which means it possesses properties of both, a metal and that of a non-metal. Free silicon is used for steel refining, aluminium casting, and in chemical industries. Highly purified silicon, on the other hand, is used as a semiconductor in the electronics industry. It has predominant and vital utility in today's computer technology and other high-tech devices.

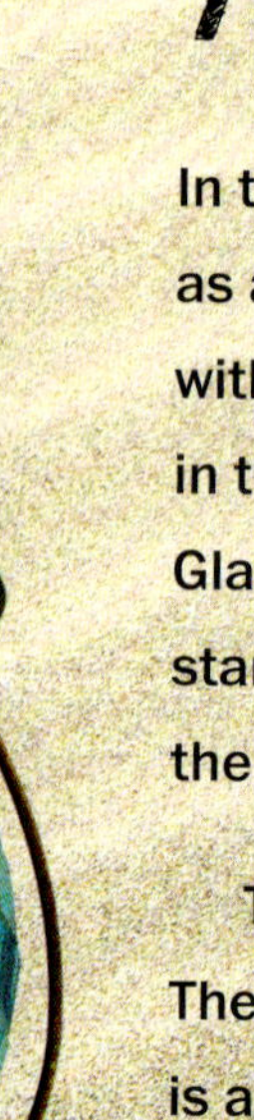

76 As Strong as Glass

In the early 1900s, a particular type of glass was developed as a solution to a major problem – the inability of glass to withstand temperature shock. A number of tragic accidents in the days of the railroads occurred due to this failure. Glass lanterns used as signals would get very hot, and if it started to rain, the rapid cooling would sometimes cause the glass to break and the signal to fail.

To prevent such mishaps, chemists worked on a solution. The resulting glass was called borosilicate. This glass is able to withstand a temperature variation of 200°C. Owing to the fact that it has greater durability than soda lime glass, borosilicate glass is utilised predominantly in laboratory glassware (beakers, flasks, test tubes, etc.) It is also used as the preferred material in glass kitchen bakeware, as it can withstand very high temperatures.

77 The Rise of MSG

Monosodium glutamate, most commonly known as 'Ajinomoto', has been extensively studied and tested for its benefits as well as adverse effects. It was discovered in 1908 by Japanese chemist Kikunae Ikeda and has ever since been used in packaged foods, soy sauces, fish sauces and other food items. It was first isolated from seaweed and was considered a flavour enhancer for some foods. It has a rather unusual flavour that comes under the category of 'umami' food tastes. Since the advent of technology, MSG can also be synthetically derived, processed and manufactured from natural foods.

78 As Rare as Astatine

Discovered in the 1940s, astatine is a dangerous radioactive element because of its unstable and reactive nature. American physicists Dale R. Corson, Kenneth R. MacKenzie and Emilio Segrè synthesised the element by bombarding bismuth, which is a chemical element, with accelerated alpha particles (helium nuclei). As a result of this reaction, astatine-211 and neutrons were produced. It is one of the rarest naturally occurring elements present in the earth's crust. Astatine is so rare that there are only a mere 30 grams of it in the earth's crust. It has also been considered as the heaviest member of the halogen family. Since astatine has no stable or long-lived isotopes (different forms of an element), its name has been derived from the Greek word astatos, which means 'unstable'.

79 Beware of Those Airbags

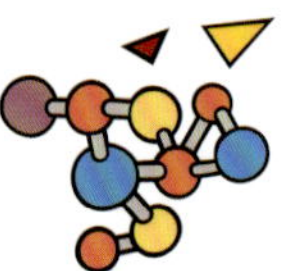

We all must have at some time or the other watched a car accident on television where when a car collides into something, an airbag gets inflated. So what is it that causes this inflation?

Airbags are packed and inflated by a rather toxic reaction produced by a chemical called sodium azide, or NaN_3. It is a stable molecule at room temperature, however, when heated it decomposes to yield nitrogen gas and sodium. It is believed that a handful of sodium azide, which is approximately 130 gm will produce 67 litres of nitrogen gas. This is sufficient to inflate a normal airbag. Secondly, sodium being a very reactive metal will react rapidly with water to form sodium hydroxide. If it finds its way into your eyes, nose or mouth, it could be dangerous. Airbag manufacturers have started mixing the sodium azide with other chemicals that will react with the sodium in such a way that they give less toxic compounds, which will minimise the intensity of exposure as well as danger.

When a collision occurs, a trigger to the car's sensors sends an electrical impulse, which increases the temperature of the salts. This sets off the chemical reaction, rapidly expanding the airbag.

Fun Fact

The 1973 Oldsmobile Toronado was the first Car with a passenger airbag intended for sale to the public.

80 ZnO - Protection from Sunburn!

A trip to the beach? Don't forget your sunscreen! What's the secret behind sunscreen? Zinc oxide! It has the ability to absorb the UV rays of the sun and hence is used in sunscreens and lotions to protect us against sunburn.

Zinc oxide, chemically known as ZnO are white hexagonal crystals or a white powder, in its pure form. It is also known as zinc white. It is used as a pigment in paints, and most importantly, it remains white when exposed to hydrogen sulphide or ultraviolet light. It is also used in creams and ointments. Not only is the use of zinc oxide confined to the cosmetics industry, the compound has also paved its way into solar cells and nuclear reactors, as it helps to prevent corrosion. Crystalline zinc oxide is a light-sensitive compound. Present naturally on earth, ZnO is primarily found in the mineral zincite. Zinc peroxide which ranges from a whitish to yellowish powder, is used in antiseptic ointments.

81 Dry Ice

Dry ice? What's that? Let's get a little more acquainted with what it is. It is carbon dioxide in its solid or frozen form. It is dense and has a snow-like appearance. It sublimes at −78.5°C and is commonly used as a refrigerant for transport and shipping of perishable products such as meats or ice cream. It is extensively used because of the ease at which it freezes and needs to be handled with the use of insulated gloves. Dry ice can be easily converted from a solid state to a gaseous state, under normal atmospheric conditions without undergoing a wet liquid state. Hence the name, 'dry ice'. It gives more than twice the cooling energy per pound of weight as compared to regular ice that is made up of water. It also provides three times the cooling energy per volume than regular water ice.

82 Thank You, Ozone!

What do you think protects us from the harmful ultraviolet radiations of the sun? It is 'ozone', a gas consisting of 3 oxygen atoms, present in the upper layers of the atmosphere. Ozone absorbs the harmful UV rays and splits into an oxygen molecule and an oxygen atom. Most importantly, it protects the earth and its population from the damaging effects of sunlight. However, substances known as chlorofluorocarbons (CFCs) have been depleting ozone, because of their increased usage. It is believed that, one CFC molecule released into the atmosphere has the ability to remain for several years without reacting with other chemicals. Once in the upper atmosphere, it is split or broken apart by UV radiation. A chlorine atom is released, which is responsible for ozone depletion.

This has led to the formation of the 'Ozone Hole', a term coined to describe the major thinning of the ozone layer in the Earth's atmosphere.

83 Of Helium and Balloons

Helium was first found in the corona of the sun. Later it was discovered in gases coming out from Mount Vesuvius. It is the second-most abundant element in the universe.

Being the second element in the Periodic Table of Elements, it belongs to the group of inert gases. It is colourless and odourless. Some very interesting uses of helium show up in semiconductors, balloons and the Large Hadron Collider. Because of its extremely low-density, helium floats in air. This 'lighter than air' property of helium allows balloons to fly. When helium is inhaled, a rather squeaky voice is produced. Owing to this low-density gas surrounding the vocal cords, cords will vibrate faster, increasing the pitch of the voice skyward.

Heard about helium superfluids? These are liquids that behave as if they have no viscosity, or resistance to flow and have been used in a number of scientific experiments.

84 A Rather Sociable Element

What could be the connection between chemistry and being sociable? Sounds rather surprising, doesn't it?

Well, we're talking about chlorine here. And why is chlorine such a sociable element? It is because chlorine is generally found in the combined form, with other elements. The primary mineral majorly mined for, is sodium chloride, also known as common salt. It is also present in the minerals carnallite (magnesium potassium chloride) and sylvite (potassium chloride). Chlorine gas is yellowish green in colour, highly toxic, and was used as a powerful chemical weapon during the World Wars.

Initially, it was used to make chloroform and carbon tetrachloride (a dry cleaning solvent). Today, PVC, a form of plastic used in window frames, car interiors, electrical wiring insulation, water pipes, is produced from chlorine. A powerful disinfectant, chlorine kills bacteria, hence it is used to treat drinking water as well as to clean the water in swimming pools. No wonder swimming pools have that unusual smell about them. Yes, that is what chlorine more or less smells like. Apart from this, chlorine is also used in textiles, dyes, medicines, insecticides and paints. No wonder it is considered to be such a 'sociable' element.

Fun Fact

It took almost 20 years for chemists to accept and claim that chlorine truly was an element.

85 I See Pink - Violet Vapours

Wondering how? Let's take a look. As part of one of his experiments in 1811, French chemist Bernard Courtois was extracting sodium and potassium compounds from seaweed ash.

Once isolated, he added sulphuric acid to these compounds, to further process the ash. It was then by accident that Courtois added a bit too much acid, and as a result of this a violet coloured cloud was formed. When the vapours condensed on metal objects in the room, solid iodine was created. In its solid state, iodine crystals are bluish black with a lustre. Iodine belongs to the halogen group in the periodic table and sublimes into violet pink coloured vapours. Iodine dissolves easily in a solution of chloroform, carbon tetrachloride, or carbon disulphide, and the result is a bright purple-coloured solution.

86 Condy's Crystals

Condy's are often used in the kitchen to disinfect veggies. What are these magical crystals that dissolve in water to give it a pretty pink colour?

Chemically known as potassium permanganate, $KMnO_4$ is the potassium salt of permanganic acid. The term 'Condy's crystal' is derived from its discoverer, Henry Bollman Condy. It is a completely odourless chemical that looks like dark purple crystals, and is soluble in water. Although non-combustible, a reaction with sulphuric acid could trigger a fire or an explosion. And when dissolved in water, the water turns pink. Due to its high oxidising property, this chemical is used as a disinfectant to treat water. It easily removes magnesium and iron from surface and deep groundwater sources. It also helps in removing rust in water equipment and pipes. These crystals are also used to treat fish diseases and cure bacterial gill infections.

87 Dear Gold

Why is the word 'karat' always used as a connotation for gold? What is a karat really?

The word karat comes from the carob seed. In ancient times, the Asians used these seeds to balance scales that measured the weight of gold.

Do you know, much of the gold jewellery we wear, isn't really made of pure gold? The amount of gold present in a necklace or ring is measured on the 'karat scale'. Pure gold is 24 karats.

Bars of gold found in locations around the world are said to be 99.95 per cent pure, 24-karat gold. When other additional metals are mixed with gold to make jewellery, the purity of gold naturally reduces, and this causes the number of karats to drop. For example, 12-karat gold is an amalgam of 50 per cent gold and 50 per cent alloys by weight.

88 Lethal Gunpowder

'Bang!' go the guns during a shootout in your favourite action movie. But what causes these loud explosions? The answer is a mixture of sulphur, charcoal, and potassium nitrate from which gunpowder is made. This mixture causes a loud explosion that is very dangerous. Invented by the Chinese, it was anciently given the name 'serpentine'. On burning gunpowder, the constituent compounds potassium nitrate (acts as an oxidiser), sulphur and the carbon in charcoal (acts as fuel) together set off a chemical reaction, forming nitrogen, carbon dioxide gas and potassium sulphide. This pressure generated is enough to propel a bullet, but not enough to destroy the barrel of a firearm. Hence it is considered to be a low explosive owing to its slow decomposition rate and low rate of explosion. But low rate of explosion or high, this is something you need to be very wary of!

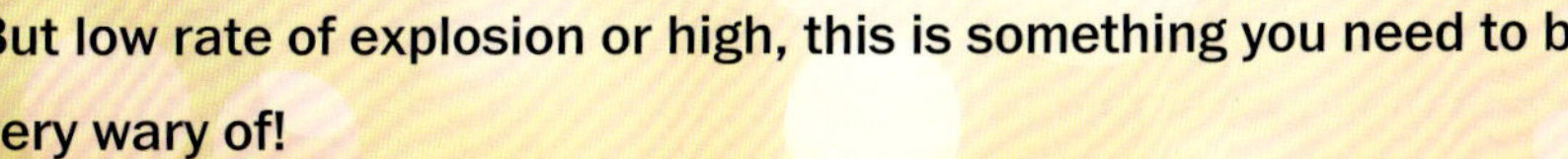

BIOSCIENCE

The world is a fascinating place that has a number of ongoing natural processes like cell biology, biochemistry, biophysics, anatomy of all living organisms. Yes, in other words, we're referring to the field of Bioscience here. This section covers some mind-boggling facts on bioscience that are sure to add to your knowledge in the most exciting way!

89 Father of Microbiology

Antonie van Leeuwenhoek, popularly known as the father of microbiology, made his own unique microscopes with specialised spherical lenses, which were responsible for offering magnification and high-resolution images. In 1674, at the age of 41, Leeuwenhoek made the first of his great discoveries, when he studied single-celled organisms, today known as prokaryotes in the world of biology. In 1674, he also examined red blood cells (RBCs). Although RBCs had already been discovered by Jan Swammerdam, Leeuwenhoek was able to give better clarity about the characteristics and morphology of the cells because of his superior lens. He was the first person to accurately determine their size. In 1676, Leeuwenhoek discovered bacteria in water, and a year later he discovered spermatozoa. A few years later, he also observed the life-cycle of maggots and fleas. He studied the different stages in the developments that occur from eggs to maggots to pupae to adults.

90 Metamorphosis

Fun Fact

The body of a caterpillar almost melts completely before it morphs into a butterfly.

Isn't it always fun to go through old pictures and look at how much you have changed from childhood, till now? The animal kingdom goes through similar changes as well. And while with us, human beings, this process is known as 'growing up', amongst animals it is known as, 'metamorphosis'. Metamorphosis is the transformation in an individual from hatching or birth, i.e., the juvenile stage, to the adult stage. Hormones play a pivotal role in regulating these changes. Apart from changes in growth and differentiation, there are modifications in physiology, biochemistry, and the behaviour of an individual.

A classic example is the tadpole in the aquatic larval stage that transforms into the land-dwelling adult frog. There are 3 types of metamorphism, namely, which is a slow increase in the size of the organism until the adult stage is reached; hemimetabolous and holometabolous, which occur in the form of life cycles.

In hemimetabolous development, the life cycle consists of the egg, nymph and adult. The immature insect resembles the adult in form and eating habits, but differs in size, dimensions and colour pattern. Complete metamorphosis called holometabolous metamorphosis occurs in insects like flies, beetles, butterflies and wasps. The life cycle in the case of holometabolous has four stages, namely, egg, larva, pupa and adult. The larval stage differs greatly from the mature adult stage.

91 There's Blood Everywhere

Iron

Heme

Polypeptide chain

Oxygen molecules

We all wonder what is in blood?
What is blood made up of? Where does it get its red colour from? What is responsible for the colour?

The red pigment present in the blood called 'haemoglobin' is the main protein in all mature red blood cells. It is made up of two parts; heme, which is iron and 'globin', which is the protein component. One molecule of haemoglobin in an adult is composed of four globin chains, two alpha and two betas. When oxygen combines with haemoglobin it forms a compound called oxyhaemoglobin. The function of haemoglobin is to carry oxygen from the lungs to the tissues and return carbon dioxide from the tissue to the lungs. Therefore, when oxyhaemoglobin is formed, the oxygen molecules are carried to all the cells and delivered so that the organs can function. If you like to maintain a healthy amount of haemoglobin in your body, beetroots should be your next best friend!

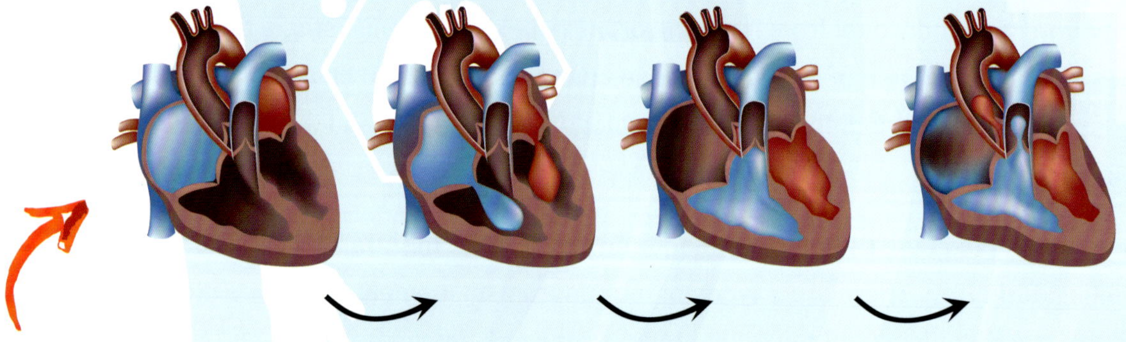

92 The Cardiac Cycle

The cardiac cycle is in layman's terms defined as the cycle of events that occur when our heart beats. This cycle consists of a series of alternate events which make up one complete pumping action of the heart and is heard as one heartbeat. Chambers called atria contract and pump blood into the next chambers known as ventricles, which relax when they receive the blood. This relaxing phase is called the diastole and the contracting phase, the systole. The different valves present in the chambers open and close during the cycle, to send blood to the different chambers. As a result of this, a rhythm or a heartbeat is formed. The heart of a human being beats at the rate of 72 beats/minute.

93 Skin, the Largest Organ

Imagine if we didn't have skin to cover our entire body. We'd just be a large population of flesh and bones moving around.

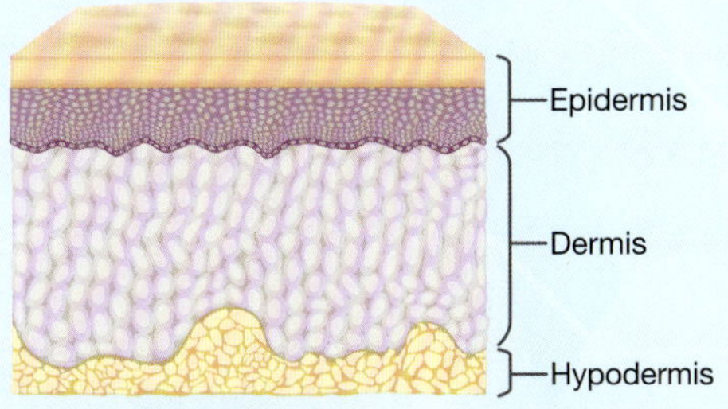

Skin is the largest organ present in the human body and consists of 3 layers, namely, the epidermis, dermis and hypodermis. The outer, superficial layer of your skin is called the epidermis. The deepest layer of your skin, called the hypodermis or subcutis contains a network of blood vessels, hair follicle roots and nerves. Skin also stores fat. The skin is said to account for about 15 per cent of your body weight. The skin helps in homeostasis that is it regulates body temperature by detecting cold and heat. The skin also has pain receptors called nociceptors. The skin protects our internal organs, muscles and bones from external diseases and infections. In order to renew itself, the skin sheds dead cells, at the rate of 30,000 to 40,000 dead cells per minute. An interesting fact is that the skin renews itself every 28 days.

94 The Longest Bone

There are a total of 206 bones in our body. But which one is the longest? Here's the answer. Femur, commonly known as the thighbone, is the longest and strongest bone in the body. Owing to its strength and rigidity, a lot of force is required to break it. The femoral shaft is the long and straight part of the femur. When there is a break anywhere along the femoral shaft, it causes a fracture. It is also considered to be the heaviest bone in the body. It serves as an attachment point for all the muscles that exert their force over the hip and knee joints. One of the earliest vertebrates to have a femur is a prehistoric lobe-finned fish. Non-walking vertebrates, such as some species of whales and snakes have femurs, which have almost become functionless with evolution.

95 A Healthy Gut

"A healthy gut is the key to a healthy life," they say. Well that's very true. So what is a healthy gut really?

For that we need to first understand what a gut is. Also known as the gastrointestinal tract, the gut is a long tube that starts from the mouth and goes on till the large intestine ending at the anus. It contains about 3.5 lbs of bacteria. Its function is to process food from the time it enters the mouth, till it is absorbed or excreted out of the body. Now, it is very essential to maintain good gut health, so as to ensure that our digestive system is in good shape, because that is what makes up about 70 per cent of our immune system.

So how can we maintain optimal gut health? A few ways are to have your meals on time and exercise. But did you know there are also certain kinds of foods that promote good gut health. These foods are also known as fermented foods or 'probiotics'. Fermented foods are foods that are rich in bacteria that produce lactic acid. These are the same bacteria that cause milk to sour. These bacteria help balance the acids in the digestive tract, thus creating an environment that promotes the growth of healthy gut bacteria.

A few examples of fermented foods are kefir, yogurt, buttermilk, kapusta, kvass and borscht. These foods hail from different parts of the world. And while fermented foods have been part of man's diet since time immemorial, today these foods are increasingly considered one of the most healing foods as per modern science.

Fun Fact

Fermented foods can easily be made at home, with basic ingredients like sea salt and plenty of sunlight.

96 Tick-Tock, Tick-Tock

Every living being has a 24-hour natural clock within them. It is this clock that is responsible for many of our physiological activities like sleep, regulation of the body temperature, hunger, etc. These rhythms that run as per our 24-hour bodily clock are known as the Circadian Rhythms. The word 'circadian' is a word coined from two different words, mainly, 'circa' which means 'around' in Latin and 'dies' that is taken from the word, 'a day'. That clearly tells us, how our rhythms go round in one whole day.

Even without a clock, our natural body rhythms could give us an idea of time. Scientists believe that certain areas of the brain, like the hypothalamus, help us keep track of time. We have interfered with our circadian rhythmic patterns owing to modern lifestyles. Animals and plants always follow the circadian rhythm, come what may.

97 My Muscles Ache!

A long day of football or some rigorous exercise at the gym can surely lead to some muscle pain! If playing is so much fun, then why is the aftermath so painful? Read on to know more.

During respiration, the body breaks down glucose to produce energy. When we perform rigorous physical activity or any strenuous exercise, respiration occurs in the absence of oxygen, i.e., anaerobic respiration. The body's ability to burn up the glucose is faster than the amount of oxygen being pumped to and supplied to the muscle cells. This leads to the production of lactic acid, which builds up in our muscles and causes the sensation of soreness. This lactic acid build-up in overworked and exhausted muscles can even lead to cramps. So the next time you've had an entire day of fun and play, don't forget to soak your feet in a bucket of warm water and Epsom salts to ease out the pain!

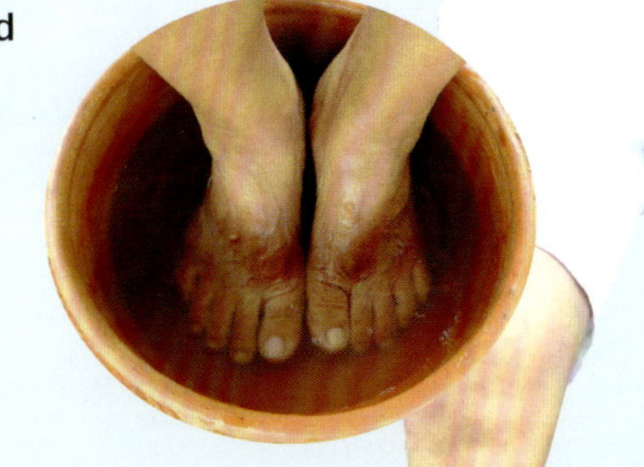

98 Brush for that Perfect Smile

We all know that brushing inadequately can result in tooth decay. But how does brushing help prevent this?

The outer visible white part of our teeth is known as enamel. It is made up of a matrix of minerals, particularly calcium and phosphate, called hydroxyapatite. Fluoride is an active ingredient in toothpaste. Its primary action is to reduce the solubility of enamel in acid by converting hydroxyapatite into fluorapatite, a less soluble compound. By acting directly on the plaque matter, it also decreases the ability of the bacteria to generate tooth-weakening acids.

Hence, it promotes remineralisation of tooth enamel in areas experiencing acid attack as well as those decalcified by acids.

99 Aflatoxins

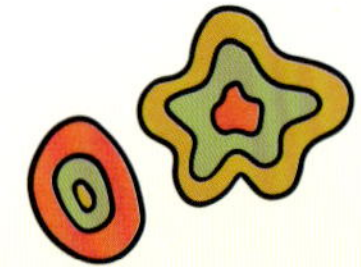

We have often read labels that say, 'toxic'. Toxins are what make a substance toxic or dangerous. Toxins are harmful substances which can cause serious diseases and sometimes even lead to death. Aflatoxins are a particular type of cancer-causing chemicals that are produced by certain moulds which grow in soil, decaying vegetation and hay. They are found on chilli peppers, corn, millet, rice, cottonseed, peanuts, sesame seeds, sunflower seeds, tree nuts, wheat, and a variety of spices, due to improper storage conditions. Through contaminated food, aflatoxins make their way into the food supply, and into feedstock for animals. Animals that have consumed contaminated food can pass these chemicals into dairy products.

Aflatoxin exposure affects children leading to retarded development and liver damage. Adults are at a lower risk to aflatoxins, as they have a higher tolerance.

100 Powerhouse of the Cell

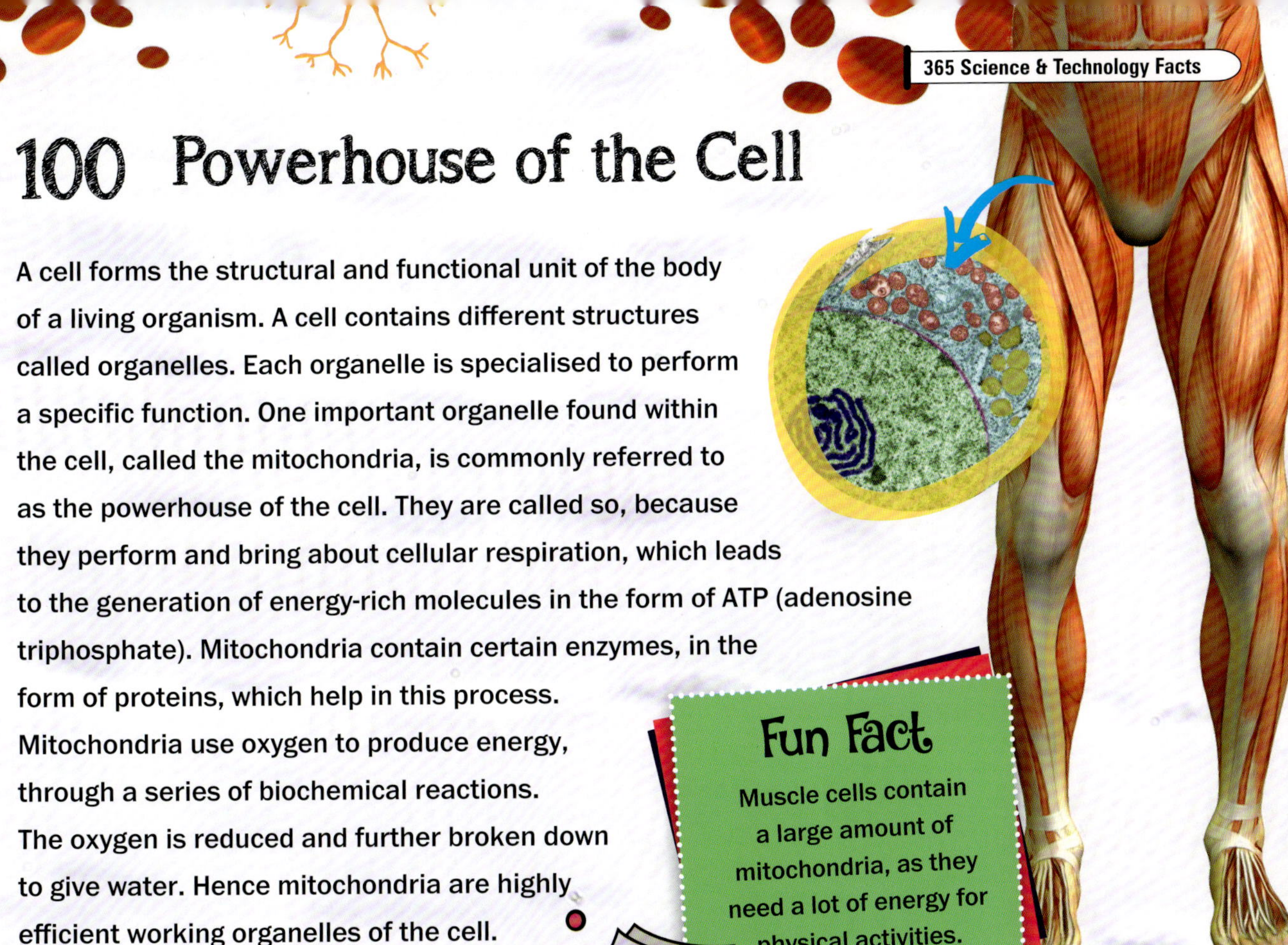

A cell forms the structural and functional unit of the body of a living organism. A cell contains different structures called organelles. Each organelle is specialised to perform a specific function. One important organelle found within the cell, called the mitochondria, is commonly referred to as the powerhouse of the cell. They are called so, because they perform and bring about cellular respiration, which leads to the generation of energy-rich molecules in the form of ATP (adenosine triphosphate). Mitochondria contain certain enzymes, in the form of proteins, which help in this process. Mitochondria use oxygen to produce energy, through a series of biochemical reactions. The oxygen is reduced and further broken down to give water. Hence mitochondria are highly efficient working organelles of the cell.

Fun Fact

Muscle cells contain a large amount of mitochondria, as they need a lot of energy for physical activities.

101 Glucose Is Important

Sugar is made up of something known as 'glucose', a term most of us have heard of. The word glucose has been derived from the Greek word 'glukus', which means 'sweet'. Glucose is used by the body to produce the energy currency of the cell, known as ATP (adenosine triphosphate). It acts as the essential source of energy and power. This energy is utilised by the body for basic biochemical, cellular, molecular activities and functions. Hence, it is important to maintain correct glucose levels in the body, in the range of 70-100. High and low levels of glucose can cause certain ill-effects to the body and affect our well-being.

Fun Fact

The normal level of glucose after a meal is below 140 and someone who crosses that level, stands a risk of diabetes.

102 What's DNA?

Deoxyribonucleic acid could sound a bit too complicated for most of us, which is why this term is so commonly referred to as DNA. And while we often come across this biological term nowadays, do we really know what it means? To simply put it, DNA is the genetic material present in all living organisms, which encodes biological information. It is a complex molecule that is made up of three main components and two strands that are wound around each other, resembling a twisted ladder. This structure is also referred to as a double helix.

When a child inherits her mother's melodious voice or his father's athletic skills, we say it is part of her or his DNA. Why is that? This is because a part of DNA is passed from the parents to their offspring during the process of reproduction. And this is exactly the reason why most of us resemble our parents, both physically and through certain other traits as well.

Although every organism's DNA is unique, DNA is composed of the same nitrogen-bases. So how does DNA differ from organism to organism? It is simply the order in which these smaller molecules are arranged that differs among individuals.

So the next time someone tells you how similar you are to your parents, you know whom to thank for it – your DNA of course!

103 Of Genes and Mutations

A gene mutation is simply a change or modification in the DNA sequence of a gene. This in simpler words means that the mutated gene sequence differs from what is found in normal people. This gives rise to a number of abnormalities, disorders and diseases. Mutations can occur anywhere in the DNA segment, hence the range varies in size. This brings us to the next question, how do genetic mutations actually occur?

There are two major causes of mutation. Mutations that are inherited from the parent to the offspring are called hereditary mutations. They are present throughout a person's life. They are also called germline mutations, because they are present in the germ cells, which are the reproductive cells, that is, the parent's egg or sperm cells. Acquired mutations, as the name suggests, occur due to exposure to certain environmental factors such as ultraviolet radiation.

For example, after the Hiroshima Nagasaki bomb blasts in Japan, thousands of people around the place suffered from gene mutations, which they did not have at birth. Apart from environmental factors, gene mutations can also occur if a mistake is made during the process of DNA replication, which if not corrected would further affect cell division. Acquired mutations occur only in body/somatic cells (somatic cells are cells other than sperm and egg cells), and they cannot be passed on to the next generation.

Fun Fact

Elizabeth Taylor, a famous yesteryears actress' dark beautiful outlined eyes were due to a rare genetic mutation that gave her 'double eyelashes'.

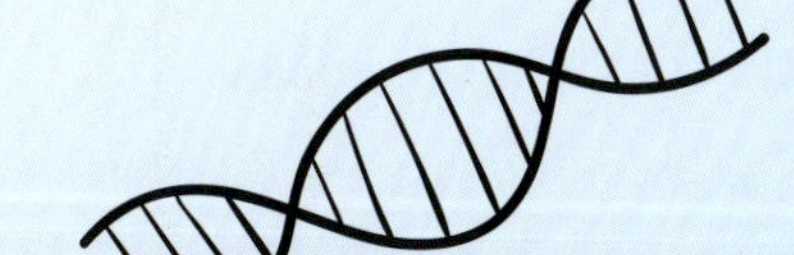

104 Broca's Area

We all wonder what happens in the brain when we talk. The region of the brain responsible for speech is called the Broca's area. It was discovered in 1861, by French surgeon Paul Broca, who studied and identified that it plays a vital role in the generation of speech. Over the years, scientists identified, that it is found in the part of the brain called frontal lobe/cortex, and more importantly it is responsible for putting our thoughts into words. Brain mapping techniques, recorded during the flow of speech, reveal that the Broca's area is most active just before words are spoken. Additionally, it is involved in language comprehension, learning as well as integration and coordination of speech.

105 A Process Called Ecdysis

Ecdysis is a process that takes place in both reptiles as well as invertebrates. Reptiles undergo this process by shedding off their old skin, whereas it happens by moulting of the cuticle in invertebrates, such as arthropods and nematodes. In invertebrates, the cuticles of animals typically form a hard inelastic outer covering called exoskeleton, which is shed during development. As a result of this a new, larger covering is formed. The process involves two main stages, apolysis and ecdysis. The initial stage apolysis, is the separation of the cuticle from the underlying cell layer, epidermis. The end stage ecdysis is the shedding of the old cuticle, which is caused by a hormone ecdysone. This hormone is responsible for the degradation of the old cuticle and secretion of materials for the formation of the new cuticle.

106 The Sea God: Amoeba

Amoeba proteus gets its name from two Greek words; 'amoeba' meaning 'change' and 'proteus' meaning 'Sea God'. This microbe is described as the Sea God, 'Proteus', since it is always changing its shape, much like the sea does. The ability to contract into any shape is attributed to a structure called pseudopodia, which are projections or extension of the cell membrane. They are present in most eukaryotic (organisms with a membrane-bound nucleus) microbes. Cycles of contraction and extension are caused by structures called microfilaments, which are present near the end of the cells, and are made up of actin proteins. Owing to flexibility of these structures, Amoeba proteus can move around freely. The size of this amoeba is as small as 0.2-0.3 mm in diameter, however, larger forms have also been identified. Amoeba proteus gets its energy from chemical sources, such as sugars, fatty acids and glycerol.

107 Very Amoeba-ish

Dictyostelium discoideum is an amoeba that lives in the soil. It is a eukaryote, which means a multi-celled organism. It has an initial unicellular phase, and as it grows, it develops a multicellular slug phase.

In the unicellular phase the amoeba feeds on bacteria, reproduces asexually through the process of binary fission, where the parent cell splits itself into half producing two new cells.

The amoeba form aggregates which develops into multicellular fruiting bodies. This complex life cycle consists of four stages; vegetative, aggregation, migration and culmination. D. discoideum serves as an ideal model organism to study a number of biological processes, including chemical signalling, chemotaxis (how different molecules are attracted to collect in a certain area), phagocytosis (engulfing of bacteria, germs and other foreign substances, during an infection) and cellular differentiation. The lifecycle of D. discoideum is relatively short, which allows for observation at all developmental stages. It is a widely-researched model organism to study genetic, cellular and biochemical mechanisms in other organisms.

108 A Fish Called Zebra!

A Zebrafish is a tiny aquatic creature that has horizontal stripes on its body that are similar to the stripes of a zebra, and hence the name. These little fish are also very useful for research.

Zebrafish are vertebrates (an animal with a spinal cord surrounded by cartilage or bone) that share a high degree of genetic similarity to humans. Extensive research over the years has shown that the Zebrafish shares structural and functional homology (similarity or identity) with mammals, including humans. For example, many proteins have been identified, that have a similar function in fish and mammals. As compared to rodents, Zebrafish produce a much larger number of offspring in each generation. Rodents have 5-10 offspring per pairing, whereas the Zebrafish is capable of 200-300 offspring per pairing. Now that's a huge number! Zebrafish embryos and larvae are transparent in nature. Therefore, the impact of any genetic manipulation or drug treatment used on them, is easy to observe and study. Zebrafish embryos are able to absorb chemicals that have been added to their water, including certain mutagens (a chemical substance that causes genetic mutation). Hence, it becomes easy to generate genetic changes and mutations in them, as is desired. Since they can tolerate high levels of chemical mutagens, in comparison to rodents, it is possible to produce and introduce a large number of mutations in their genetic structure. The Zebrafish have a biological make up that is as interesting as their name.

Fun Fact

Unlike most other fish who prefer mating in the dark, Zebrafish generally mate during the break of dawn.

109 A Swimming Bladder

A swim bladder is a gift of nature to fish, and this is what helps them swim with ease without sinking.

This bladder is responsible for the effect of buoyancy (ability of something to float in water), is present in the body cavity, and is an extension of the digestive tube that is present in fish. It contains oxygen gas, which keeps the density of the fish the same as that of water, ensuring that the fish does not sink, even if it stops swimming. The fish alters the amount of air inside the bladder, depending on the depth at which it is swimming. It is also considered to be a chamber which is capable of producing or receiving sound. In certain species of fish it acts as a lung for respiratory function. However, the swim bladder is absent in all cartilaginous fish such as sharks, skates and rays, as well as in some deep-sea bony fish.

110 Stars of the Sea

Starfish, commonly known as the 'sea star', belong to the echinoderm group. Around 2,000 species of sea stars exist in the world's marine habitats. The most common is the five-arm variety of starfish, but species with 10, 20 and even 40 arms have been identified. They can consume prey outside their bodies, with the help of specialised tube feet. In order to protect themselves from predators, sea stars have evolved a bony, calcified outer covering of skin.

However, the most interesting fact of all is that sea stars have no brains and no blood. Their nervous system spreads through their arms, and their blood is actually filtered sea water. However, what is most interesting about the starfish is that it has the ability to regenerate its entire body.

111 People Are Like Flies

NASA plans to send fruit flies (Drosophila Melanogaster) into space to learn what space travel does to the genes of astronauts. But why are fruit flies being sent into space and not astronauts? The little fruit fly that hovers around food, shares a lot in common with human beings, in terms of its genetic make-up. Studies conducted by the National Human Genome Research Institute (NHGRI) show that 60 per cent of the genes are common between humans and flies. 75 per cent of the genes that cause diseases in humans are also found in fruit flies. In fact, the fly is being used as a genetic model for research on several human diseases, including neurodegenerative disorders like Parkinson's and Alzheimer's disease. Flies have been used in studies involving aging, immunity, diabetes and cancer.

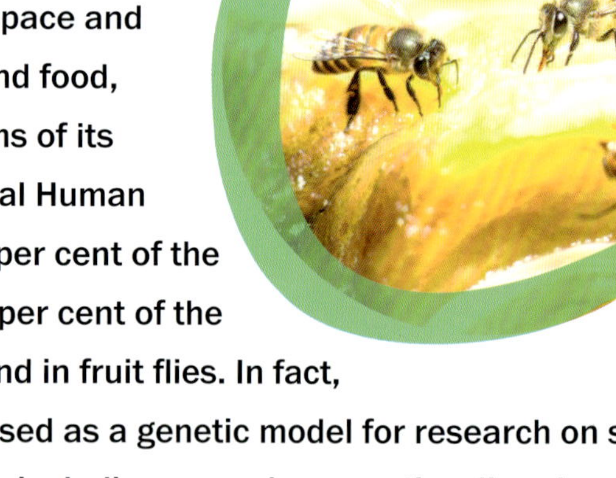

112 Mysteries of the Brain

The fruit fly is in reality quite tiny, but it has a highly complex and developed brain just like humans. Studies have been performed on the Drosophila brain that provide a great deal of information about how the human brain functions, even in an abnormal or diseased state. Neurons in Drosophila show molecular similarities to that of humans. Another reason would be because the fly brain consists of molecules that are related to those of humans, including the toxic proteins that accumulate in the brain causing certain neurodegenerative diseases. So as time goes by and science develops, better treatments for any issues with the human brain, we must not forget to thank the tiny little fruit fly for it!

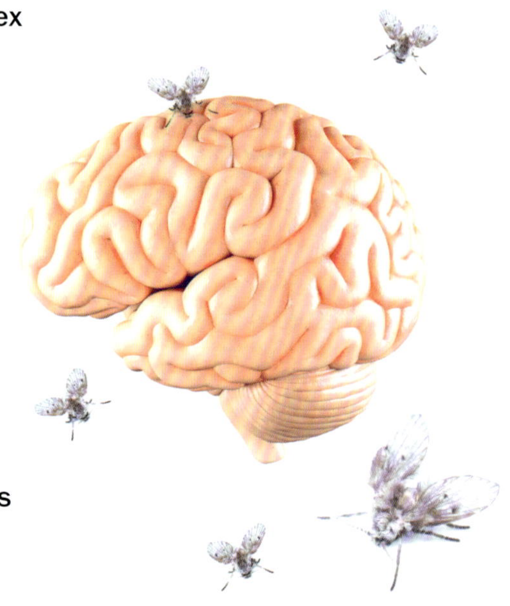

113 Ant Alarms and Trails

The sense of community displayed by ants is simply astounding. Did you know that pheromones have a huge role to play in this? Pheromones are chemicals that are released by an organism into the environment of its own species. These chemicals also affect the behavioural responses of other organisms. For example, when an ant is disturbed, it releases a pheromone that can be captured by other ants at several distances. Because of this, they get attracted by the chemical and begin to move towards the ant. They get alarmed by higher concentrations of pheromone. This causes them to run about the disturbed ant, so that they can resolve the disturbance. Isn't nature truly amazing?

Fun Fact

Ants are able to carry twenty times their own weight! Like seriously? Wow!

114 The Model Plant

Plants and flowers have extensive value in science and research. Let's look at an important one. Arabidopsis thaliana is a small flowering plant, belonging to the mustard family. It has several traits that make it very desirable for laboratory study. It has a rapid life cycle, short generation time, can be cultivated in very limited space requirements and is easily grown in a greenhouse chamber. It has a small, tractable genome that can be genetically manipulated more easily and rapidly than any other plant genome. Hence, mutations can easily be introduced, by irradiating the seeds of Arabidopsis thaliana or treating them with mutagens. The life cycle of these plants is about six weeks from germination to mature seed. It can produce up to 10,000 seeds per plant, thus making it easy to carry out genetic studies.

115 Photosynthetic Bacteria

Yes, certain kinds of bacteria can perform photosynthesis in unique ways. These bacteria are capable of converting light energy derived from the sun into chemical energy. Photosynthetic bacteria are unique bacteria that contain light absorbing pigments for the process of photosynthesis.

A classic example of photosynthetic bacteria is Cyanobacteria that contain chlorophyll. These bacteria are bluish green in colour. Other types of bacteria contain a pigment called bacteriochlorophyll, which is similar to chlorophyll but absorbs light of a longer wavelength as compared to chlorophyll. Bacteriochlorophyll-containing bacteria do not produce oxygen during the process of photosynthesis, i.e., they undergo what is called anoxygenic photosynthesis. In contrast, cyanobacteria perform oxygenic photosynthesis, that is, they release oxygen during the process of photosynthesis.

116 Sulphuric Bacteria

Sulphur and bacteria? Sounds like an odd combination, doesn't it? But the fact is that there exist certain types of bacteria, which you will now learn about, that have a close association with sulphur. Let's take a look.

A group of bacteria called purple bacteria have been extensively studied as they release sulphur particles outside their cells. These bacteria generally reside in stagnant water or hot sulphur springs. However, purple non-sulphur bacteria do not produce sulphur, since they can withstand only very small amounts of sulphur. They have also been found underwater near Indonesia. These bacteria can tolerate extreme conditions of heat. Another interesting class of bacteria is green and red filamentous anoxygenic phototrophs (FAPs). These bacteria use sulphur and its compounds during photosynthesis.

117 An Important Fungus

Fungi are not always bad. They have been widely used in the biotechnology industry for many purposes and have been widely researched.

Aspergillus niger also known as A. niger, is a filamentous fungi, which is being used today in biotechnology and waste treatment. The fungus most commonly grows on decaying vegetation, soil and plants. Genetic studies that were performed on this fungi reveal that it has about 13,000 genes. It is also a thermotolerant organism, which means it can tolerate or bear high amounts of heat and is capable of growing at high temperatures. The fungi can also tolerate freezing temperatures. A. niger is a very important microbe used in the field of biotechnology, as it is capable of producing citric acid, and enzymes such as amylases, lipases, cellulases and proteases. But it causes a disease called 'black mould' on certain fruits and vegetables such as grapes, apricots, onions and peanuts, and is a common contaminant of food.

118 Good Fungi

We all know that fungi's are generally divided into categories of good fungi and bad fungi. We will now learn a little more about Saccharomyces cerevisiae, considered to be a good type of fungi.

Saccharomyces cerevisiae has been widely used in the field of research and technology, majorly for alcohol fermentation in wine manufacturing. The fungi have been used for various cell cycle studies, gene analysis, different budding patterns, and biochemical analysis. It is a yellowish-green yeast that is most commonly found in areas where fermentation occurs. It is a very good 'model organism', as it has an extremely rapid growth rate. In normal yeast medium, it takes 90 minutes for the yeast population to double. It reproduces asexually on its own through the process of budding.

119 What is Microevolution?

They say, we humans were monkeys at one point of time. The science behind this finding is known as evolution. Evolution studies the changes that have occurred over years together, from one phase to the next. It studies the biological changes that have evolved in organisms through time. This evolution has occurred at various levels for different life forms.

Microevolution is defined as a change in gene frequency within a population of a species. For example, from one generation to the next, the frequency of a gene for pesticide resistance in a population of crop pests increases, over a short period of time. Since the time house sparrows were introduced to North America, they have evolved different traits in different geographical locations. Sparrow populations in the north are larger-bodied than those in the south. Larger-bodied birds can survive and adapt to lower temperatures more often than smaller-bodied birds can. Because of the cold weather in the north, larger-bodied birds adapt better.

120 Kiwis – Not a Fan of Evolution

A group of researchers from the Universities of Birmingham, Lincoln and Auckland, found that kiwi birds that are native to New Zealand, have very small eyes and their visual fields are the smallest among the nocturnal birds. The regions responsible for vision in the kiwi's brain were virtually non-existent. Hence the kiwi brain was considered unique among birds. However, the parts of the brain devoted to touch and smell are large. Kiwis hunt for prey in the night, in order to avoid other birds that come out in the day, to whom the kiwis were prey. Thus, as part of evolution, they preferred abandoning vision as a key sense. While most birds receive information through their eyes, kiwis receive the same through the tip of their beak and whiskers. Although they have developed wings, kiwis are flightless birds.

121 Birds Were Dinosaurs!

The first known Archaeopteryx was discovered in the early 1860s. Like any other bird it had feathers too, but unlike other birds, it also had teeth and a long bony tail. Though similar to the bones of birds, many of the bones in Archaeopteryx's hands, shoulder girdles, pelvis, and feet were distinct, and exhibited reptilian looks. Therefore, the Archaeopteryx was considered as a cross between birds and reptiles, which makes us wonder, which reptiles?

In the 1970s, palaeontologists noticed that the Archaeopteryx shared certain common features with small carnivorous dinosaurs called theropods. Due to these observations and progress and developments made in the field of evolution, theropods are now considered to be the ancestors of birds. Quite interesting!

122 Good Gibberellins

Gibberellins, also known as gibberellic acid (GA), are major plant hormones responsible for stem elongation, shoot growth and increased leaf growth. GA inhibits or breaks long periods of dormancy (under development). Examples are seed dormancy, dormancy of potato tubers and dormancy of certain parts of the shoot. GA also induces flowering of short-day plants like chrysanthemums. GA exerts its effects on cell growth as well. In many plants which are photo periodically sensitive, GA simulates light. In cold-requiring biennials (plants that take up to two years to grow), GA replicates the cooling of the seed during germination so that flowering is accelerated when it is planted.

123 The Acid Hormone

Abscisic acid (ABA) is often referred to as an inhibitory, rather than a hormone, as it is responsible for the closure of stomata, bud and seed dormancy and can inhibit the actions of other plant hormones like gibberellins. In order to conserve water during stress-related conditions of droughts, large amounts of ABA are produced in the leaves of plant, which causes the stomata to close. This decreases the rate of transpiration, and prevents excessive water loss from the leaves during times of low water availability.

Abscisic acid delays seed germination in many plants, as it induces and maintains dormancy. It inhibits shoot growth and cell division in the vascular cambium. However, it may or may not promote growth of roots. In response to environmental stimuli like cold, drought, salt and mechanical wounding, plants trigger the synthesis of ABA.

124 Plants Are Sensitive Too

Although plants do not have a nervous system like we humans do, they do react or respond to certain changes and factors in the external environment known as a stimulus. Hence they also show sensitivity. They do so by growing or moving specific parts toward or away from a stimulus. This movement is biologically known as tropism.

There are two types of stimulus. Positive stimulus is the movement or growth towards the stimulus. Negative stimulus is the growth or movement away from the stimulus. There are many types of tropism. Hydrotropism is the response and movement of roots towards water. Geotropism is the response and growth of roots towards the Earth or gravity in order to absorb the water and nutrients. Therefore, roots grow down towards the soil.

Phototropism is the response and growth of shoots towards light, more specifically sunlight. Haptotropism is the response to touch or contact, seen in venus fly trap. When an insect comes in contact with the sticky hair of the sundew plant, they curl around the insect as a part of the response. Lastly, photoperiodism is the response of the plants to the length of day or night. For example, long night plants produce flowers if the night is long, and short night plants do so if the nights are short.

Fun Fact

A hormone called florigen, produced in the leaves, sends a message to the relevant area in the plant to produce flowers.

125 Xenopus - The Frog

Haven't you often read about frogs in fairy tales? Of course, you have! But let us now take a look at frogs from the science point of view.

Xenopus, commonly known as the African clawed frog, is a valuable, model organism because it can produce eggs all the year round. The embryos are a good model system for studying vertebrate development and human disease as they show genetic similarity to humans. Frog eggs are large, transparent and produced in multitudes. Furthermore, Xenopus eggs and embryos can be subjected to extensive genetic manipulation. It is easy to inject a range of materials (e.g. nucleic acids, proteins, whole nuclei) into a complete embryo or into certain cells. Xenopus's eggs and embryos are an important source for biochemical studies, cell and molecular biology, developmental biology and physiology studies. The oocytes (immature egg cells that are still in the ovary) are widely used in the field of environmental toxicology. Hence, Xenopus is greatly used in biological research.

126 Those Compound Eyes

The eyes of insects and crustaceans (lobsters, crabs, crayfish, etc.) are very different from those of mammals. Arthropod eyes are called compound eyes. They are made up of repeating individual units, called ommatidia. Each separate unit functions as a separate visual receptor. It consists of a lens, a cone, visual cells and pigment cells. The visual cells are known to be light sensitive. The lens system refracts light onto a structure called rhabdom, which is a rod-like structure, surrounded by the light-responsive visual cells. After receiving information from all the ommatidia, the brain assembles a response in the form of a mosaic image, a sequence of light and dark dots. A compound eye is excellent at detecting motion and movement.

127 As Ancient as a Cockroach

Cockroaches have been on Earth for over 300 million years. They are considered one of the most notable and successful group of animals living on planet Earth. Nearly 3,500 species of cockroaches exist over the world. The most widely scattered, and found in urban areas, houses and other institutions, is the German cockroach. German cockroaches produce a larger number of eggs per capsule, and the time taken from hatching until the mature adult stage is very short. This results in a rapid population growth. The German cockroach has three developmental stages: egg, nymph and adult. The life span of the adult female varies from 20 to 30 weeks. Over 10,000 descendants can be generated in a year. German cockroaches are smaller than most other cockroaches hence they can hide in many places inaccessible to those of the larger species.

128 Nephridium

Waste is something that almost every living being releases from its body, be it a human being or a little worm. In certain organisms, such as the earthworm, metabolic nitrogenous wastes are excreted out of the body by special excretory organs called nephridium, a tubular, coiled structure. They are considered the waste collecting tubules. A connecting funnel-shaped structure called the nephrostome, opens into a coiled tube called the nephridial tube. The metabolic waste enters the nephridium through the nephrostome and passes into the nephridial tubule, where the useful substances are absorbed. The waste to be excreted out of the body passes through a small opening called the nephridiopore. The nephridia are found on the septa (the membrane that divides soft tissue in the body) and in the skin.

129 What Is Gemmation?

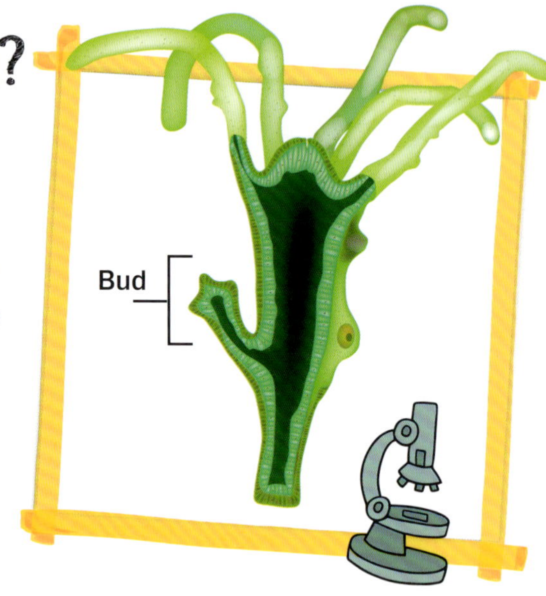

'Gemmation', which is a bodily function of the gemmae, involves the formation of an aggregation of cells, which grow out of the parent organism and develop into a new organism. Now that we have understood this, let us take a look at what a gemmae is.

Gemmae is a tiny, budlike mass that can separate on its own to form a new gemmae altogether; in other words, gemmation is a form of asexual reproduction which is also known as budding. It occurs in certain animals and plants like the hydra. The new organism then either separates itself from the parent, like corals do, or it may stay on as a self-contained autonomous organism. For example, in hydra, the bud forms and grows on the parent organisms, and then detaches itself.

130 The Gift of Regeneration

Regeneration is a miraculous way to replace or rejuvenate lost or hurt body parts. Many invertebrate animals such as sponges and hydra are capable of regeneration from a collection/aggregation of cells called totipotent stem cells. When a certain species of flatworms have their heads cut off, they are able to regenerate a new head.

Amphibians like newts and salamanders can also regenerate a missing tail. When the tail of a salamander is cut off, a sequence of re-growth events are followed by it. A layer of epidermal cells grows around the severed region, covering it. Underneath, a mass of cells, called the blastema develops. Muscle and cartilage and spinal cord also develop in the re-growing tail. A new, fully functional tail is formed after a few weeks, which marks the end of the process of regeneration. Echinoderms such as starfish can regenerate the entire body from just one arm and the central disk. Isn't that amazing?

131 The Ripening Hormone

As ripening begins to occur, some fruits produce ethylene gas. Apples and pears are classic examples of fruits that generate ethylene on ripening. The gas is also responsible for the changes in texture, softening and colour associated with the process. Fruits such as cherries and blueberries do not produce much ethylene, and it doesn't influence their ripening. The effects of ethylene extend to fruit ripening, loss of chlorophyll, abortion of plant parts, and stem shortening. Ethylene is an odourless hydrocarbon gas. It can be produced when plants are injured, either mechanically or by disease. It can also cause damage to crops, yellowing of vegetables and leaves and cause flowers to drop off (abscission). Post-harvest, ethylene gas is used commercially to ripen tomatoes, bananas and pears.

132 It's a Tough One

Yes, there are millions of bacteria in the world. They are of different types too. But one of them wins the award for the strongest of all. Deinococcus radiodurans was first discovered in 1956, in a can of ground meat. The can had to be irradiated with large doses, for the purpose of sterilisation to remove all the bacteria from the product. Since then, this species has been considered to be radiation resistant. Its name has been derived from Latin and it literally means, 'strange little berry that withstands radiation', owing to the fact that if looked at through a microscope, it has a berry-like shape.

It has been widely researched upon, and can tolerate radiation levels of up to 1,000 times, which could kill a normal human being. It can also survive intense conditions of drought and lack of nutrients. D. radiodurans is so powerful that it is even capable of breaking down solvents such as toluene, a colourless water insoluble chemical compound, which has a paint-like odour.

133 Viruses – Here They Come!

Every now and then, we hear of 'viruses' in the news. So, what are viruses really and where did they originate from? A virus is an organism that cannot reproduce autonomously. Viruses infect a host cell, to replicate and produce more viruses. Viruses can infect a wide range of organisms, including animals and plants.

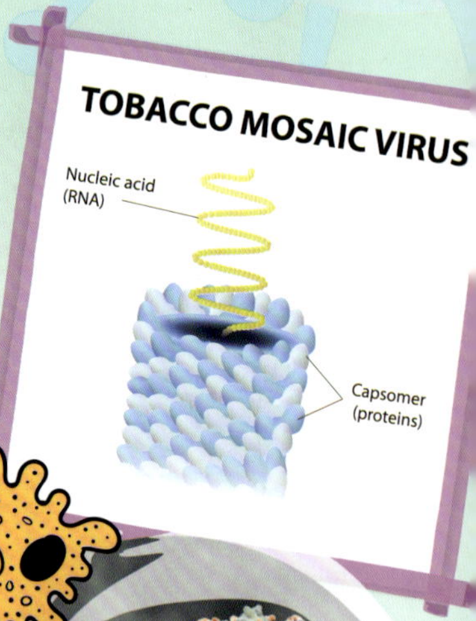

Fun Fact

SV40 also known as simian virus 40, was accidentally discovered in kidney cell cultures from wild monkeys and was used in the production of poliovirus vaccines.

Research on plant viruses paved a way and marked the beginning for some of the first experiments in molecular biology. In 1935, Wendell Stanley purified and partially crystallised Tobacco Mosaic Virus (TMV). As research progressed, other plant viruses were crystallised too. Thereafter, the characteristics of viruses were discovered.

134 A Cow's Stomach

The stomach of a cow has 4 chambers and is very different from the stomach we humans have. The rumen is the first and largest chamber, into which food passes un-chewed. The rumen contains bacteria, which can digest and ferment fibre, starch, cellulose, sugars and proteins to yield chemicals such as volatile fatty acids and proteins. Another important function of the rumen is the nutrient absorption of volatile fatty acids (VFAs) that are absorbed and serve as a major energy source. The partially digested food from the rumen then enters the second chamber, the reticulum. From the reticulum, it passes into the third and fourth chamber, the omasum and the abomasum respectively. Here the food contents are further processed.

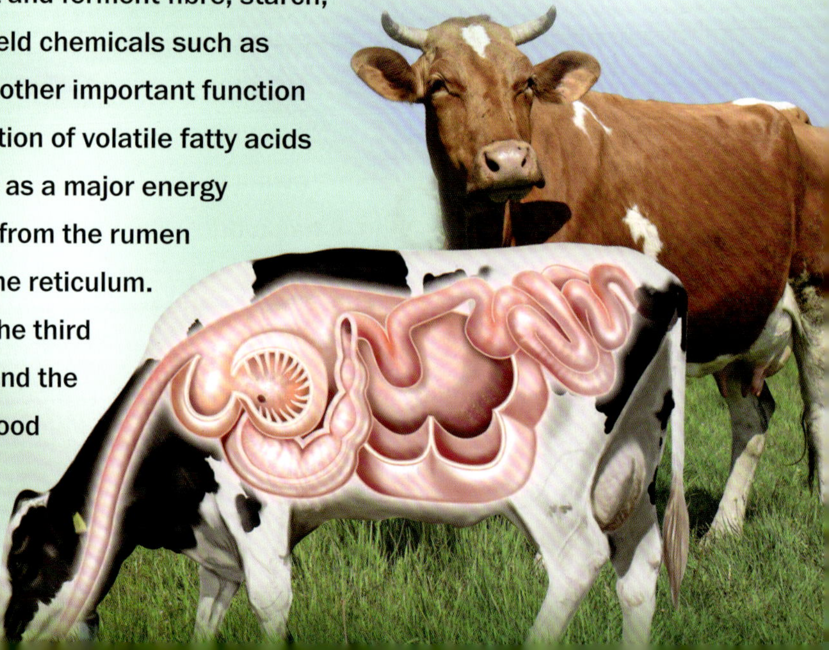

EARTH SCIENCES

Science can explain so many things about our planet. It has an explanation about how the continents were once together in a single super continent but are now separate. It can explain why strange things happen in the Bermuda Triangle and how creatures survive deep in the Mariana Trench. This section explains things about our planet and how humans have used science and technology to improve their lives by modifying geographical features.

135 Our Home

The name 'Earth' is derived from the English word 'eartha' and Anglo-Saxon word 'erda', which means ground or soil.

For a long period of time, astronomers believed that the Earth was the centre of the Universe as it was static and had other objects and bodies orbiting around it. This was proven otherwise in time to come, our planet has a very strong magnetic field due to the presence of nickel and iron in the Earth's core. And even though the Earth is around 150 million km away from the Sun, the radiation of the Sun is strong enough to reach it.

However, because of this powerful magnetic field, the Earth is protected from the harmful and harsh effects of the solar winds. The tides caused on the Earth are because of the gravity between Earth and the moon. The surface of our planet contains 70 per cent water. The remaining is landmass, that is, islands and continents.

Fun Fact

Earth is the only planet that has an atmosphere that contains 21 per cent oxygen.

136 The Big Five

What is the Earth's atmosphere made up of? The Earth's atmosphere is made up of five different layers.

The layer closest to the Earth is known as the troposphere. It contains air and oxygen. It is the layer that is responsible for weather conditions. The layer above it is called the stratosphere. This is where the ozone layer is present. The next layer is known as the mesosphere, which has low and cold temperatures. Then comes the thermosphere, which is again a cold, thin layer. This layer is considered to be outer space. The final layer of the atmosphere is known as the exosphere and it extends into outer space. This is the highest layer of all.

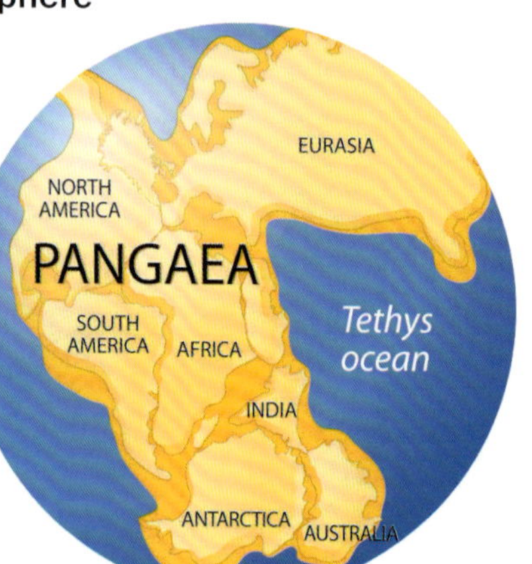

137 Pangaea the Great

Pangaea was a supercontinent that comprised all the landmasses on Earth, as one complete body. It was surrounded by an ocean called Panthalassa. Around 200 million years ago, during the Early Jurassic Period, the supercontinent began to break apart. This eventually gave rise to the modern continents and the Atlantic and Indian oceans.

The name 'Pangaea' is derived from the Greek word pangaea which literally means, 'all of the Earth'. The theory of plate tectonics states that Pangaea did not break apart all at once but rather fragmented in a series of events. Plate tectonics also claims that the continents came together and broke apart several times in the Earth's geological history.

138 As Time Goes By

Almost every New year's eve, we catch ourselves thinking, *How fast this year has gone by!* But, contrary to what we feel, science claims that each year, the days on Earth have only been getting longer.

Moon

Research has found that the Earth's rotation is slowing down with each passing day. Due to this, the days on Earth will increase by 1.8 millisecond every 100 years. That sounds strange, doesn't it? Well, as strange as it sounds, it is also true. Now you're thinking, *Why is the Earth's rotation slowing down?* It is because of a natural phenomenon called 'tidal braking'. According to this phenomenon, the tidal pull of the moon acts as a drag on our planet, slowing it down.

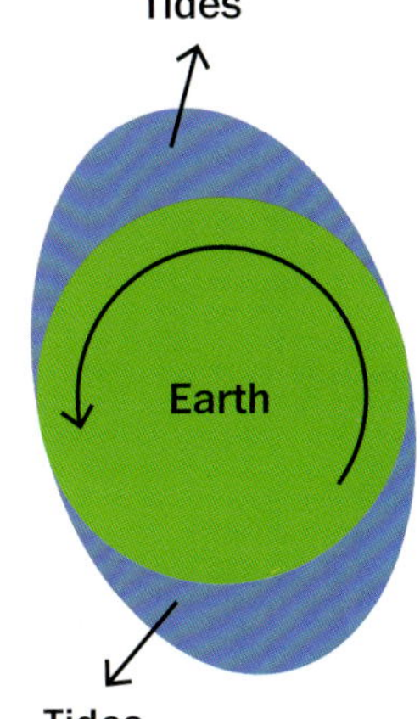

139 A Slow Spin

We are all aware that the Earth spins on its axis once every 24-hours. This is the reason why we experience day and night; the part of the Earth facing the Sun, experiences day and the part that faces away from the Sun, experiences night. In spite of these facts, why is it that we can never feel the Earth spinning?

The Earth spins at the rate of about 1,000 miles per hour and orbits around the Sun at a speed of about 67,000 miles per hour. We do not ever feel any of this movement, because these speeds are always constant, i.e., since man has known it, these speeds have never changed. Thus, if we don't know what it is like to move faster or slower, we do not feel any acceleration or deceleration. It's not just the Earth that spins, but we spin along with it too. It's like you being on an airplane. You don't feel the plane move since you are moving with it. But should you be stationary while only the plane moved, you would certainly feel the movement. This is exactly the case with the Earth and us. Isn't nature an interesting piece of creation? Never fails to intrigue us!

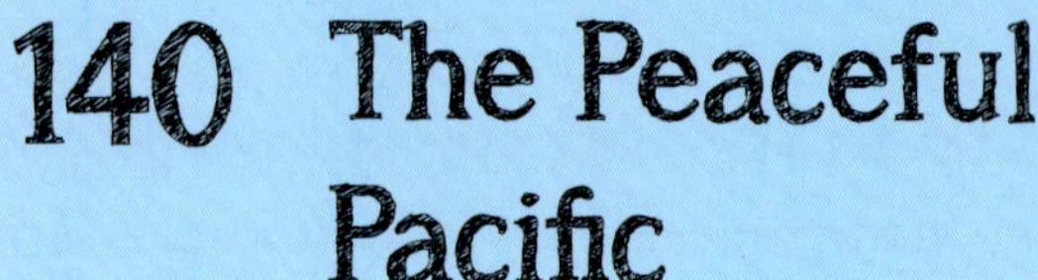

140 The Peaceful Pacific

The Pacific Ocean is the Earth's largest and deepest ocean basin. It is also considered to be the largest water mass on the planet. It extends for more than 30 per cent of the 71 per cent of the Earth's surface that is covered with water. With a surface area of more than 60 million square miles, it contains nearly twice as much water as the Atlantic Ocean. The Pacific Ocean has a depth of approximately 13,000 feet. Hence it has also come to be known as the Earth's deepest water body. The name 'Pacific' was given to this ocean by explorer Ferdinand Magellan, in 1520. Pacific means peaceful. And due to the calmness of its waters, the ocean earned this name.

141 Spicy Islands

The Spice Islands are the small group of islands to the north-east of Indonesia, between Celebes and New Guinea. They are also called the Maluku Islands. They were the largest producers of many different spices in the world, such as mace, nutmeg, cloves, and pepper. This abundance of spice production called for the wide trade of spices over the world. In the 1520s, the Portuguese started buying spices from the Spice Islands. Hence, they had good control over the trade.

It wasn't for another 80 years that the Dutch and English ships reached the islands. Other than spices, the vegetation found on the Spice Islands includes rainforests, sago, and rice. Some of these islands have mountains and even show the presence of active volcanoes. But there is some amazing beauty to look for on these islands.

142 Great Barrier Reef

Considered to be one of the seven natural wonders of the world, the Great Barrier Reef is the largest living structure in the world. So large, that it beats even the Great Wall of China in its length and is the only living thing on our planet that is visible from space.

Located in Queensland, Australia, the reef consists of 2,900 separate reefs and about 900 islands. It is also considered to be the largest coral reef system in the world. The reef spans around 2,600 km in length. Corals are marine animals that are found in abundance in the reef. More than 400 different kinds of corals have been recognised on the reef. These corals form calcium carbonate which gives them their hard shell-like structure.

Apart from these beautiful corals, the reef is also home to a diverse and unique number of species of living organisms and life forms. 30 species of whales, dolphins, and porpoises have been identified in the Great Barrier Reef. More than 1,500 species of fish, 330 species of ascidians and 17 species of sea snakes reside in the reef. 215 bird species (including 22 species of seabirds and 32 species of shorebirds) visit the islands. The reef is also a breeding ground for six rare species of sea turtles and humpback whales.

Owing to its vast natural life and its stunning beauty, the reef is very popular and is a sought after tourist destination in the world.

143 The Galapagos Islands

The Galapagos Islands, located in the Pacific Ocean, is an archipelago of exotic islands. And we say 'exotic', not just because of the stunning views and blue oceans it has to offer, but also because the kind of life the islands are home to, is simply mind-blowing. Situated at a distance of 1,000 km from the coast of Ecuador, certain volcanic activity has played a role in its formation.

In spite of this, it is home to one of the richest marine reserves in the world. It houses unique species of plant and wildlife. The islands are diverse and unusual with respect to the land and marine species found here. Some of them include corals, sharks, penguins (the most northerly species of penguin in the world), whale sharks, rays, cetaceans, giant tortoises, marine iguanas, land iguanas, etc.

Plant life consists of different species of giant daisy trees, huge cacti, endemic trees, and about 500 vascular plant species. A number of unique birds like mockingbirds (different species of them) and finches also reside on these islands. The area has 127 islands, islets and rocks, with 19 major large islands. The islands are surrounded by the Galapagos Marine Reserve, created in 1986. It extends over a vast area of 133,000 square km. Hence, along with so much life on it and its inland waters, the islands are considered to be not just a hot spot for travel and nature lovers, but also one of the largest thriving marine ecosystems in the world.

Fun Fact

The Galápagos Islands have the highest abundance of sharks known in the world.

144 A New Continent

While most of us are aware of the seven-existing continents of Africa, Asia, Antarctica, Australia, Europe, North America, and South America, there is something new that has come up in the list of continents.

According to a latest geological study, the Earth also has an eighth continent, which has always been there, but was never discovered. Researchers behind this theory have come to the conclusion that New Zealand and New Caledonia aren't part of an island chain. The two of these are instead, a part of one single continent known as Zealandia. This continent span over 1.89 million square miles, i.e., it is larger than Madagascar, New Guinea, Greenland, or other microcontinents and provinces. We can't wait to officially welcome this new continent!

145 Mid-ocean Ridge

The longest mountain range on Earth is the mid-ocean ridge. It spans 40,389 miles around the globe. 90 per cent of the mid-ocean ridge is under the ocean. It is formed by the movement of the Earth's tectonic plates. When the plates move apart, gaps are created. Magma rises and fills these gaps. As a result, mountains and valleys form along the sea and a new ocean floor is created. The mid-ocean ridge consists of thousands of volcanoes that erupt periodically. Not only is it considered the longest, but also, the only unbroken mountain chain in the world, running through the middle of the Atlantic Ocean. The wonders of nature never cease to amaze us!

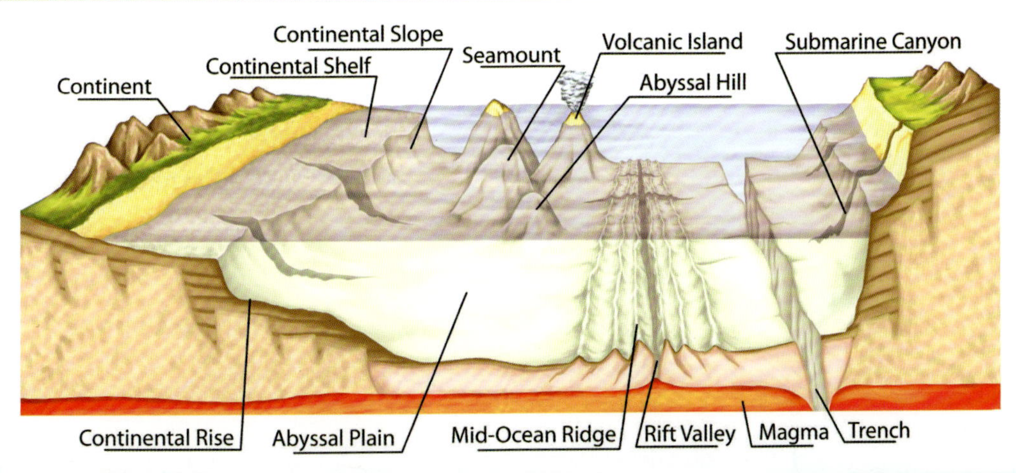

146 Mysterious Triangle

What if you went somewhere never to return? Sounds spooky, doesn't it? Well, that is how strange the Bermuda Triangle can also be!

One of the most mysterious places on Earth, the Bermuda triangle, which is located in the Atlantic Ocean, between Bermuda, Puerto Rico and Florida, is one place where the maximum number of disappearances have occurred. A large number of ships, boats and airplanes have been known to go missing while travelling on or over the Bermuda Triangle. So what is the great mystery behind this triangle?

Different people have different theories for these disappearances. Some people associate them with paranormal activities. However, research indicates that bad weather is one of the main causes of these strange incidents. Some famous incidents to have occurred in the Bermuda Triangle were the USS Cyclops and its crew of 309 that went missing in 1918. In 1958, a Douglas DC-3 aircraft containing 32 people, disappeared, while in 1955, a yacht was found, but its entire crew was missing. The explanation for these disappearances includes a number of reasons such as pirates, hurricanes, rough weather, huge waves, human error and sinking.

147 The Mariana Trench

The Mariana Trench located in the Pacific Ocean just east of the 14 Mariana Islands near Japan, forms one of the deepest parts of the Earth's oceans. It is also identified as the deepest spot on Earth.

The deepest region of the Mariana Trench is called the Challenger Deep or the Abyssal Zone. It is extremely cold and has a high amount of pressure. The floor consists of hot water vents (created by the spreading of tectonic plates), where the temperatures can rise to 300° Celsius.

This trench is home to thousands of invertebrates and fish, such as the Anglerfish, that use bioluminescence (light) to attract its prey. Apart from the Anglerfish, the trench is also home to a particular species known as the 'vent crab' that is especially found in hydrothermal vents.

Arrays of bacteria that can withstand extremely high temperatures also reside near the vents. These organisms consume hydrogen sulphide released from the vents of the Mariana trench. These deep sea creatures are considered to have a lifespan of over one hundred years. So, even though the temperatures are quite sweltering down in the trench, that doesn't stop some gorgeous aquatic life from flourishing there.

And while many climbers have successfully scaled Mount Everest, which is the highest point on Earth, only two people have descended into the Mariana Trench so far! Well, we don't blame them for not trying, considering the depth.

Fun Fact

In 1960, a 'deep boat', called the Bathyscaphe Trieste, was the first ever vessel to reach the bottom of the Challenger Deep.

148 Deadly Lakes

There are some deadly lakes found around the Earth. One of them is Lake Nyos, found in Cameroon. It is an active crater lake that was formed by an eruption about five centuries ago. Like Lake Nyos, lakes Monoun and Kivu also contain large amounts of carbon dioxide dissolved at a depth. As these lakes rest above extinct volcanoes, the magma chambers present below the lake bed are still active and continue to release carbon dioxide. The carbon dioxide that rises up, dissolves into the groundwater and is transferred to the lake. When the dissolved gases reach higher concentrations, the carbon dioxide could result in explosions. In August 1986, the Lake Nyos Disaster caused 1,700 deaths, while the Lake Monoun Disaster was responsible for 37 deaths. The gas killed all life forms within a 15-mile radius of the lake.

149 A Sea Named 'Dead'

Floating in the Dead Sea is a task that even a non-swimmer could achieve without much struggle! The Dead Sea, known as the salt sea has been recognised as one of the saltiest water bodies on Earth. Owing to this environment, no fish, birds or plants can survive the high salinity conditions.

Salinity increases as we go deeper and the water becomes so concentrated with salt that there is a salt build up on the seafloor. Salt builds up and accumulates into rocky ridges, peaks and towers along the shore. People with skin diseases like psoriasis, visit this place to find relief in the mineral-rich water and soothing mud.

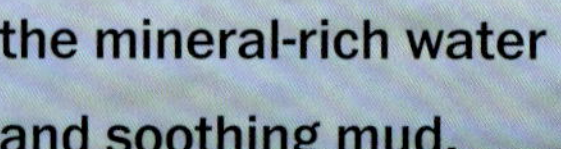

150 A Dam on the Nile

The Nile is the longest river on Earth. Around 5000 years ago, the ancient Egyptian civilisation flourished on the banks of the Nile. Today, the Nile provides water, food and transportation to a large population of Egypt residing near it. Every year the river would flood and deposit fertile black silt on its river banks. This nutrient-rich soil would be used to grow crops. However, the construction of the Aswan High Dam in 1970 put an end to this annual flooding.

The dam controls the flow of the Nile and stores its waters in a reservoir called Lake Nasser. The dam is used to generate electricity, irrigate fields and provide drinking water. The reservoir is used to breed fish. However, one of the unintended negative consequences of the dam's use is a decline in fertility of soil. This is because the nutrient-rich silt brought by the river is held back in the reservoir and doesn't reach the fields.

151 Amazon Rainforest: Carbon Sink to Source

The Amazon rainforest is the largest rainforest in the world that extends across nine countries. During photosynthesis, trees use carbon dioxide, sunlight and water for their growth. They store carbon in their trunks and branches. Owing to climate changes, the Amazon suffered terrible droughts in 2005, 2010 and 2015.

Scientists have found that a single drought hampers the rainforest's ability to absorb carbon for years even when the rains return, turning it from a carbon sink to a source. They found that from the drought year 2005 to 2008 the Amazon basin lost an average of 270 million metric tons of carbon per year. Trees start dying under continued drought and tall trees, which store more carbon dioxide, die first as they need more water, which has to be pumped to greater heights. The decomposing trees release the stored carbon into the atmosphere. The rainforest makes 50 per cent of its rainfall itself through transpiration and evaporation. However, loss of leaves and dying trees diminish rainfall thus extending the drought.

152 A Waterfall that Defies Gravity

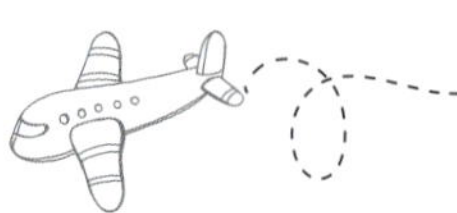

The highest waterfall in the world, Angel Falls also called 'El Salto Angel', is located in Canaima National Park on the Churún River in Venezuela. The waterfall drops from a flat-topped plateau called Auyán-Tepuí from a height of 979 metres. Angel Falls is 19 times the height of Niagara Falls. Often, its water doesn't reach the bottom. This is because the fall is so steep and long that the air pressure exceeds the water pressure of the waterfall. So, the water changes to mist before reaching the bottom. The mist can be felt a mile away. The waterfall was discovered by a US pilot Jimmie Angel in 1935, who was flying over the area in search of gold. It was named after him.

153 Oxygen-filled Lake Baikal

The world's deepest (1,632 mt), oldest and largest freshwater lake by volume (23,013 km^3), Lake Baikal, extends 400 miles through the southeastern part of Siberia. Formed 25–30 million years ago, Lake Baikal is unique because unlike other deep-water lakes, its waters are rich in oxygen even near the floor of the lake with more than 80 per cent relative saturation of dissolved oxygen.

Oxygen is added to lake water when aquatic plants release oxygen as a by-product of photosynthesis and when oxygen from the atmosphere diffuses through the surface water. Living organisms in a lake use the dissolved oxygen to breathe. It is also used up during decomposition of dead plants and animals at the bottom of the lake. But Lake Baikal is the only lake to have such high concentration of dissolved oxygen even near the lake bed.

154 Amundsen's Quest for the North Magnetic Pole

Norwegian explorer Roald Amundsen became the first to sail through the Northwest Passage (1903-06) while searching for the North Magnetic Pole (NMP). During his expeditions he collected scientific data in fields such as meteorology, oceanography, botany, zoology, terrestrial magnetism, palaeontology. To find the location of the (NMP), he studied terrestrial magnetism. Building a magnetometer laboratory and an astronomical observatory at King William Island, he took meteorological observations and measurements of the earth's magnetic field for two years. He calculated the exact location of the NMP and found it had moved since its previous calculation in 1831. He proved that the NMP keeps moving.

155 The First Ascent of Mt. Everest Without Supplemental Oxygen

Reinhold Messner and Peter Habeler, were the first to summit Mount Everest without any supplemental oxygen. As we ascend in height the oxygen supply lessens. This affects our breathing and can sometimes prove to be fatal without a supplementary supply to aid us. Now, isn't that fantastic? Their very first attempt was on 21 April 1978. This was not successful, as Habeler got extremely ill from food poisoning at base camp. Although Messner attempted the summit himself, he was unable to complete it as he could not withstand the extreme weather conditions. Messner and Habeler made a second attempt which turned out to be successful on 8 May 1978.

156 World's Largest Observatory

Mauna Kea (White Mountain) is a dormant volcano in Hawaii. It is the world's tallest mountain, as it is over 9,750 metres tall as compared to Mount Everest which measures 8,850 metres. It is also Hawaii's tallest volcano, and has an altitude of 4,205 metres. The base of Mauna Kea is about 6,000 metres below sea level, and the summit is about 4,000 metres above sea level, so the summit rises above 40 per cent of the Earth's atmosphere.

The summit of Mauna Kea is home to the world's largest astronomical observatory and 13 telescopes used by astronomers from 11 countries. The University of Hawaii operates the observatory, which was constructed in 1964 after American astronomer Gerard Kuiper's suggestion.

Mauna Kea is an ideal location for astronomical observations. This is because the atmosphere above it is extremely dry, which is an essential for measuring infrared and submillimeter radiation from heavenly bodies. This is because water vapour in the atmosphere can block infrared radiation. Further, due to its high altitude the atmosphere remains cloudless and free from pollutants thus offering clear skies for observations. Since, it is quite far from city lights, a darker sky enables observation of faraway dimly-visible galaxies.

Fun Fact

Mauna Kea last erupted about 4,500 years ago and is the only Hawaiian volcano that was covered by glaciers during the Ice Age.

157 Longest Cave Is Home to Rich Biodiversity

Most caves are generally products of natural occurrences and the Mammoth Cave National Park, in Kentucky is no different. Considered to be the longest cave system in the world, these natural caves and underground passageways, are a result of limestone formations. It is home to a rich variety of flora, fauna and also a number of endangered species that include mammals, gastropods, birds, crustaceans, fish, insects, mussels, plants and reptiles. The cave system comprises stalagmites and stalactites, a beautiful array of stunning gypsum flowers, delicate gypsum needles and other natural features. Apart from these, the caves house a vast variety of sulphate minerals. UNESCO recognised it as a World Heritage Site in 1981.

158 Speleology

The scientific study and exploration of caves is called speleology. The deepest cave in the world Krubera in Georgia is more than 2,000 metres deep. The cave is named after the Russian geologist Alexander Kruber. It is a kaist, which means that it is formed from the dissolution of soluble rock. First explored by French speleologists in 1956, over the years many brave divers, such as Ukrainian caver Alexander Klimchouk and diver Gennadiv Samokhin, have undertaken expeditions inside the cave and tried to go deeper to find its potential depth. Cavers and speleologists use dye traces to mark where they have been and to measure the depth of the cave.

159 Stalactites and Stalagmites

Stalactites and stalagmites are different types of geographical rock formations typically found in caves, created by the precipitation of minerals from water.

These unusually shaped structures, which are formed by calcite, derive their names from the Greek words, 'stalagma' and 'stalaktos' which means 'dripping'. The major difference between the two of them is that stalactites hang from the ceiling, much like icicles, while, stalagmites, grow from the floor. In spite of their differences, stalagmites and stalactites are generally found in pairs. The world's longest stalactite is in Lebanon, in the White Chamber of the Jeita Grotto and stands at a length of 27 feet, while the world's longest stalagmite stands at an astonishing height of 204 feet in the cave of Cueva Martin Inferno, Cuba.

160 Mount Augustus

Mount Augustus, in Australia, is an inselberg or island mountain, which means the only mountain lying on a plain. The rock is 8 km long and spans an area of 4,795 hectares within Mount Augustus National Park. About one-third of the rock is said to be visible, the remaining lies below the surface. It is an 'asymmetrical anticline'. An anticline means that the layers of rock have formed an arch-like structure with the oldest layer at the centre. 'Asymmetrical' means that all the sides of the arch are uneven. The rocks on Mount Augustus are composed of sand and gravel that was brought by a prehistoric, south-east flowing river system that existed about 1600 million years ago. The river deposits compressed, and formed sandstone and conglomerate, and then buried it beneath marine deposits.

161 Most Destructive Earthquake

On 22 May 1960, an earthquake rocked areas near Valdivia, in southern Chile. It had a magnitude of 9.5 on the Richter scale and was the world's largest earthquake. It was preceded by four foreshocks above magnitude of 7. It is often called the 'Great Chilean Earthquake'. Scientists say that the earthquake moved the Earth's axis and reduced the length of a day by 1.26 microseconds.

The quake occurred beneath the Pacific Ocean off the coast of Chile. It caused great damage and destruction to buildings and settlements, leaving 2,000,000 people homeless. It caused subsidence or sinking of the ground that led to flooding. The earthquake also shifted the shorelines of the affected areas.

A series of tsunamis generated in the Pacific Ocean by the earthquake inundated areas as far as Hawaii, Alaska, Philippines and Honshu island in Japan. In fact, it was the tsunamis that caused greater damage than the earthquake itself. Near Hilo, Hawaii, 61 people were killed because of the waves. Twenty-two hours after the quake, waves up to 18 feet high hit the island of Honshu, Japan.

Fun Fact

The Valdivian Earthquake was a megathrust earthquake that is, it occurred at a subduction zone (place where one tectonic plate moves under another).

162 Yellowstone: Ideal Site for Scientific Research

The Yellowstone National Park lies in the states of Wyoming, Montana, and Idaho in the United States. It is famous for its rich biodiversity of flora and fauna and geothermal features like geysers, hot springs, fumaroles, and mud pots.

Home to many ecosystems, it is one of the last well preserved areas where human activity has not hampered natural processes. It also has archaeological records of human activity dating back to 11,000 years before. Therefore, scientists regularly conduct research in the park.

In a year, 150–200 scientific researchers are allowed to use study sites in the park. The earliest written accounts of the wildlife and geothermal features of the park by settlers, trappers, Indian scouts in letters and journals in the 1860s-70s inspired the first government scientific expedition led by geologist Ferdinand Hayden in 1871-78.

Today, the park issues research permits to scientists for studies and collections after a formal process of research review. The researchers need to submit an annual report about the progress of their study. Publications of the conducted research can be found in the park's library.

An example of successful research is when in 1966, the researcher Dr Thomas Brock discovered *Thermus aquaticus* in a Yellowstone hot spring. An enzyme found in the microorganism was later used to quickly reproduce DNA.

Fun Fact

Yellowstone has about 1,000 to 3,000 earthquakes every year.

163 Measuring Electricity Over an Active Volcano

Often lightning occurs in the ash plumes of volcanoes, when ash particles rub against each other and generate static electricity. Wanting to study how electrical charge builds up in plumes that contain no ash, scientists released balloon-borne instruments to measure electricity over Stromboli, one of the most active volcanoes on Earth, whose plumes comprise only gases and no ash. It doesn't produce lightning but its plumes are electrified. Situated on the island of Stromboli, Italy, it has been constantly erupting since 1932 and erupts every 20 minutes. The scientists found that radon, the radioactive odourless gas, which is spewed out during eruptions releases charged "daughter" elements upon decaying. These elements decay and in turn generate charged particles, thus electrifying the plume.

164 A Volcano that Changed the Weather

The largest and deadliest volcanic eruption occurred on 10 April 1815, when the Indonesian volcano Mount Tambora blew up. The eruption released 150 cubic km of ash, pumice and around 60 megatons of sulphur into the atmosphere, which dimmed the sunlight and reduced global temperatures by about 3°C. Ash rained for weeks in the surrounding areas, destroying houses and contaminating fresh water bodies. The death toll was round 90,000. The next year saw unseasonably cold weather such as snow and frost during June-to-September in eastern US and western Europe which destroyed crops leading to famine and rising prices. Scientists speculate that the Tambora eruption was one of the factors responsible for this cold climate.

165 The Ring of Fire

The Ring of Fire is a 40,000 kilometre area along the Pacific Ocean where active volcanoes and regular earthquakes occur. This is because the boundaries of several tectonic plates are found in this region, such as the Indian-Australian, Nazca, Cocos, Pacific, Philippine, Juan de Fuca and North American Plates.

The boundaries of most of the plates overlap and are pushed down under the other plate, thus creating subduction zones. This movement causes earthquakes. When rocks are subducted they melt and form magma, thus resulting in volcanic activity.

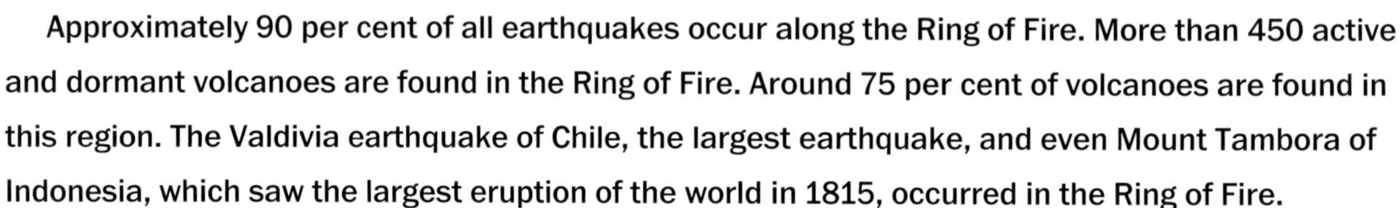

Approximately 90 per cent of all earthquakes occur along the Ring of Fire. More than 450 active and dormant volcanoes are found in the Ring of Fire. Around 75 per cent of volcanoes are found in this region. The Valdivia earthquake of Chile, the largest earthquake, and even Mount Tambora of Indonesia, which saw the largest eruption of the world in 1815, occurred in the Ring of Fire.

166 Mystery of the Sailing Stones

The Death Valley National Park in US is amongst the hottest places on Earth but is also home to the mysterious 'sailing stones' in Racetrack Playa, a dried up lake bed. Scientists were puzzled how stones weighing upto 300 kg would move across the dry lake bed on their own while leaving tracks behind in the mud. The mystery was solved in 2014 when scientists used weather stations to monitor wind speeds and attached motion-activated GPS units to stones. They found that a combination of ice, water and wind was responsible. During winter, a pond would form after rainfall with the stones partially submerged. It would freeze at night and start melting the next day by afternoon leaving floating sheets of broken ice, which surround the stones. Winds would push the sheets which would, in turn, propel the stones forward.

167 Fire Resistant Trees

Hyperion, a coast redwood tree, is the world's tallest tree. With a height of 379.1 feet, the 600-year-old tree was discovered in the Redwood National Park, California, in August 2006, by Chris Atkins and Michael Taylor.

Coast redwoods, found in the states of California and Oregon in the US, are able to grow so tall because of several factors: the favourable moderate climate with temperatures ranging from 8°C to 16°C, abundant rainfall, nutrient-rich soil, regular fogs in the area during summer which reduce transpiration and evaporation and allow the leaf pores (stomata) to remain open longer to take in carbon dioxide for photosynthesis and thus enable growth, and high content of tannin in the bark which is insect-and-fire resistant.

168 Pollinator or Pollen Thief?

The size of bees determines how much pollen they deposit on flowers and thus help in seed and fruit production. So, to properly pollinate flowers, bees should be the right size in relation to the flower. The better the bee fits the flower and is able to touch the male and female sexual organs of the flower, the more pollen it is able to transfer and is an effective pollinator, scientists have found. When a bee is smaller than the flower, it acts like a pollen thief, taking a lot of pollen from the flower but depositing very little on other flowers. Often pollen thieves visit fewer flowers and use the pollen (a source of protein) to feed their larvae.

169 Global Warming: A Man-made Phenomenon

In recent years, the entire planet has been heating up and the main reason for this is the previously predicted global warming. So what is global warming?

Global warming is a phenomena where there is an increase in temperature on Earth, as a result of what is known as the 'greenhouse effect'. Greenhouse gases like carbon dioxide are emitted from burning fuels. Rise in the levels of carbon dioxide, water vapour, methane, etc., are responsible for the rise in temperature. This is because these gases tend to trap the heat in the atmosphere and warm up the planet. And it is none other than man-made activities that are responsible for this phenomenon.

One of the major contributors to the greenhouse effect is deforestation. Since trees take in large amounts of carbon dioxide and purify the air, the more we cut down trees, the more carbon dioxide tends to remain in the atmosphere.

170 The Hottest Place on Earth

Global warming is becoming a reality. This is clearly evident by the temperatures recorded in 2004, 2005, 2006, 2007, and 2009, where the highest surface temperature recorded on Earth was found in the Lut Desert in Iran.

The Lut desert is one of the hottest spots on Earth and during the year 2005 had the highest overall temperature of 70.7°C (159.3°F). Temperatures at El Azizia in Libya have also been constanthy rising in the summer. The highest temperature on Earth was recorded at Death Valley was 93.9°C (201.0°F).

171 Water that Kills Life

The Atacama Desert, Chile is the driest place on Earth, with an average of less than 0.01 cm of rain per year. It can go without rainfall for years. The Atacama is considered to have conditions similar to Mars. Its harsh weather conditions don't support animal or plant life except for some species of algae, lichen, bacteria and fungi. These microbes live under the desert's surface and seem to go in a state of inactivity for several years till it rains again in the desert. However, unexpectedly the Atacama witnessed two rainstorms in 2015 and one in 2017, which resulted in lagoons forming in the desert. But scientists were surprised that instead of resulting in a burst of life, the deluge had destroyed most of the microbial communities living in the soil. Scientists took samples from the three lagoons and found that most of the microbial species had been killed. This is because the ability of these microbes to store water, which helps them to survive during the dry periods, led to their downfall as they couldn't switch off this mechanism at the molecular level during a surplus of water. Consequently, they continued to accumulate water until their membranes exploded from inner pressure. This puts a question mark on the presence of life on Mars, which is believed to have had water a billion years ago.

Fun Fact

The remains of mummies, estimated to be about 800 years old, were found in the Atacama Desert.

172 An Expanding Desert

The Sahara Desert, the world's largest desert, has been growing by about 10 per cent since 1920, a scientific study found in 2018. The research involved studying changes in the desert's boundaries over the last century and implies that other deserts could also be getting bigger. Deserts usually receive average annual rainfall of less than 4 inches of rain per year. The researchers studied rainfall data records of Africa from 1920 to 2013. They observed that during the 93-year period the Sahara expanded the most during the summer, with almost a 16 per cent rise in the desert's average seasonal area. The scientists suggest that global warming and climate change due to human activity and natural climate cycles are causing the desert's expansion.

173 A Toxic Plant that Can Kill

The yew tree is considered to be one of the most toxic plants found on Earth. As the tree grows, it builds up harmful substances or toxins, which accumulate within the plant, making it dangerous. The Yew tree is poisonous and is capable of killing a number of animals.

Yew poisoning causes cardiac (heart) diseases. The oil of yew, found in the sap, causes intestinal problems. Death occurs 1-3 hours after consumption of the plant. Animals such as cattle die 1-2 days post ingestion of the plant. The Yew tree belongs to the Taxus baccata species. Some of the most common varieties include European Yew, Japanese Yew, American Yew. The chemical composition of the plant has a large number of naturally occurring substances, namely, flavonoids, esters, and taxines, which are the toxins responsible for the deaths.

174 Honey Fungus

Although it sounds like the name of a little girl, this plant is far from that.

Armillaria, also known as the 'honey fungus', is a huge fungus, and recent studies based on findings have shown that it can span up to 2,200 acres. It is considered to be parasitic on trees, mainly the wood of conifers and is a harmful forest pathogen. It is responsible for causing 'white rot' root disease in forests. But how is it that this fungus has the ability to grow acres and acres wide? That is because it grows and spreads underground, in the soil, completely out of sight. And, it is only once in a while, during the fall season that this fungus lets its golden coloured honey mushrooms sprout on the surface of the Earth.

175 Corpse Flower

The Earth is filled with some fascinating species of animals and plants, some that can even make us want to run miles away from them. We're talking about the Corpse Flower.

Also known as the stinky plant, the corpse flower is one of the world's largest and rarest flowers. As it blooms it gives out a strong pungent odour, which smells like decaying meat or a dead body. Matching its name, the flower is green on the outside and a deep hue of red on the inside that gives it the appearance of rotting meat. The flower blooms for a very short time. Studies reveal, the reason for these unique features is mainly to attract pollinators such as dung beetles, flesh flies, and other carnivorous insects, as they feed on dead flesh.

The temperatures of these flowers could even reach as much as 98°F. The plant is chemically composed of many substances which are responsible for the stench. Also known as titan arum, the plant can grow to a height of 10-15 feet, and the leaves are 13 feet wide. The scientific name of the corpse flower is *Amorphophallus titanum*.

It has been studied that corpse flowers can take as long as seven years to bloom. Some bloom once in a few decades. It was first discovered in Sumatra in 1878 by an Italian botanist Odoardo Beccari. The plant grows only in the equatorial rainforests of Sumatra, Indonesia. The tallest bloom of a corpse flower that measured a little more than 10 feet was cultivated in Gilford, New Hampshire. It bloomed on 18 June 2010.

Fun Fact

The Corpse Flower was featured in *Dennis the Menace* – the movie.

176 Moon Trees

To the moon and back is what really happened in the case of these trees! In 1971, Apollo 14 astronaut, Stuart Roosa took some seeds to orbit around the moon and on his return to Earth, germinated and planted the seeds at different places in the USA. The trees are called Moon trees.

Five different types of trees were chosen, namely, redwoods, loblolly pines, sycamores, Douglas firs and sweetgums. Many of these Moon trees can be seen growing at national landmarks, such as the Washingtion Square in Philadelphia. 'Half-moon' trees are second-generation trees or by-products that are planted from seeds or cuttings from an original Moon Tree and are thriving well.

So, where did this idea of Moon trees come from? Roosa formerly worked with the US Forest Service, and when he was selected to go into space, Astronaut Stuart Roosa as his way of paying tribute to the Forest Service, packed the seeds into his space kitty upon the request of the chief of the Forest Service.

177 The Smallest Bats

Also known as the bumblebee bat, the Kitti's hog-nosed bat is considered to be the smallest of all the species of bats in the world and also one of the smallest mammals on Earth. It derives its name from the little snout it possesses. These little creatures are bestowed with very strong claws and legs. In order to sense the environment, they use echolocation (the use of sound waves and echoes to navigate) to find food in the dark. Discovered in the early 1970s, these bats are found along the southeast part of Burma and in the western areas of Thailand.

They are generally found in colonies at an average of 100 bats per cave. They reside in areas such as limestone caves and bamboo forests. Their diet consists mainly of flies and spiders. Their predators include birds, snakes, squirrels, and cats. The bat weighs approximately 2 grams and measures 29 to 33 mm in length.

178 Easter Island Stone Masons

Easter Island, also called Rapa Nui, lies in the Pacific Ocean, near Chile. It is famous for its mysterious Moai or gigantic stone statues of disproportionately large heads. They were built by the Rapa Nui people between AD 1250 and 1500. In 2018, archaeologists analysed the chemical composition of stone tools discovered during excavations on the island. They wanted to know from where the basalt used to make these tools was sourced. An instrument called mass spectrometer checked the amount of various chemical elements in pieces of the stone tools, which indicate their geology. They found most of the tools were sourced from the same quarry on the island. Since most of the stone-carvers were using one type of stone, this indicates they worked together and had high levels of cooperation to build so many statues.

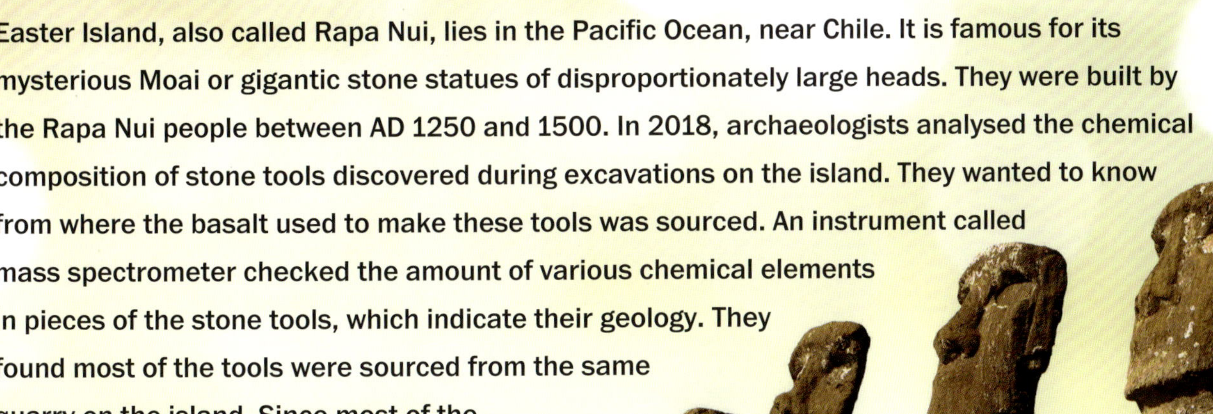

179 The Desert Beetle

The darkling beetle found in the Namib desert in Africa has a unique way of drinking water. The Namib desert receives less than 1.3cm of rainfall every year but it does experience fog around six times in a month. When the fog rolls in from the Atlantic ocean, the desert beetle raises its back at a 45 degree angle to harvest water from fog! This behaviour is called fog basking. Its dark shell is covered with several bumps which are made of hydrophilic (attracting water) substances and the valleys between the bumps are made of waxy, hydrophobic (water-repellant) material. The fog condenses into tiny water droplets of few microns in diameter on the bumps and when a large enough water droplet has formed it rolls through the valleys between the bumps towards the beetle's mouth. Scientists have studied this mechanism of the darkling beetle and tried to create fog-harvesting materials or surfaces that mimic the desert beetle's exoskeleton in order to help drought-prone areas. NBD Nano is a startup that has been developing a self-filling water bottle inspired by the desert beetle's behaviour. Its prototype had reached proof-of-concept stage. Taking inspiration from the beetle's mechanism, researchers from Virginia Tech also developed a surface pattern to prevent frost formation, which can damage equipment such as wind turbines and aeroplane wings. Their anti-frost technology was successful at a small scale during lab tests.

Fun Fact

The red sand dunes of the Namib desert get their colour from the layer of iron oxide that covers the sand.

SPACE

Made up of some of the most mysterious phenomena, space is a vacuum zone that is about 100 kms above planet Earth. And here no air, light or sound exists. While space is generally perceived to be empty, it is far from that. As a matter of fact, it is made up of some of the most interesting phenomena known to man.

180 The Red Planet

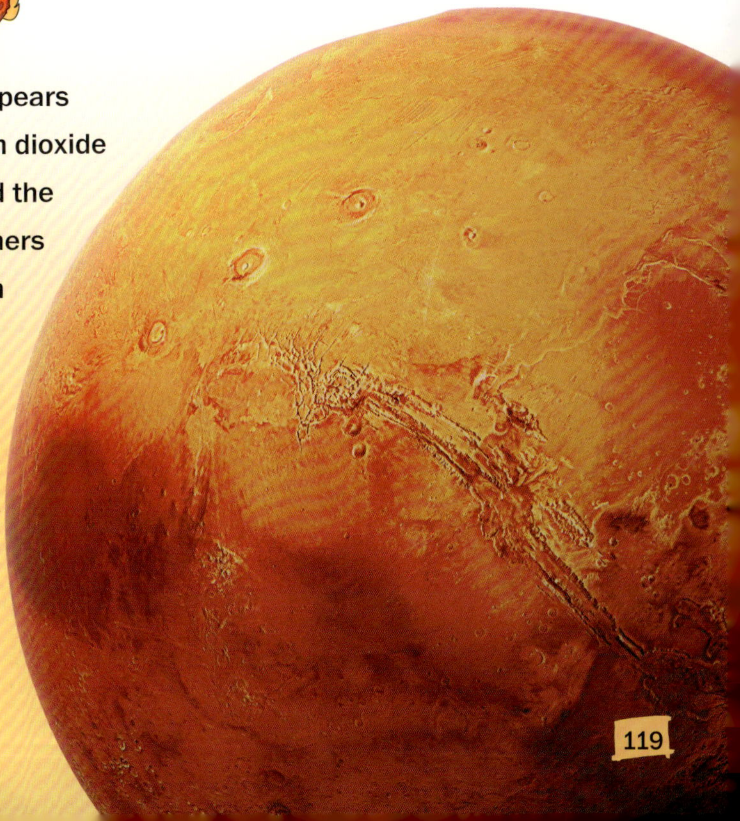

Mars, named after the Roman God of War, appears reddish and contains large amounts of carbon dioxide in its atmosphere. It is a terrestrial planet and the fourth planet from the Sun. Chinese astronomers considered it 'the fire star', while the Egyptian priests named it Her Desher, or 'the red one'. The red colour of Mars is due to the iron-rich rock and dust covering its surface. The planet is surrounded by extensive dust storms, which last for months together. Water in the form of ice is also present on the planet. Mars has two moons, Phobos and Deimos.

181 Gas Giant

Jupiter is known as a gas giant as it is a planet composed of gases. It is the fourth brightest object in the solar system and has 67 moons, the largest being Ganymede, Calisto, Lo and Europa. The moons are sometimes called Jovian satellites. It is one of the five visible planets from Earth. It has the shortest day of all the planets as it rotates once every 9 hours and 55 minutes. Jupiter's atmosphere shows the presence of cloud belts and zones, composed of ammonia crystals, sulphur, and mixtures of the two compounds.

The atmosphere on Jupiter comprises 90 percent of hydrogen gas. Below the atmosphere, there are layers of compressed hydrogen gas, liquid metallic hydrogen, and a core of ice, rock, and metals. Jupiter has three rings, which are made up of dust particles. Its atmosphere contains small amounts of gases, such as ammonia, methane and water as well.

182 Pluto and Charon

Pluto's largest moon called Charon was discovered in 1978, by astronomer James Christy. It has a mass that is one-eighth of Pluto. The planet was named after the Greek mythological figure, Charon. The surface of the moon is surrounded by ethane and nitrogen ice, and small quantities of water ice. It is believed that the majority of the mass on this planet is ice, although it may have a rocky core. Observations made by the Gemini Observatory in Hawaii, suggest that the moon could have ice-volcanoes or ice-particle geysers. The surface of Charon has thousands of kilometres of cliffs and troughs. Also found are canyons seven to nine kilometres deep. There is a noteworthy theory about the creation of this moon. According to the theories, Charon is supposed to be formed as a result of a collision between an object neighbouring the Kuiper Belt and Pluto. Due to the destruction caused, debris was released into the orbit around Pluto, which eventually led to the formation of Charon.

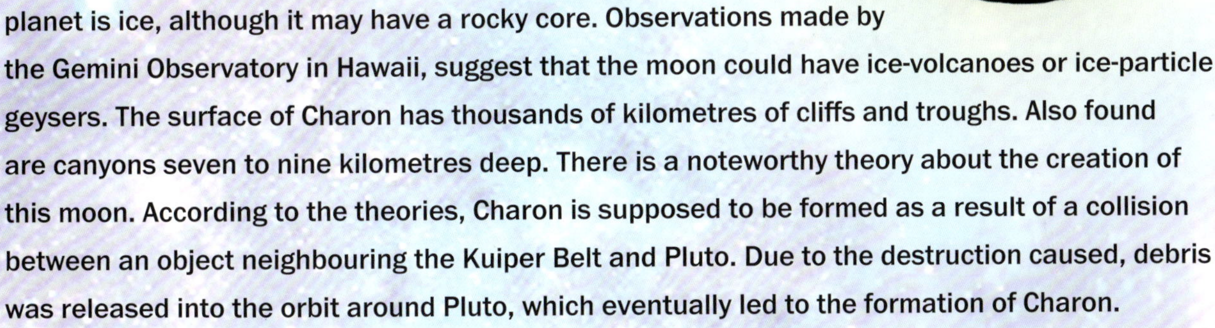

183 The Titan

The second largest moon in our solar system, Titan, could have been considered a planet since it is larger than Mercury. It is the largest moon belonging to Saturn, having a thick, heavy and hazy atmosphere. One of the major gases found here is nitrogen, accompanied by clouds of methane and ethane and a thick organic smog. It was discovered in 1655, by Dutch astronomer Christiaan Huygens. Titan is primarily composed of ice spread over a rocky core. The surface of this moon contains liquid hydrocarbon lakes and the vents of cryovolcanoes (a kind of volcano that releases substances like methane, ammonia and water, instead of molten rock).

184 The Red Dwarf

Red dwarf stars are small in size but have a long lifespan. Since they are much smaller than the sun, they are low in mass, and burn very slowly. In fact, some red dwarfs live for trillions of years. They do not have high temperatures like other stars. Also, red dwarf stars are not as bright or luminous as the other stars we see. These stars cannot be easily seen with the naked eye. They make up the largest population of stars in the galaxy, and experience temperatures of 3,500 °C. A famous example of a red dwarf star is the Proxima Centauri, which is also the star closest to the sun.

185 Alpha Centauri

Alpha Centauri is the star system that is closest to the sun and consists of 3 stars, namely Alpha Centauri A, Alpha Centauri B, and Proxima Centauri, at a distance of 4.2 light years away. Alpha Centauri A is the third brightest star, at a distance of 4,300 light years away. The star 'Yellow Alpha Centauri A' is a little bigger. Being close to Earth it appears bright in the night sky. The surface temperature at Alpha Centauri is a little less than that of the sun. However, it has a larger diameter as compared to the sun and is luminous. The orange coloured Alpha Centauri B, is one of the smaller stars in the system. It also has a lower temperature than the sun and does not shine as brightly. Although we see Alpha Centauri as a single bright star, it is actually a multiple system, considered to be a double or triple star. It is located in the constellation of Centaurus, also known as 'The Centaur'.

186 Magnetic Mercury

Mercury, apart from Venus, is the only planet in the solar system that does not have a moon. Let us learn a little more about this planet.

Mercury, named after the messenger of the Roman Gods, is the smallest and the closest planet to the sun. The very thin surface of the planet is covered with impact craters or holes, created by rocks falling from space. As the rocks come towards Mercury at a fast rate, they hit the planet, leading to the formation of holes. As a result, the planet is heavily cratered. It has a density higher than the moon, hence it is considered the second most dense body in the solar system. The interior of the planet has a rich iron core, and the outer shell is a relatively thin layer (mantle and the crust) mainly composed of silicates. Other light elements such as sulphur have also been found in the core. It has been proposed that these light elements prevent it from becoming fully solid. Hence Mercury does not have a majorly solid core but mostly a molten core, since the iron in the core changes from a liquid to a solid state. This is responsible for Mercury's powerful magnetic field. Some interesting features have been observed on the planet, the largest being the Carlos basin which spans a large diameter. Due to past volcanic activity, regions of heavy craters and smooth plains have been found on the surface of the planet. Extreme changes in temperature are also a characteristic trait of Mercury's environment.

187 The Largest Moon

Ganymede is not only the largest moon in the solar system, but is also Jupiter's largest moon. In fact, it is bigger than Mercury. It was discovered in 1610, by the renowned astronomer Galileo Galilei. The moon derives its name from the Greek son of a King who was carried to the sky by the God Zeus. Ganymede is the only moon in the solar system known to have a magnetosphere. This means that there is a certain component inside the moon which is able to produce and maintain a strong magnetic field. Below the liquid iron and nickel core of the moon, is a subsurface ocean. It is this core which is known to be responsible for the generation of the magnetic field. The surface of Ganymede is considered to be icy. Two types of landscapes cover the surface of Ganymede, the lighter regions and the darker, cratered regions, which have clay and organic material.

188 The Ocean Moon

Did you know Enceladus, which is one of Saturn's most well-known moons resembles the ocean? It was discovered by William Herschel, in 1789. The moon has a cold icy crust below which is an underground ocean and hydrothermal vents and plumes releasing water vapour, ice particles, organic compounds, volatile gases, carbon dioxide, carbon monoxide, salts, and silica. These eruptions generate huge amounts of fine ice dust around Enceladus. It reflects almost 100 per cent of the sunlight that falls on it, because of which the surface temperatures go as low as 201°C, making it extremely cold. Enceladus, which is Saturn's sixth largest moon, is also characterised by craters.

189 Andromeda Galaxy

Also known as Messier 31 (M31), the Andromeda Galaxy is the galaxy that is closest to the Milky Way. It is considered to be the brightest of all the galaxies. It is a spiral galaxy that is about 2.3 million light years away from Earth. Its name has been derived from the mythological princess Andromeda. The Andromeda Galaxy is recorded to have as many as one trillion stars, and it was created nearly 10 billion years ago because of the collision and merger of smaller protogalaxies.

190 Kuiper's Belt

The Kuiper Belt, also known as the Edgeworth-Kuiper Belt, is the outer region or area of the solar system. It is home to small objects of the solar system, which are generally made up of ice, i.e., frozen gases such as methane, ammonia, nitrogen, and water. It also has certain dwarf planets like Pluto, Haumea, and Makemake. The Belt is named after the astronomers Gerard Kuiper and Kenneth Edgeworth. The largest objects recognised in the Kuiper Belt are known as Trans-Neptunian objects. These are Pluto, Quaoar, Makemake, Haumea, Ixion, and Varuna.

191 Largest Star

Our universe is home not just to billions of stars shining in the night sky, but also billions of galaxies. However, the largest star recorded till date is UY Scuti in the Milky Way. Not only is it the largest star, but it is a supergiant luminous star. It is located in the Galactic Centre (centre of our galaxy), close to the Black hole Sagittarius A*. UY Scuti is a red pulsating variable star. Although it is 30 times the mass of the sun, it has a radius 1,700 times the sun's radius. UY Scuti is nearly eight astronomical units (AU) across, that's eight times the distance between Earth and Sun and it is 9,500 light years away.

192 A Black Hole

A black hole is among the most interesting things found in the universe. It is an area containing matter that has collapsed in such a way that large quantities of mass become concentrated in an extremely small region. The gravitational pull in black holes is enormous and overpowering. Although black holes do not have a surface, they may be surrounded by layers of material. These layers orbit like discs around the black holes and become very hot. Black holes exist in many sizes. Stellar-mass black holes are a little larger in size than the sun. They are formed when a star which is about 10 times heavier than the Sun, ends its life in a supernova explosion. What remains of the star are solar masses. These collapse into an area only a few kilometres across. Just like other galaxies, the Milky Way galaxy has massive black holes at its core.

193 From a Mill to Space

Hailing from a tiny village in Russia, Valentina Tereshkova worked in a textile mill as a young girl. However, with all the interest she showed in jumping parachutes back then, it was no surprise that Tereshkova, became the first woman to fly into space in 1963. She was selected for erstwhile USSR's space program that sent her aboard Vostok 6 into space. When Tereshkova married astronaut Andrian Nikolayev, and had her first child, 'Elena', their baby caught the attention of the medical world, since doctor's thought that the exposure of both parents to space might have an effect of some kind on their offspring.

194 Callisto – The Moon

Although it may sound like the name of a little boy Callisto is one of the many moons of the planet Jupiter, more precisely, the second largest. Discovered by Galileo Galilei, its size is almost similar to that of Mercury. The surface of Callisto contains a large number of elements including water ice, carbon dioxide ice, silicate dust and rock particles, and hydrocarbon compounds. Hence it is considered to be semi-icy and semi-rocky. The surface of the moon has a large number of heavy craters. It has a thin atmosphere mostly containing carbon dioxide. The moon has an outer rigid layer and interior ocean made up of water plus salts and ammonia. The most striking feature on Callisto is an impact basin called Valhalla that extends beyond 1800 km and was formed around two to four billion years ago. The missions to have studied and explored this moon are Pioneer, Voyager, Galileo, Cassini and New Horizons missions.

195 A Unique Moon

An exotic moon that is visible only from the European region, is called Europa. Discovered in 1610 by Galileo Galilei, Europa was a moon that was named after the daughter of a king in Greek mythology. Europa is Jupiter's smallest moon, the same size as Earth's Moon. It is also said to be the sixth largest moon of the 181 moons in the solar system. The moon has large amounts of water. It has also been found to have a magnetic field. The smooth surface of the moon shows some bright and dark markings, along with a few craters. The largest crater is called Pwyll. Other features observed include features called, 'freckles'. These are created as the water melts and is released due to the moons warm interior. Under its cracked surface, Europa has a water ocean, which covers a small rocky core. Traces of clay-rich minerals have also been found here. Planetary scientists consider Europa's ocean to be salty. Scientists think that life could exist on this moon, because of its particular characteristics. Images of Europa have been obtained and recorded by the Voyager and Galileo space crafts. Two missions, a NASA mission called Europa Clipper, and an ESA mission called Jupiter Icy Moon Explorer (JUICE), are yet to visit the moon in the near future.

Fun Fact

The radiation from Europa is so strong that it can kill a human being in just one day.

196 Ceres – The Dwarf Planet

Although the name Ceres takes after the Roman Goddess of Agriculture, we are neither speaking of agriculture here, nor of goddesses. What we are speaking of is a small planet with a diameter of only 950 km and the first object to have been identified in the asteroid belt between Mars and Jupiter. Although initially it was considered the largest asteroid in the solar system, it now comes in the league of the dwarf planets like Pluto, Eris and Makemake, and it is the smallest among all of them. It occupies approximately one-third of the mass in the asteroid belt. The planet was discovered by Italian astronomer Giuseppe Piazzi in early 1801. Images taken by the Hubble Spacecraft and photos by the spacecraft, Dawn, show the presence of a unique white spot on Ceres. Dawn was the first to visit Ceres in 2015. Ceres does not have moons. According to observations recorded by the Herschel Space Telescope, the presence of water vapour was seen on Ceres. Jets of water vapour are seen streaming out from the planet's surface. They may be formed as the icy surface of the planet warms and water is converted from solid to vapour. This indicates that Ceres has an atmosphere that contains an icy surface. Evidence shows the presence of good amounts of ice under the surface of the planet.

Fun Fact

Ceres loses 6 kg of its mass in steam each second.

197 Aqua Satellite

A satellite by the name of Aqua that orbits the Earth was launched in May 2002, to study the earth's physical processes in relation to the water cycle. It is considered to be a multinational satellite that studies various phenomena on Earth, such as precipitation, evaporation, and cycling of water. It is the second in the series of EOS (Earth Observing System) after Terra Satellite. It has six instruments to study water on Earth's surface and in Earth's atmosphere. A few of its studies among many include measuring cloud properties as well as aerosol properties (a mixture of fine solid particles and liquid droplets in air). Other areas of study include the measurement of land and sea surface temperatures on the Earth, ocean evaporation, atmospheric water vapour, clouds, terrestrial snow, land ice, sea ice, and soil moisture.

198 Hey Pluto!

Pluto is known to be the largest dwarf planet, discovered on 18 February 1930 by the Lowell Observatory. However, in August 2019, Pluto being a planet was again the point of discussion. Its name has been derived from the Greek God of the Underworld. Pluto has five known moons, namely, Charon, Hydra, Nix, Kerberos and Styx. The planet contains large amounts of water; one-third of it is water and the remaining two-thirds is rock. The surface of the planet contains ice. As Pluto approaches the Sun, the ice present on the surface thaws and forms a thin atmosphere, made up of nitrogen, which slowly leaves the planet. As Pluto moves away from the Sun, the atmosphere freezes and returns to its solid state.

199 Terra Satellite

Named after the Latin word for Earth, Terra Satellite is the first in the 'series of EOS' (Earth Observing System), followed by Aqua and Aura. Its remote sensors study the environment of Earth and the current ongoing climatic changes. Remote sensors collect and obtain information, mainly from satellites and aircraft. They do so by measuring the amount of energy that is reflected from Earth. It has helped scientists to study the spread of pollution around the globe, particularly pollution caused by harmful gases such as carbon monoxide as well as aerosols.

200 Sputnik

The first artificial satellite to be launched by the erstwhile Soviet Union on 4 October 1957, was Sputnik 1. It was just about the size of a beach ball, weighed only 83.6 kg and was pressurised with nitrogen. Sputnik took barely about 98 minutes to orbit Earth. The sphere of the satellite had antennae that looked like whiskers and were responsible for generating data and information with regards to the density of the upper atmosphere. The Soviets then launched Sputnik 2 on November 3, in the same year. The events directly led to the formation of National Aeronautics and Space Administration (NASA) as of 1 October 1958. The launch of Sputnik 1 marked the beginning of the space age and race.

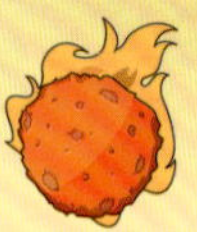

201 Martian Moons

Mars has 2 moons that are called Deimos and Phobos.

Deimos is the smaller of the two moons. The surface of the moon consists of dusty and rocky materials. Deimos does not have an atmosphere. As the moon does not contain any gases, it cannot create an atmosphere, and the low gravity on the moon will be unable to maintain it. This moon has certain features which make it identical to an asteroid. The moon has a smooth surface marked with the presence of a few craters, Swift and Voltaire being the largest. The larger moon, called Phobos, contains heavy craters. Much like Deimos, Phobos also shares characteristics that are similar to asteroids. The surfaces of the two moons are covered with a layer of dust called regolith. A project called Phobos and Deimos and Mars Environment (PADME), is scheduled to be launched to Mars in 2021.

202 Forever on the Moon

When astronauts visit the moon, they leave back their marks forever. As long as the moon lasts, the footprints astronauts have left on it, will last. In other words, forever.

Unlike Earth, there is no atmosphere on the moon thus there is no erosion by wind or water. In fact, all the water on the surface of the moon is frozen. Also, there is no volcanic activity on the moon to change the lunar surface features. Due to these reasons, once astronauts visit the moon, they leave their mark there forever!

203 A Mystery Named Nibiru

Theories of a new planet called Nibiru are flying all over the place. Also known as the 'shadow planet' or 'planet X', Nibiru is considered to be a humongous planet with a vast orbit. In fact, Nibiru is considered to be about nine times the size of Earth and is somewhere near the edge of our solar system. A number of theorists also claim that very soon Nibiru shall pass very close to Earth, and its strong gravitational pull could trigger earthquakes and other catastrophic events, ten times stronger than what they currently are, thus causing havoc to life on Earth. In fact, there was a point in time when Nibiru was expected to collide with planet Earth in the year 2012.

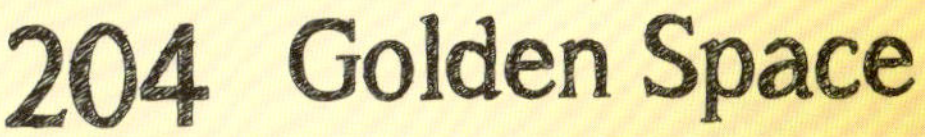

204 Golden Space

It is believed that around 4 billion years ago, a meteor bombardment brought 20 billion tons of a gold-rich space rock to our planet Earth. Tracing gold's origin even further takes us into deep space. A 2013 study proposed that the collisions of dead stars known as neutron stars, gave birth to the majority of the gold in the universe.

According to the American Museum of Natural History (AMNH), the gold mined from Earth, is a result of hot fluids flowing through gold-bearing rock. Further on, as the liquid flows, the rock picks up and collects gold, concentrating it in the fractures between rocks.

205 The Heaviest Star

R136a1 is the heaviest star, and is a part of a rare set of stars called Wolf - Rayat stars. It has a mass that is 265 times the Sun's mass. It is located in the Tarantula Nebula in the Large Magellanic Cloud, (a galaxy orbiting the Milky Way) and is at a distance of around 160,000 light-years away from Earth. Its surface temperature rises as high as 100,000 degrees °F. It is considered to be the most luminous star, around 8 to 10 million times brighter than the Sun. It is suggested that the star is capable of causing or creating a powerful explosion that may lead to a black hole being formed. It is believed that this star has been burning for 4.57 billion years, and gives off a large amount of energy.

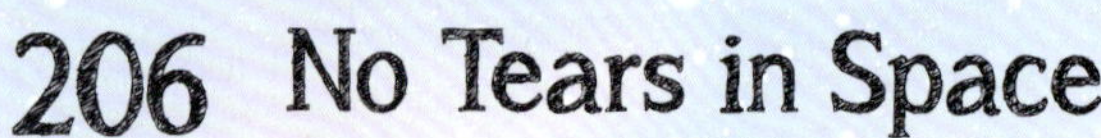

206 No Tears in Space

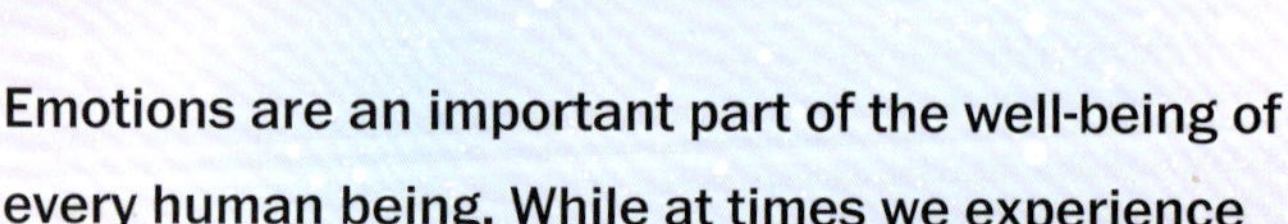

Emotions are an important part of the well-being of every human being. While at times we experience happy emotions, at other times, our emotions can be sad and make us cry. Astronauts are no different. In fact, being in space so often, they miss family and are bound to get teary-eyed more often. But if astronauts do cry when in space, the one thing they can be assured is that the tears will not fall off their eyes! Since there is no gravity in space, tears stay in the eyes of the astronaut crying. If he is really sad and keeps on shedding more tears, it will form a big liquid ball and stay right there, in his eyes!

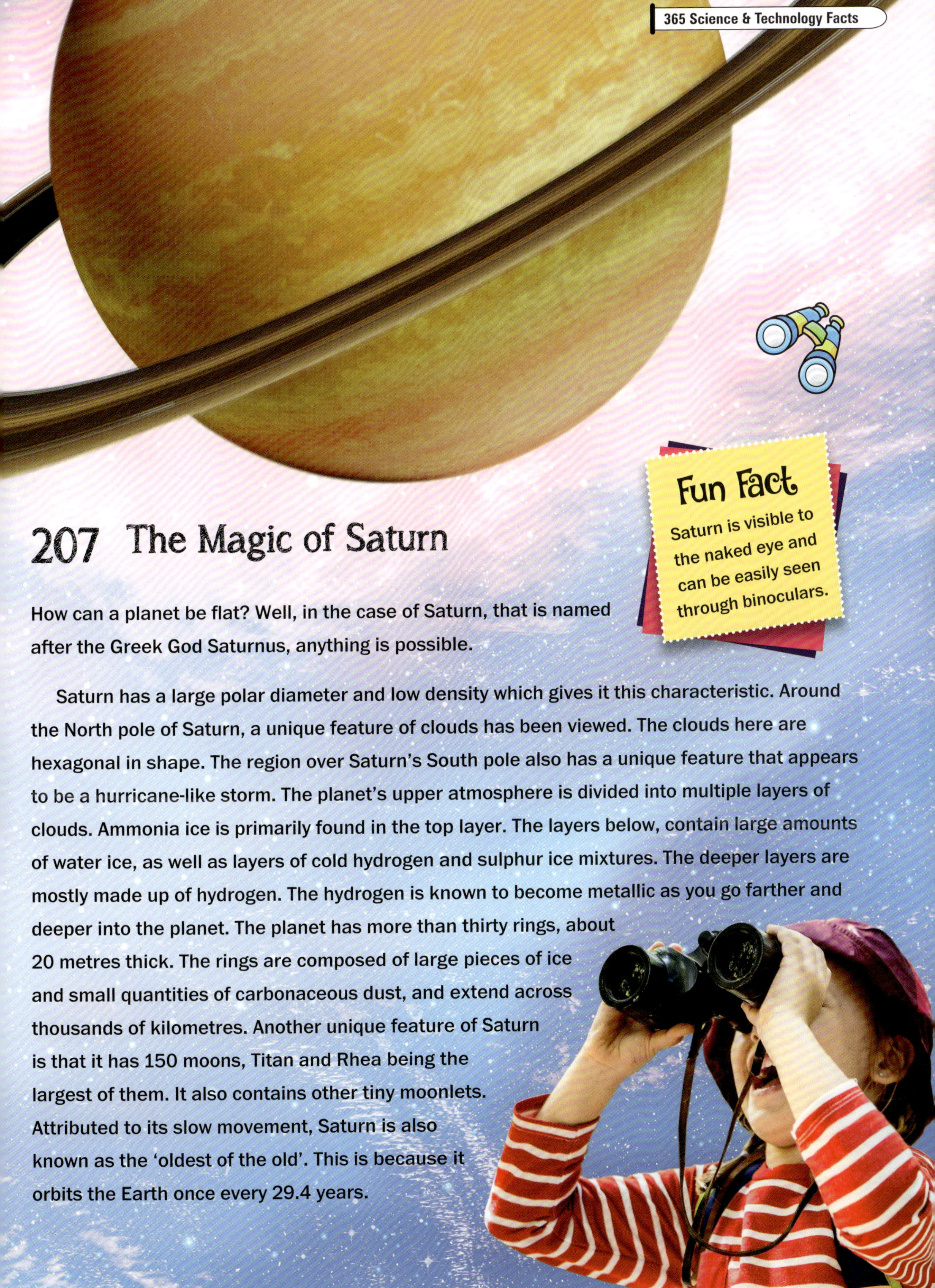

207 The Magic of Saturn

How can a planet be flat? Well, in the case of Saturn, that is named after the Greek God Saturnus, anything is possible.

Saturn has a large polar diameter and low density which gives it this characteristic. Around the North pole of Saturn, a unique feature of clouds has been viewed. The clouds here are hexagonal in shape. The region over Saturn's South pole also has a unique feature that appears to be a hurricane-like storm. The planet's upper atmosphere is divided into multiple layers of clouds. Ammonia ice is primarily found in the top layer. The layers below, contain large amounts of water ice, as well as layers of cold hydrogen and sulphur ice mixtures. The deeper layers are mostly made up of hydrogen. The hydrogen is known to become metallic as you go farther and deeper into the planet. The planet has more than thirty rings, about 20 metres thick. The rings are composed of large pieces of ice and small quantities of carbonaceous dust, and extend across thousands of kilometres. Another unique feature of Saturn is that it has 150 moons, Titan and Rhea being the largest of them. It also contains other tiny moonlets. Attributed to its slow movement, Saturn is also known as the 'oldest of the old'. This is because it orbits the Earth once every 29.4 years.

208 A Fireball

If you are among a lucky few you could get to witness a phenomenon as rare as a fireball!

Chunks of metallic matter from outer space frequently enter our atmosphere. These metallic chunks that travel at lightning fast speeds, tend to burn up due to friction with the air. And this combustion, leads to some beautiful displays of light. These are known as meteoroids. However, there is another kind of meteoroid that burns so bright, that it feels like something you have never seen before or will never see again. It is almost surreal. This brightly burning ball meteoroid is known as a fireball. Bolides are a type of fireball that explode in mid-air and sound like thunder, sending pieces of meteoroids onto the Earth.

209 Kepler

Kepler is one of the major space crafts or space observatories of NASA. It was launched to discover exoplanets, which are Earth-sized planets that orbit around other stars, in or near habitable zones (areas that can support life). These zones are called Goldilocks's planets. Found deep in space, they are considered to be Earth's twins. A Goldilocks zone is a range that is neither too hot nor too cold. The main aim was to determine the size and shape of the orbits of these planets. Kepler also studied the properties of the stars that have planetary systems. In May 2016, NASA confirmed the discovery of 1284 new planets or exoplanets. The 3 types of exoplanets that have now been classified are gas giants, hot-super-Earths in short period orbits, and ice giants. Thanks to Kepler, we are now aware of so much more!

210 Nebula

Nebula is the Latin word for 'cloud'. They are giant clouds made up of dust, hydrogen and helium gas, and plasma. They are referred to as 'stellar nurseries', the site where stars are born. They are large and are classified into four categories. Most of them belong to the group of Diffuse Nebulae, which means they do not have strict well-defined boundaries. They are further divided into sub-categories called 'Emission Nebulae' and 'Reflection Nebulae'. Emission Nebulae emit visible light and are largely composed of ionised hydrogen. Reflection Nebulae do not emit large amounts of visible light. Dark Nebulae cannot emit visible light, and they are unable to reflect the light from the stars.

211 Meteorites Are a Mess

When a piece of rock or metal from an outer space object like a comet, asteroid or meteoroid enters the Earth's atmosphere and falls with an impact on the Earth's surface or any other planet, it is called a meteorite. About 90 per cent of the debris material is rock, while the remaining consists of iron, nickel or both. Meteorites are classified based on their chemical composition. Besides this, they are also classified as stony, metallic and mixtures of rock and iron. The Earth has witnessed the fall of many asteroids, the most famous being Allende meteorite. Another 60-tonne rock meteorite named Hoba fell in Africa about 80,000 years ago. It is declared a national monument in Africa and is a famous tourist spot.

212 The Ice Giant

Uranus is also known as one of the ice giants, besides Neptune, owing to its rocky, iron core that is surrounded by a thick icy mantle. The planet was discovered by William Herschel in 1781. It rotates opposite to the direction of Earth's rotation called retrograde. It has been observed that the axis of the planet is unusually tilted, a possible cause for which, would be a collision. The planet's core is mostly made up of rock and ice, and the mantle consists of water, ammonia and other volatile elements.

The planet appears to be blue in colour because of the presence of water, ammonia and methane ice crystals in the upper atmosphere. Studies suggest that methane cloud layers absorb light in the wavelength of red colour and reflect in the wavelength of blue colour. Below the methane layer, is a layer of hydrogen, helium and trace amounts of acetylene and methane. It is the coldest planet of all the eight planets in the solar system. The surface temperature measures as low as –224 °C. Uranus has 13 rings, two of which are extremely narrow just a few kilometres wide. The rings are made up of ice as well as dust and debris.

Fun Fact

The chemical element Uranium, discovered in 1789, was named after Uranus.

213 Mimas Is a Moon

Saturn's second moon was discovered on September 17, 1789, by English astronomer Sir William Herschel. Commonly referred to as the 'Death Star Moon', Mimas is one among Saturn's many moons. The Herschel crater (a huge impact crater on Mimas) gives it this distinctive look. Apart from the Herschel crater, Mimas is known to have many other craters. Although it is close to Saturn, the water ice on Mimas does not melt, which is not the case in other distant moons. Scientists believed that there might be a liquid ocean beneath Mimas' surface. Though it is one of the larger moons in Saturn's inner ring, yet it is the smallest of Saturn's large moons. Apart from ice, Mimas is also known to have very small amounts of silicate rock.

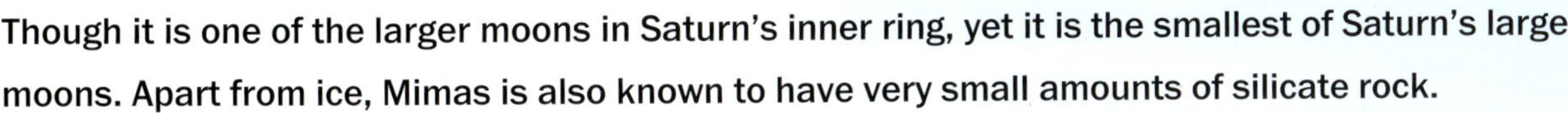

214 One-sided Moon

We are all aware that Earth rotates on its own axis and so does the moon. Under these circumstances, aren't we supposed to see the entire moon then? Why is it that we always see the same side of the moon?

While many moons ago, the moon spun at a much faster pace, the gravitational force of the Earth kind of slowed this spin down to 27.3 days approximately to match that of its orbit. Had the moon not spun at all, its far side would be visible to the Earth while it orbited. However, since the rotational time and orbital time of the moon are the same, we are always able to see the same side of the moon.

215 The Milky Way

The Milky Way is a large spiral galaxy that is made up of billions of stars, gas, dust and dark matter held together by gravity. It has about 100-400 billion stars. It keeps losing stars through supernova events and also keeps producing new ones. It is also home to the sun and other planets, including Earth. It is a part of a large group of galaxies called the Virgo Supercluster. The Milky Way resembles a huge whirlpool and comes across as a hazy band of white light in the night sky. Unlike the Earth, the Milky Way rotates only once in 200 million years.

216 Io Moon

Discovered, by Galileo Galilei in 1610, Io is the innermost moon, and the second smallest of Jupiter's four Galilean moons, namely Europa, Ganymede and Callisto. More than 400 active volcanoes are found on the surface of Io. Hence, it is considered the most active volcanic part of the solar system. This leads to the creation of volcanic plumes and lakes that cover vast areas of the landscape. The volcanic plumes of Io generate large amounts of sulphur, sulphur dioxide particles, and rocky ash, which rise up to 200 km. Io also has many mountains, some of which are as tall as Mount Everest. Research has shown that tidal heating is responsible for the occurrence of volcanoes on Io. The surface and atmosphere of the moon is considered to be highly toxic and dangerous because of the radiation in its environment.

217 Great Red Spot

The Great Red Spot is in the Southern Hemisphere of planet Jupiter. It is a continuous anti-cyclonic storm, blowing for hundreds of years. It is different from the Great Dark Spot observed near the northern pole of Jupiter. What causes the reddish colour of the Great Red Spot is not confirmed. It may be due to complex organic molecules like red phosphorous or sulphur compounds. Images taken during a period of 20 years have shown that the Great Red Spot is shrinking and changing its shape from an oval to a circle.

218 The Silence of Space

Space, like the name suggests, is that vast expanse where nothingness could go on for miles and miles at the end. Not only is space vast, but it is also eerily silent. This is because, a major portion of space is empty. And in this emptiness, there is also a complete lack of air. Due to this, sound, which is vibrations produced in air, also fails to exist. Well then how do astronauts speak to each other in space? While in a spacecraft, they are able to speak with each other normally because there is air in the spacecraft. But while they spacewalk, they make use of radios that are installed in their helmets, in order to communicate with each other.

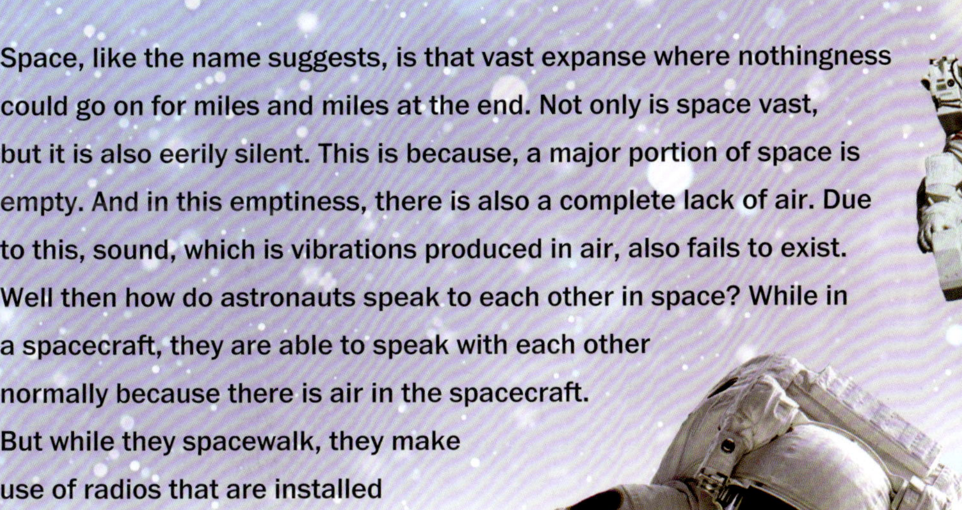

219 Asteroid

Asteroids are small, rocky objects of the solar system that are rich in metals, water and some precious metals too. They are commonly found in interplanetary space (space between planets). Millions of asteroids have been recognised and classified on the basis of composition. They are also known as minor planets or planetoids. They are bodies that are smaller than the moons. Some asteroids have their own moons. Asteroids mostly orbit the sun between Mars and Jupiter and are categorised into three classes. The first class, called C-types, are largely composed of clay and silicate rocks. S-types, which are the "stony" asteroids largely contain silicate rocks and nickel and iron mixtures, and M-types that are made up of metallic nickel-iron.

220 Look, It's an Eclipse!

Every time there occurs an eclipse, people over the world are excited to see it. So, what exactly is an eclipse? An eclipse is a phenomenon where one spatial body such as a moon or planet moves into the shadow of another spatial body. There are 2 types of eclipses, solar eclipse and lunar eclipse. In a solar eclipse, the moon is in between the Sun and Earth. It is known as occultation and the moon casts its shadow onto our planet. Because of this, it blocks the light from falling on to Earth. On the other hand, in a lunar eclipse, Earth lies in between the moon and the sun. The Earth blocks the light from reaching the moon. As a result of this, the moon does not receive any light. A lunar eclipse can last for a few hours, unlike a solar eclipse, which can go on for only a few minutes.

221 Hyperion

Hyperion is one of the small moons of Saturn and the last one to be discovered. It resembles an elongated potato rather than a sphere. Scientists believe that due to an impact the round moon might have lost its shape. It has low density and a porous surface. This sponge-like moon of Saturn is the largest moon in the solar system, which is not spherical in shape. Its rotation is always changing because of the pull by its neighbour Titan, which keeps it away from its circular orbit. Though small, it has a huge amount of interaction with the magnetic environment of Saturn. Hyperion has also been found to have many craters. Neptune's moon, Proteus, is the only irregularly shaped moon, which is larger than Hyperion.

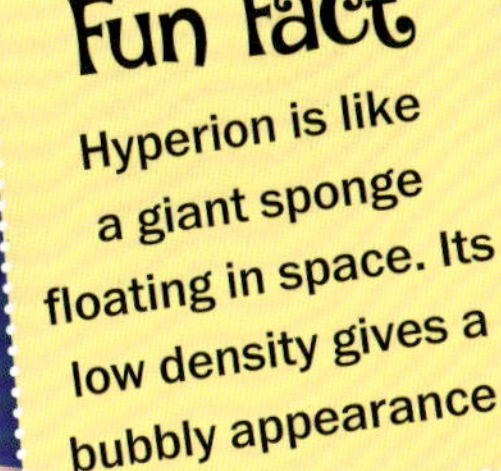

Fun Fact

Hyperion is like a giant sponge floating in space. Its low density gives a bubbly appearance.

222 Like a Comet

A comet is a very small object present in the solar system that is made up of a mixture of large amounts of ice along with small quantities of dust and rock. The core or main body of the comet is called the nucleus. It has water, methane, nitrogen and ice. When a comet comes too close to the sun or even to the planets, it breaks apart or disintegrates. Comets contain super cold methane, ammonia and carbon dioxide ice, combined with rock, dust, and bits and pieces of solar system debris. Comets have two tails; a dust tail, which can be seen with the naked eye, and a plasma tail, which is generally invisible to the naked eye. Comets are usually created in the outermost regions of the solar system, namely the Oort cloud and Kuiper belt.

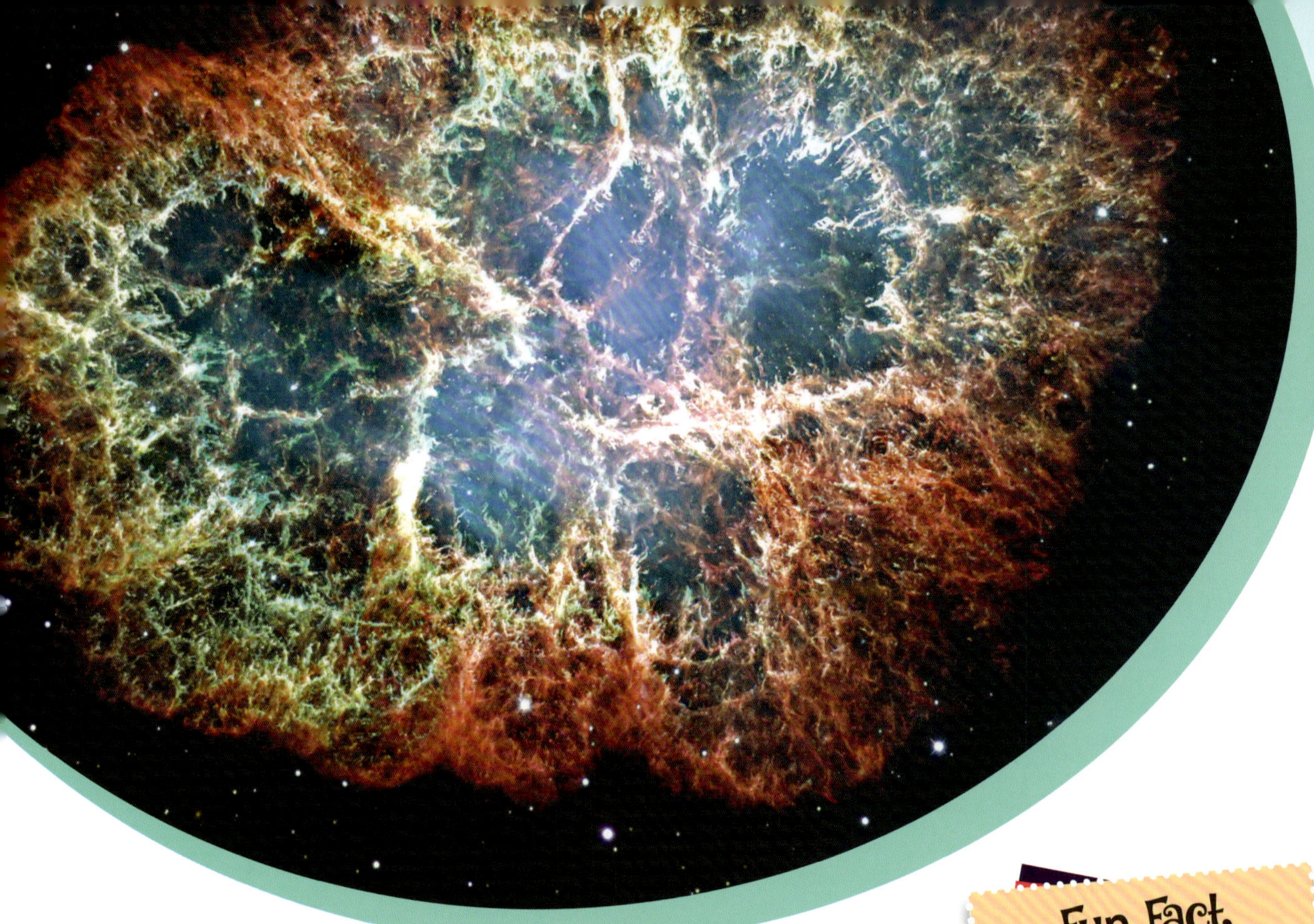

223 The Super Supernova

When there is a change in the core of a star, the star explodes causing a huge explosion in space. The brightness of the star suddenly increases immensely, because of the explosion. This phenomenon is known as a supernova. Every second a supernova occurs somewhere in the universe. A supernova is so bright and powerful, that an entire galaxy of stars seems to fade in comparison to the brightness of this explosion, and it releases as much energy as our sun in a period of 10 billion years. This celestial event occurs at the end of a huge star's life that is destroyed by the explosion of extreme proportions. Yet, the average spotting of a supernova in the Milky Way is two per century and the last one was some 400 years ago. Some explosions do not destroy the parent star, because they are not real supernovae. At times supernovae create beautiful displays of light. The oldest supernova recorded is SN 185. It emits vast amounts of radiation. If it were to occur close to Earth, it would rob our atmosphere of ozone.

Fun Fact

When a supernova explodes it ejects large amount of elements like oxygen and iron. Many chemical elements are also made in a supernova.

224 Galactic Galaxies

When we talk about space, there are so many things that come to our mind like stars, moons, planets, and many more interesting heavenly bodies. And we know that all of this exists in space. But thinking from a broader point of view, what forms all of this? The answer is galaxies!

Billions of stars, the solar system, a large number of gases and dust make up a galaxy. Galaxies are of different shapes, sizes and colours. There are billions of galaxies in the universe. Some are spiral, elliptical (smooth and oval-shaped), and there are others with irregular shapes. Let us understand a little more about different galaxies. An elliptical galaxy contains up to one trillion stars but little dust and interstellar matter. A small galaxy of this type is called a dwarf elliptical galaxy. Irregular galaxies, as the name suggests, have no distinct shape or form new stars. They were formed some 10-20 billion years ago, after the 'big bang' that started the universe. Then we have the whirlpool galaxy, which is one of the brightest and most beautiful galaxies and is a close neighbour of the Milky Way. Our galaxy, the Milky Way, is spiral with around 100 billion stars.

Fun Fact

There are close to 200 billion galaxies in the observable universe.

225 Wonderful Venus

Named after the Greek God of Love and Beauty, Venus is the brightest planet ever known. It is considered both a morning star as well as an evening star, visible to the naked eye. Venus shares some similarities with planet Earth as it is almost similar in size (only slightly smaller than our planet), composition and density, and both the planets contain craters. However, research shows that Venus cannot be hospitable to life because of certain factors, such as the high pressure of the atmosphere, presence of large amounts of carbon dioxide, multiple thick layers of clouds of sulphuric acid. Hence Venus is capable of producing a greenhouse effect, because of its dense atmosphere. Although Mercury is closest to the Sun, it is not the hottest. It is Venus that is the hottest planet, as the surface temperatures can rise to 450°C. The surface of the planet has areas of depression as well as a few highland areas. Evidence and certain findings on the surface of Venus also indicate the presence of lava flows, many large shield volcanoes. The planet's interior has an iron core which is large in radius and a rocky mantle which is molten. Recent studies suggest that the crust of Venus is strong and thick. A few hotspots have also been identified on Venus. These are the volcanically active regions, which show a range of many interesting features.

Fun Fact

Venus does not have a magnetic field.

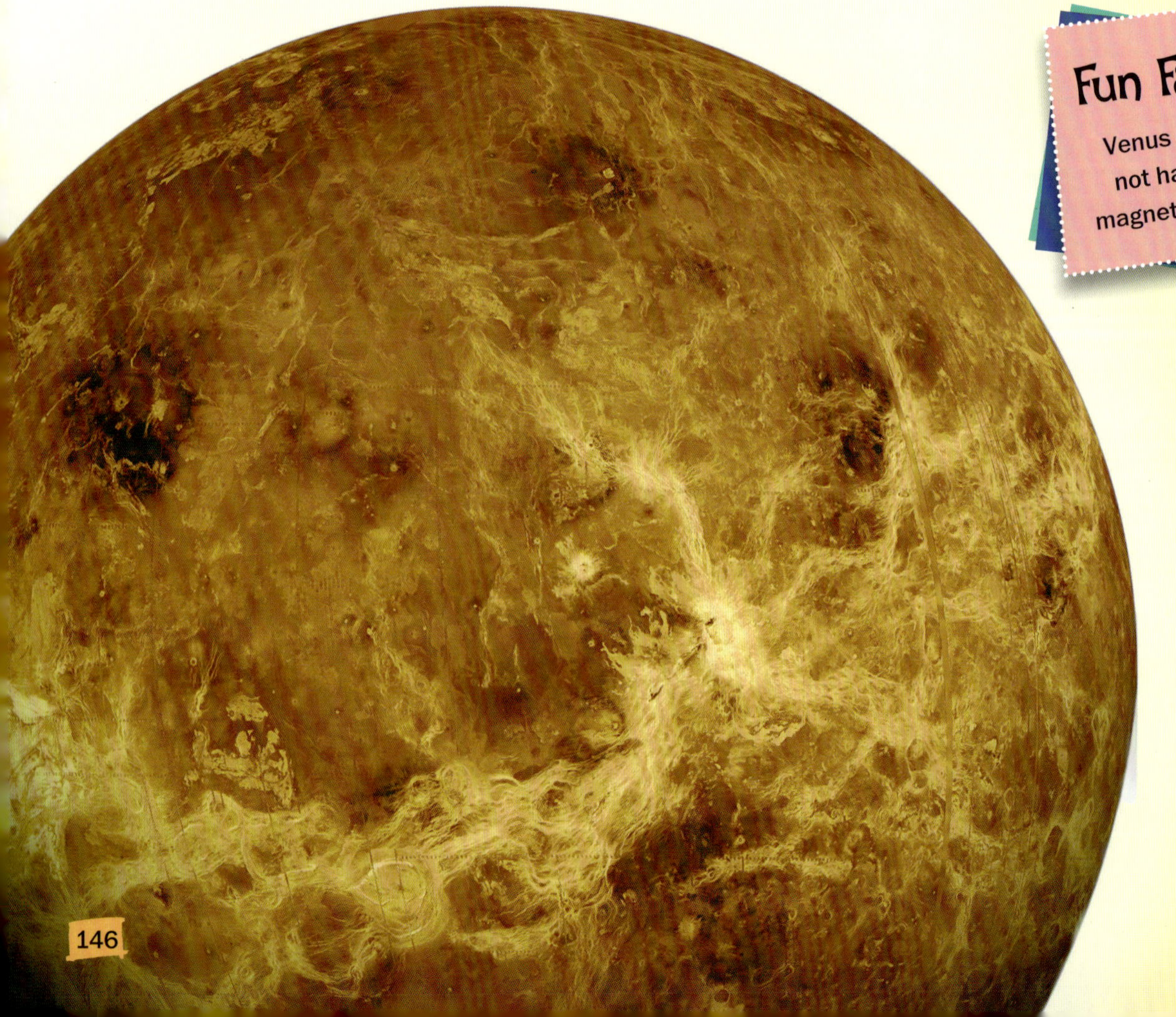

TRANSPORT

From the time that the wheel was invented, transport has been at the heart of technological progress made by humans. From travelling on land and on water to travelling in the air and in space, humans are moving from one place to another like never before.

226 From Bullock Carts to Auto Rickshaws

In prehistoric times, man was known to travel long distances on the backs of animals like horses and mules. Bullock carts and horse-drawn carriages came as technology progressed. Inspired by horse-drawn carriages, the rickshaw, that is, a two or three-wheeled cart pulled by hand to carry passengers was first invented in Japan around 1869. Soon it spread to other Asian countries like Singapore, India, China and Korea as it became a form of employment for migrant peasants. Reverend J. Fordyce first introduced rickshaws in India in the city of Shimla around 1880.

Later, auto rickshaws or mechanised versions of rickshaws were invented during the 1950s when the Piaggio company in Italy introduced the Piaggio Ape. It began to be used as public transport in Asian countries. During the 1960s the Bajaj Company got the licence to manufacture and sell the Piaggio Ape in India. It began selling a modified version of the Ape in India and thus the auto rickshaw came to India.

227 The Good Old Times

Prehistoric humans walked from place to place. As they began domesticating animals, they realised that larger animals like donkeys, horses and camels could be used for transport. And so, these animals began to be used for road transport.

Even before the wheel was invented, the prehistoric humans had begun to ski. The oldest skis ever discovered were built between 8000 and 7000 BC and were found in Russia. Hundreds of pieces of prehistoric skis have been discovered in Sweden, Finland and Norway. A 4000-year-old rock carving found near the Arctic Circle in Norway shows skiing. Many human societies living in cold climates where snowfall was common came up with some form of skiing.

The wheel was invented around 3500 BC in Mesopotamia to be used as a potter's wheel. It was several years later that wheels began to be used in wagons for long distance travel and to transport goods.

When chariots began to be built, the wheel with spokes and axle came into being. Before that doughnut-shaped wheels were being used, which were heavier. Horse drawn chariots were used by Romans, especially by the nobility. Besides transporting people these chariots were used for hunting, racing and games. Later bullock carts and ox carts began to used.

One of the earliest modes of water transport were canoes, a kind of boat, the wood for which was obtained from the trunk of a tree. Later, the Egyptians built sailing boats out of bundles of papyrus reeds which were tied together. Subsequently, wooden ships for trade began to be used by Egyptians.

228 The Ship of the Desert

The camel is also known as 'the ship of the desert' because it is an effective mode of transport in deserts as it is the only animal that can sustain the harsh desert conditions.

The camel can go without water for days together. It stores fat in its hump, which it metabolises when it needs energy.

Besides this, camels have thick, wide hooves, which keep them from sinking in the sand. These tough and leathery pads protect their feet from burning in the hot desert sands. They can also close their nostrils to block blowing sand.

Further, they don't sweat often. Consequently, their bodies conserve the water that they drink for long durations of time. Their long, thick lips also help them to eat the thorny plants found in the desert.

In hot climatic conditions, camels can carry up to 160 kgs of load. Camels can be harnessed to a cart as well. A series of camels carrying passengers and goods is called a camel train or a caravan.

Single humped camels are also used as a mode of transport in the deserts of Arabia, Middle East, North Africa and the Thar Desert. There are double humped camels as well-known as 'Bactrian' camels, which are used extensively in places like the Gobi desert in China, as well as Mongolia.

Fun Fact

Camels have two rows of thick eyelashes that protect their eyes from the desert sand.

229 Up, Up and Away!

Imagine if you had wings. Instead of travelling by car, bus or train, you could fly to your destination. We're talking about jetpacks. You may have seen these on sci-fi TV shows, but they are no longer a thing of the future. Commercially available jetpacks are here. Jetpacks work on the principle of Newton's third law (every action has an equal and opposite reaction). They are worn on the back and strapped on tight. Fuel in the tank ignites and creates propulsion that launches a person upwards.

The technology is still in its early stages and therefore jetpacks are very expensive and can only be flown for around 30 minutes before they run out of fuel. However, more work is being done on this amazing mode of transport and perhaps this will enable us to zip around our city in the future.

230 Rulers of Sand

As the name suggests a sand rail is a vehicle that is built for travel on sand. In fact, it is specially built for sand dunes, and hence is also called a dune buggy. These vehicles can also be operated on dirt, mud and even snow. However, a sand rail is unsuitable for rocky regions.

These bare-boned vehicles are off-road vehicles, and travel in those areas where normal cars cannot go, for example, in the desert. These vehicles can also be modified to traverse on roads. However, to do this, they need to have a windshield and a license plate. A word of caution here; since collisions are the most common form of accidents in the case of a sand rail, one must take utmost caution while driving these beasts.

231 Carting It Along

Cart is just a four-lettered word, but the kinds of carts that exist are several. Before we understand the kinds, let us take a look at what a cart is.

A cart is a vehicle with two wheels to carry passengers and goods pulled or pushed by muscle power. A cart may be pulled by one, or a pair of draught animals, or by a man. A cart that is pulled or pushed by one or more than one person is called a handcart. A handcart is used to transport agricultural products like grain, cloth, furniture, etc., for transporting over short distances. With the invention of wheels and domestication of animals animal carts came into existence. Draught animals like donkeys, horses, camel, etc., were harnessed to the cart for transportation purposes. A cart with two wheels is called a spring cart and is used as a sporting vehicle.

A shopping cart or a trolley is provided in supermarkets to put in the load of merchandise and carry it to the payment counter. After the payment the customers can take their goods in this cart to their cars. A shopping cart for the disabled is an electric chair with a basket attached. It has an electric motor and navigational control is offered by some supermarkets.

The shopping cart enables the customer with difficulty in moving around a large area, or pushing a regular cart, to move around the store picking up the required items and keeping those in the cart. These carts move at a speed of around 2 miles an hour.

A golf cart is usually a two-seater vehicle that is used to carry golfers around the golf court.

232 Farm Tracks

A tractor is a farm vehicle used for carrying out agricultural tasks like tilling or transporting agricultural equipment, which can be towed behind or mounted on it. A farm tractor is an open vehicle but the recent models have enclosed cabins for safety and comfort. Older tractors ran on steam but later gasoline engines with kerosene and ethanol were used. However, diesel is the common choice for fuel.

Countries like Germany use biodiesel as a source of energy. Modern tractors have electric switches and levers to carry out different functions. Small tractors are put to work for lawn mowing, orchard work and truck farming (growing one or more types of vegetables for export) and for landscaping. Fields where bulk crops like wheat, maize and soya are grown use large tractors. The speed at which a tractor moves on a farm, is usually less than 1 mile/hour, while on road it is 25 miles/hour.

233 A Few More Tractors

Green tractors are used in private gardens for cutting grass or cultivating small patches of land. Road tractors are heavy-duty vehicles that transport freight over a distance. Pushback tractors are used to push aircrafts away from their parking bays.

Space agencies like NASA use very large tractors to move space shuttles. Tractors are the only viable option for transporting supplies in the Arctic. Mines sometimes use tractors for transporting dirt and ores, and for transporting fresh supplies and digging.

234 An Electric Skate

Electric skateboards move as fast as 25 miles per hour, with the help of an electric motor. They are usually controlled with a radio frequency remote and look exactly like normal unpowered skateboards. The only difference between the two is noticeable when the skateboards are lifted, and you look underneath. You will observe the batteries and an electric motor.

As far as operating an electric skateboard goes, you'd hardly be doing much. This is because while in a normal skateboard, you'd use your foot and body weight to push the skateboard forward, in the case of an electric skateboard, all you'd be doing is riding with the help of a remote control.

Fun Fact

The first electric skateboard was produced in the seventies.

235 The Big Yellow Bus

The colour yellow on school buses across the world is not a coincidence. This is because yellow does a great job at attracting our attention. In fact, this colour is so eye-catching that human beings can perceive it even from the corner of their eye. Research has shown that yellow is 1.24 times more eye-catching than the colour red. Therefore, it is used on school buses. The bus can easily be detected in dim light, bad weather and in the rear-view mirror. This increases the chances of safety of the bus on the road, which is extremely important as the safety of children is top priority to each one of us!

236 Never Stop

What if we told you, that you could hop onto a train that never stops? Sounds unbelievable, right? But, a train like this actually does exist.

Proposed by Chinese designer Chen Jianjun, this is the train of the future. How it works is that passengers get onto a compartment which acts like a platform above an incoming train. This compartment then gets attached to the train as the train moves past the platform, and passengers from this compartment are transported into the moving train. At the next station, those who want to get off move up into the attached compartment. Thus while the train never stops, the compartment does a great job of acting as a platform.

237 Maglev Trains

Maglev is a term that is coined from the concept of magnetic levitation. The technology of magnetic levitation makes use of magnets and their working principle – likes repel, opposites attract. Using electromagnetic suspension, a maglev train runs along special rails called guideways. These high speed trains run between 350 km/hr to 500 km/hr. They have magnets on their tracks as well as on board. This creates a magnetic field and the force of attraction and repulsion from the magnets lifts the train anywhere between 8 mm-12 mm above the tracks.

This magnetic field helps to propel the train, making it run without direct contact with the track. This helps the trains to run smoothly and they are comparatively less noisy than conventional trains. The best part of these trains is that they do not cause air pollution, as there is no burning of fuel.

Fun Fact
The average delay of a Shinkansen is not more than 36 seconds.

238 Shinkansen

Shinkansens are trains that run at super high speed, reaching up to 220 km per hour. They are mostly powered by electricity, except for a few that run on diesel. These long-distance trains are used by passengers travelling to work in metros from suburban areas. These trains, due to the shape of their nose-cone resembling a bullet are also called bullet trains. And like the Japanese themselves, these trains are punctual and frequent too. They have food carts and vending machines on board. The trains also offer various advantages like taking along foldable bicycles, pets like dogs, cats and birds on-board. There are also special provisions and seating arrangements made for the handicapped.

239 The Caterpillar

With its long, caterpillar like, compartmentalised body, trains are a convenient means of transport for both man and goods.

In 1970, the British developed steam locomotives. Electric trains came into being sometime in the 1880s. Diesel electric trains began taking over steam engines from the 1940s. Rail transport is a major form of public transport. Trains operate in different ways; for example, metros, subways and monorail are all specialised railway modes for local transport. They operate in tunnels or on elevated structures. A passenger train consists of several coaches. Long distance passenger trains have sleeping facilities too. Freight trains have wagons or containers to transport goods and animals.

Fun Fact
There is a famous cartoon character who is a train known as Thomas the Tank Engine and is very popular with children.

240 Elevators

Since time immemorial, man has been in search of better vertical transport machines, to move people and goods from ground level to a height and vice-versa. In earlier times, elevators or lifts were called hoists. They were human powered, animal powered or water powered. During the 1800s, elevators evolved from steam power to hydraulic power. They were mainly used in factories and mines. The first electric elevator was installed in 1889.

With the advent of electricity, technology in every field was revolutionised. Elevators were one of them. Electricity, together with motor transport raised the speed of elevators. Today, in times of high-rises they are a necessity and not a luxury.

Space elevators are a proposed idea in space transportation that could be used to transport people to space stations. This idea could soon become a reality!

241 Up and Down

Going up and down an escalator is always fun!

Escalators are a type of conveyor transport that makes use of a conveyor belt, for the movement of goods and people between floors. They are moving staircases and have a device for vertical transport. Here, people do not climb up or down, but the escalators moves, eliminating physical effort. Escalators work with the help of chains that rotate and pull a set of stairs, in a constant cycle, creating a moving staircase. Escalators are used when elevators are not practical.

Escalators are expensive machines that are used in departmental stores, malls, subways, theatres, etc on a regular basis these days.

242 Up in the Air

While most cars run on the road, there are some cars that you also find up in the air. Yes, that's true. And as strange as it may sound, cable cars are what we are talking about. Also known as ropeways, cable cars are a type of aerial transport where cars are permanently fixed to and suspended from cables. Yet, there are some which can be detached from the cables. They are installed mainly in mountainous regions, ski resorts and waterscape areas. Besides moving people they can also carry goods.

The city of New York and Portland have adopted this transport system for public utility. A double deck cable car in France called the Vanoise Express carries 200 people in each car and stretches about 5,900 ft between the two resorts it connects. The longest cableway is in Sweden which is 42 km long.

Cable transport has two main elements. These are the use of pulleys, and balancing of loads that go up and down. This system relies on cables that are rotated by a motor outside to pull or lower vehicles at a steady speed. The vehicle in this system does not have a motor or an engine and hence, there is no use of fuel. This in turn, is good for environmental health. Modern technology has made cable transport one of the safest modes of transport with very rare occurrences of accidents.

243 Let's Catch a Flight

Like road transport, there exists a variety of modes of air transport, like airplanes, helicopters and sea-planes. Besides these, you have hot air balloons that are used for recreational purposes. Air transport is the fastest mode of transport second only to space transport.

Commercial aircrafts can carry hundreds of passengers. Sea planes can take off and land on water. They are mainly used while travelling to islands and can accommodate only a few passengers.

Helicopters are useful forms of air transport but carry only a few passengers at a time. They are also used during emergencies for rescue operations.

244 Supersonic Jets

Supersonic jets can travel about five times faster than the speed of sound!

Supersonic aircrafts include fighter jets, and Concorde by the Franco – British and Tupolev TU-144 by the Soviets, were the only two supersonic jets used for commercial flights. Both these aircrafts were grounded permanently in 2003 and since then there have been no supersonic civilian aircrafts in service. The high cost of fuel consumption, expensive tickets and limited seats, lead to their discontinuation. As these jets travel faster in air than sound does, they create shock waves or a sonic boom, which is a loud deafening sound, like that of an explosion. This is one of the main reasons for their ban for civilian use.

245 Flights of the Future

Keeping in mind the technological innovations that have taken over the world of transport, innovations that were previously even unthinkable, have now become a reality.

Take for example the Airbus 2050 concept plane. A plane that travels across the globe, just like any other except for the frills and fancies it offers. This giant, apart from offering the most comfortable flying experience, will also have dedicated fun zones that have gaming zones, panoramic windows and seats that make use of our body heat to power these in-cabin features. There will also be massage seats that serve passengers what they require, while filling the air with a scent of fresh pine or sea breeze.

Apart from these, the plane will also have ambient sounds and special shades where passengers can control how much light is let into the cabin. The cabin's bionic structure will be based on the bone structure of a bird so as to keep it light, yet strong. The inbuilt fittings and furnishings of the plane are built in such a way so as to take care of their own repair and maintenance. And all this thanks to innovation and technology.

Truly, this one is a flight of the future!

246 Pull that Sledge

A sledge is a vehicle that slides across snow or ice or surfaces having no friction. They have long pieces of wood called runners, fitted to the bottom, to slide across the surface. They are used to transport passengers and cargo in snow laden regions. Sledges could be moderate or large sized with open roofs, and are drawn by horses or dogs.

Royalty in earlier times preferred moving about in these vehicles. During 19th and 20th century, man powered sledges were used on expeditions to the Arctic and Antarctic regions. As there is no engine they do not use any fuel, thus causing no pollution.

247 Hagglunds

Of Swedish origin, Hagglunds are huge vehicles that are designed to move on snow, sea and ice. These vehicles are powered by turbo diesel engines and have rubber tracks. They have a light body which helps them to move on snow without sinking. Only a person qualified to drive a Hagglund can do so.

The Hagglund BV 206 is an all-terrain amphibious vehicle which can move on sand, boulders, swamps, marshes, roads as well as water. It can carry personnel as well as equipment and hence is put to use for civilian and military transport. Besides being a transport vehicle it is also used for rescue and relief work.

248 A Snowmobile

With improvements in technology, man has come up with more than one technique to travel in the snow. A snowmobile is a small vehicle used for travelling over snow and ice. Snowmobiles are also used for recreational activities and can accommodate 1-2 persons at a time. They are powered by combustion engines. Snow mobiles do have a negative impact on the environment and also can cause noise pollution.

They are however, very handy in rescue work as they move fast and with ease on snowy terrain.

249 Winter Wonderland

Travelling on snow on sleighs or similar means of transport is always fun.

A dog sleigh is one such vehicle pulled by dogs for carrying people or goods over snow. A toboggan is a small vehicle without wheels, used for moving over snow. A snow coach is a passenger transport vehicle that can accommodate ten or more passengers and have either a rubber track or a ski system.

Snow coaches with rubber tracks can move over thin snow. A bobsleigh is a small vehicle which can seat 2 people. It is used for sliding over snow and ice and is also used in races called bobsleigh races. Another snow vehicle called Hagglund is used for transporting equipment and passengers from one country to another. This vehicle can float on water if it breaks through ice, making it perfect for frozen landscapes.

250 Fly, Don't Drive

A four-seater flying car is all set to fly into the markets very soon. This car with wings makes use of ducted fans in order to take flight.

For the last 40 years, Paul Moller has been working at building a car that flies, and from the looks of it, it doesn't seem like that day is very far. So far, only the prototype (a test model) with the name Moller 400, has hit the skies. However, knowing the brilliance of Paul Moller who built his own sports car at age 15, and then tried building his own helicopter too, time means nothing. We wish him all the best in his endeavour and hope to see a flying Moller very soon!

251 Wonder Bikes

While we are all familiar with the concept of car sharing, here's something new – a bike (cycle) sharing network known as Mobike.

This is a smart move not just towards saving time and money but also towards saving the environment. All the user needs to do is to open the Mobike app, and scan the QR code on the bike with the help of a smartphone. This unlocks the smart lock and an automatic timer comes on. This brilliant concept is the brainchild of a former Uber employee, Wang Xiaofeng, who is now the CEO of Mobike. The unique feature of these bikes is their distinct orange coloured rims.

252 The Waterways

One of the most ancient forms of transport are through which waterways have played an important role between countries. Since times immemorial, people sailed to trade, to explore, to settle and sometimes to even conquer distant lands through these waterways.

Besides being convenient for transporting large amounts of goods like grains, logs and metals, it is also cheaper as compared to the airways. However, it is a slower mode of transport and adverse conditions at sea can result in loss of goods. There are different types of vessels that sail on water like boats, ships, ferries, tankers, etc. During the Stone Age, hollowed tree trunks were used as boats for travel and fishing. They were called canoes. They are used for recreational sports and short distance travel for locals living around waterscapes even today. Another form of water transport in those days was rafts, in which logs of reeds were tied together and used to travel on water.

253 Ro-ro Ships

Ro-ro ships are sea vessels that carry passengers as well as cars and trucks. Ro-ro stands for, 'roll on, roll off'.

MS Color Magic, the largest Ro-ro passenger ferry built in Finland, is 223.70 metres long, 35 metres wide, and can carry 550 cars. The development of these ships was boosted during World War II, for transporting military equipment, which after the end of the war were converted to merchant ships. These vessels are speedy and efficient, and have helped boost tourism. Passengers on vacation can take their vehicles on a Ro-ro ship to another country. However, before the ship sets sail, it has to be thoroughly checked, since if the loading door is not properly secured and water enters the ship's deck, the ship could sink.

254 Air Boats

Also known as swamp boats or fan boats, an airboat is a flat bottom vehicle which moves forward with the help of an aircraft or automotive engine. It has a large fan at the back that helps move the boat.

Airboats are a popular means of transportation in marshy or shallow water areas. They are used during floods and ice rescue operations. The military and coastguard also make use of these airboats. Fishing, hunting and ecotourism are some of the activities undertaken with the help of these boats. Airboats travel at high speed and the only negative factor is that they make a lot of noise.

255 Hovercrafts

A hovercraft is a boat, like the name suggests that hovers or moves across water. It is capable of travelling over land, water, sand, swamps, mud and ice. It can travel on other surfaces as well. It is a hybrid vessel and is manoeuvred by a pilot. Besides being used for sports and transporting passengers and vehicles, they are also employed in coastguard and military operations. Very large hovercrafts can carry soldiers and other large equipment. They are used in rescues at sea and also to rescue people from thick mud, ice and floods. Remote places on islands are accessible by hovercrafts. Small hovercrafts are used for cruising on inland lakes, rivers or marshy areas as well as for inland racing. They use less fuel and travel at a speed of up to 145 km/hr.

256 From Boats to Ships

Over time, different modes of water transport have evolved. The most commonly used mode is a boat. Boats may be motorised or have ores, paddles and sails. They are used to sail on inland waterways like lakes, rivers and bays. Around a hundred years ago, steam boats transported people and goods along rivers.

Today, ferries carry passengers across rivers. A catamaran is a type of ferry that moves at a high speed on sea and lakes. Cargo ships are ships that carry goods from one place to another or even from one country to another. There are different types of cargo ships too. Tankers carry liquid goods like petroleum and its products. Container ships transport finished goods and products. Refrigerated ships, also known as 'reefer ships', carry perishable goods. Another category are the dry bulk carriers that transport grain, ores and sand.

257 The Solar Sailor

Solar energy is the energy of the sun that is harnessed for further use in vehicles and household appliances. Solar energy is captured with the help of solar panels, and the best place to install these would be some place that does not obstruct the rays of the Sun falling onto it. Bearing this concept in mind, Dr. Robert Dane created the solar sailor.

A solar sailor is a boat that makes use of solar energy to propel itself. A device called a solar sail, is attached to the boat at an angle where it gets an ample amount of sunlight. The solar sail concept can be used for all kinds of water transport including yachts, shipping vessels and ferries.

258 Golden Quadrilateral

A very mystical sounding name, the Golden Quadrilateral is a high-strung network of highways that connect four of India's metropolitan cities, namely Delhi, Mumbai, Chennai and Kolkata.

This highway connection ends up forming a quadrilateral. The project, which was launched in 2001, is one of the largest highway projects in India. It is a part of the National Highways Development Project (NHDP). The Golden Quadrilateral that spans 5846 km in length and consists of six highway lanes, was completed in 2013. Anticipating the success of the Golden Quadrilateral, the Diamond Quadrilateral, which is a project for the Indian railways will soon be launched.

259 Runs with the Sun

Yes, a car that runs with the sun! And by that we don't mean a car that runs 'along' with the sun, but a car that is powered by energy from the sun. In other words, a Solar Car is what we're talking about.

The technology used in solar cars is a mix of three industries – aerospace, bicycle and the automobile industry. Here, sunlight is converted into electricity by photovoltaic cells that are present in solar panels. These photovoltaic cells are made up of semiconductors, mostly silicon, that help in absorbing the sunlight.

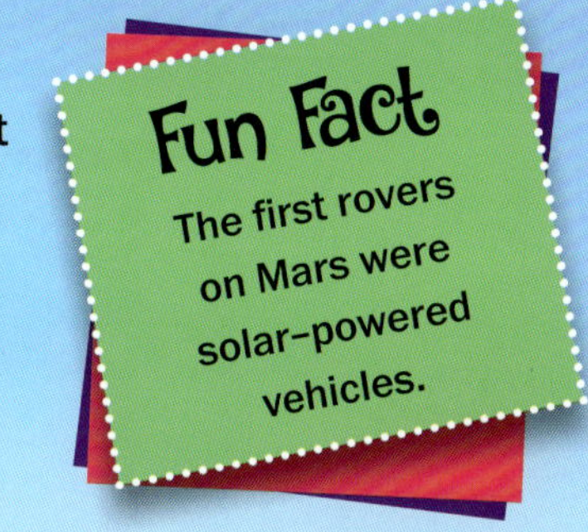

The energy of the sun then frees electrons in these semiconductors, thus leading to a flow of electrons. It is this flow that generates electricity to power the battery and the specialised motor in solar cars. Solar cars have solar panels on the car itself. There are some solar cars that do not use batteries. The power to run the solar car goes directly to an electric motor, but solar cars have to rely on a battery in times of need, like driving at midnight, or in the rainy season, when the sun is rarely seen. A solar car does not cause pollution when it is driven.

Fun Fact

The first rovers on Mars were solar-powered vehicles.

Thus, the use of solar cars may lead to overall diminished levels of carbon dioxide.

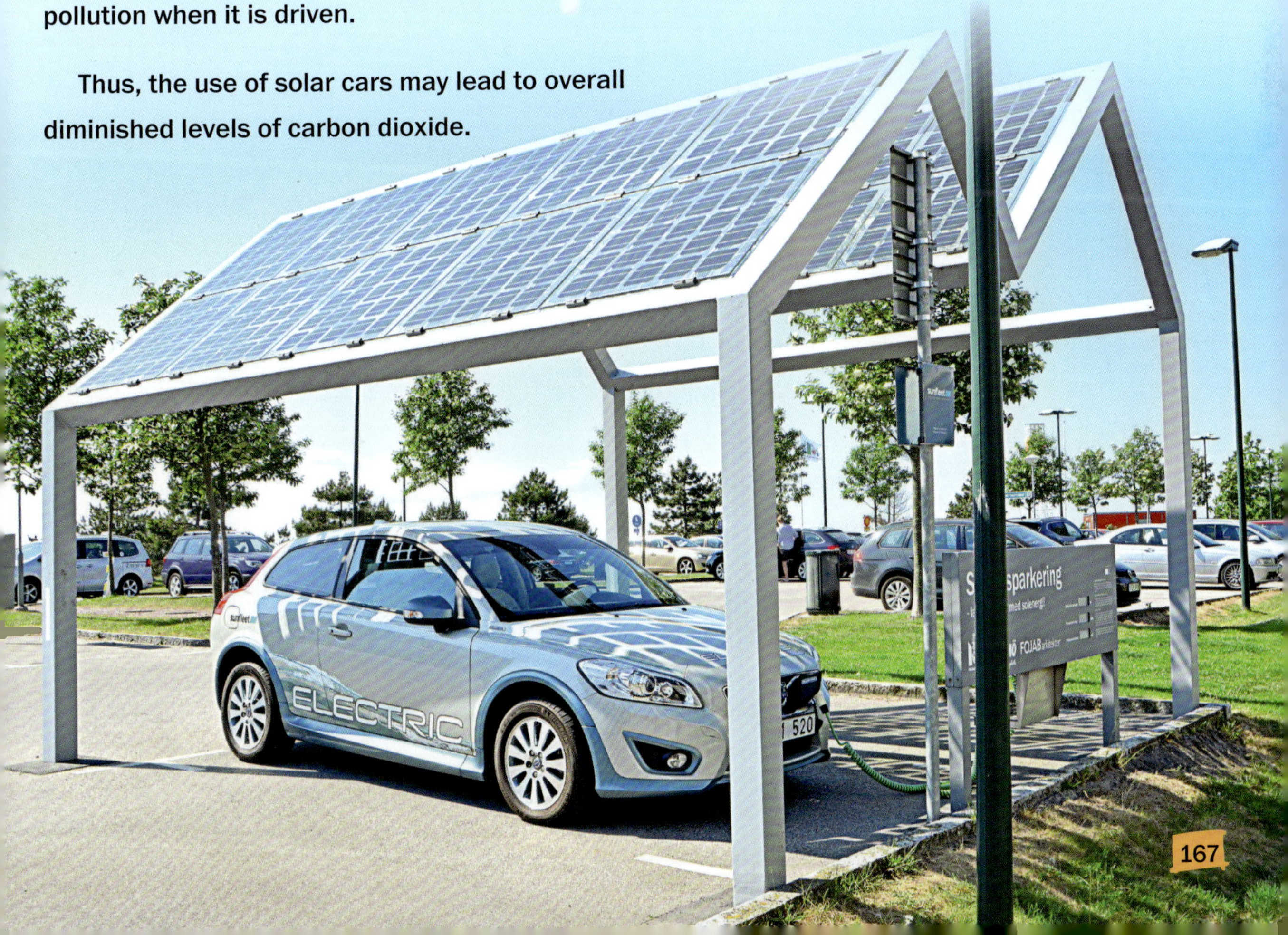

260 A Driverless Drive

Imagine a long drive in the privacy of your own car, with no one else in the car but you. Not even a driver. Yes, you read that right! With the latest automated cars, this is now possible.

These cars have no steering wheel, paddles or brakes and are equipped with artificial intelligence which helps them to identify obstacles and navigate with ease. These cars have laser lights, GPS and computer vision. They eliminate the risk of accidents due to human error. These cars also have the option of being driven by a driver in case of emergencies. Thus today, the disabled and even the old can experience the joy of driving, without driving!

261 Smart Roads

Researchers have proposed that roads of the future need to make use of innovative technology, like glow in the dark road markers. Here, a photo luminous powder is used in the paint which allows the markings to glow in the dark. They get charged during the day and glow for nearly eight hours at night. Another proposition would be technology that involves the use of motion sensor lights. As a car approaches, the stretch of road will light up brightly, and as the car passes, the light slowly dims away. The future of traditional roads is indeed bright!

262 Straddling Bus

Also called the 'trans-elevated bus', a straddling bus is one of the latest concepts in the field of transport. This bus is built on an extremely futuristic concept and is the brainchild of China. The model is such that the bus is raised over the road so cars can drive beneath it.

The main idea behind the straddling bus was to avoid cars being stuck behind huge vehicles like a bus, especially in countries like China, where traffic poses to be one of the biggest problems. The first bus that was created for a road test was called, *batie.* The bus runs on electricity, another great move towards protecting the environment, while making life a little more convenient.

263 Mono Tracer

It looks like one of those futuristic vehicles that one would think they'd only see in movies. But today, the MonoTracer has become a reality. It is an enclosed motorcycle. It has four wheels altogether, two large wheels with two small wheels on both sides of the vehicle that protrude from the body of the vehicle at slow speeds or when it comes to a halt.

The MonoTracer has an inbuilt aerodynamic cockpit, with a 130 horsepower engine, that helps it travel at about 120 miles per hour. It has enough space for just two passengers. It also has an all-electric lithium-ion battery, and hence is another great mode of transport that helps protect the environment. However, starting at about $82,000, the price of it is high enough to burn a deep hole in your pocket.

264 Hybrid Vehicles

Vehicles that use two or more types of power modes or fuel sources are called hybrid vehicles. These include a combination of internal combustion engine and an electric motor. The power sources used in hybrid vehicles could be gasoline, hydrogen, ethanol, biomass, electricity, muscle power, etc. Today we have hybrid bikes, cars, trucks, trains and even submarines.

Steam-powered ships were earlier a famous mode of hybrid transport. A non-nuclear submarine, when underwater, runs on batteries and when on the surface uses diesel. These dual powered vehicles have the advantage of gasoline engines and electric motors. When the vehicle comes to a halt the engine shuts off automatically and restarts when the accelerator is pressed down. Hybrid powertrains make use of diesel, electric or turbo-electric power sources. Hybrid vehicles do not use fossil fuels. Hence, they do not give out large amounts of harmful gases. Besides reduced emissions, these vehicles are fuel efficient.

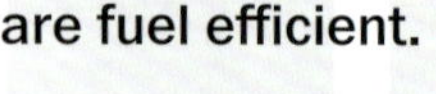

265 Your Traffic Jam Assistant

One of the most time consuming and annoying parts of road transport is a traffic jam. To make life easier, Ford is in the process of inventing something called a Traffic Jam Assistant.

This concept uses a semi-automatic technology that sometimes requires the driver's assistance. It gathers information about how far the car ahead is, thus keeping itself at a safe distance, and moving as and when it is able to. Traffic Jam Assistant gets activated with the help of a tiny button the driver presses as soon as he notices an oncoming traffic jam. This technology senses how the driver interacts with the steering wheel, and should there be a lack of steering activity, it issues acoustic and visual warnings. The best part is that the driver can take over at any time by using the indicators, the steering wheel or the pedal. Can't wait to get into this one, can we?

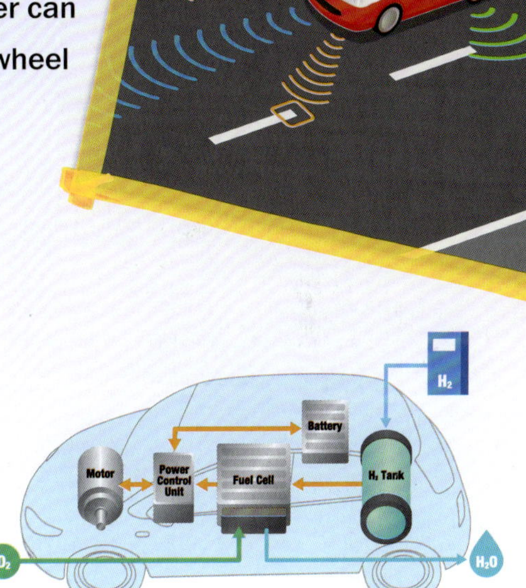

266 Fuel Cell Vehicles

While conventional vehicles run on gasoline or diesel, the technology in fuel cell vehicles is different. Fuel cell vehicles combine hydrogen stored on board, and oxygen from the air to produce electricity, which powers these vehicles. These are a type of electric vehicles. But they use a stack of fuel cells instead of a battery. These vehicles give out less harmful emissions. They only give out heat and water. They are quieter, smoother and require less maintenance than vehicles that run on diesel or gasoline. Hydrogen can be obtained from nature, gas, coal, water, biogas and agricultural waste. However, in spite of this, fuel cell vehicles are expensive. Apart from being excellent for the environment due to their minimal emission of carbon dioxide, these vehicles can be refuelled in a very little time.

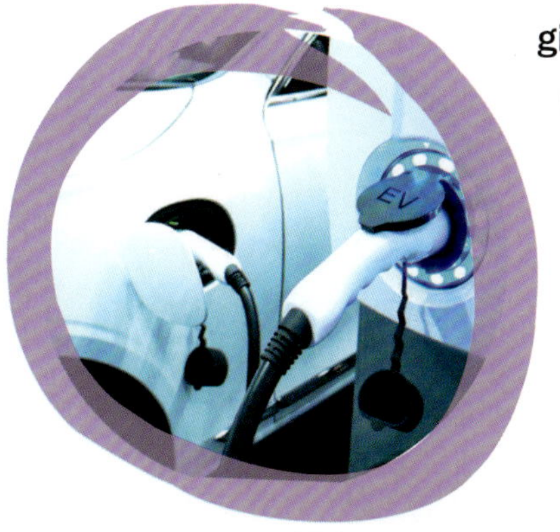

267 Save the Planet

The transport systems around the globe are one of the major causes of emission of greenhouse gases, leading to global warming, health problems, etc. Hence, adopting a means of transport that is environmentally friendly is the need of the hour.

For this, public awareness is necessary, apart from merely producing vehicles which run on renewable sources of energy like wind, solar, biofuels and hydroelectricity. Such systems of transport are called green transportation. And although the production of such vehicles on a mass scale is not immediate, we have alternate means of transport like bicycles, electric bikes, green trains, electric water cycles, etc., that help save carbon footprint.

Apart from being cost-effective, cycling is also an excellent form of exercise that offers numerous health benefits. Electric vehicles include cars, motorcycles, boats and scooters. These vehicles run on electricity and do not emit any harmful gases, thus making them environmentally friendly. Green trains are modern electric trains that run at high speeds and have high safety levels. Some trains have hybrid locomotives (a specialised type of electro-diesel locomotive) too. Hybrid cars emit very low harmful emissions.

268 As Tiny as a Peel

A tiny little thing that stands barely 54 inches long and just 41 inches wide, the Peel P50 is the smallest car in the world.

The car was created in the 1960s, on the Isle of Man, by Cyril Cannell. The original design allowed the car to run at barely 40 miles per hour and was comfortable only for a single adult and a briefcase. However, in the year 1964, the production of these cars stopped. Only 50 Peel P50s have ever been produced. It was only a few years ago, in about 2012, that the production of these cars started once again. This time around, the car was fitted with a better engine, with electric models of the same available as well.

269 Get Driven

Wouldn't it be amazing if you could just sit in a vehicle and get driven around? Although this may seem similar to Google's driverless cars, it is different. What we speak about, is less of a car and more of a vehicle! And that is the reason why this bubble-like vehicle is also known as EN-V which stands for Electric Network Vehicle. A product of General Motors, this two-wheeled, battery-powered vehicle drives on its own and has just about enough seating for two. With the help of its inbuilt sensors it detects its surroundings and wireless communications, thus positioning itself accordingly to the city. Ideal for urban driving, isn't it?

MEDICINE

Since time immemorial, healing has been an integral part of every culture. However, with the passing of time and advancements in science, these healing techniques have come to be known as 'medicine'. Thus, medicine is the practice of diagnosing, treating and preventing disease–all three of which are essential to promote good health.

270 The Oath

The Hippocratic Oath is something that is undertaken by physicians before they officially start their own practice. So what does this oath say?

Well, while the oath is a bit too long to be mentioned, here is a gist of what the oath says: The physician shall be indebted his entire life to his teacher of medicine, prescribe to his patients the best dietary regimen, shall never try and perform the role of a surgeon, since he is a physician and a physician he shall act like, shall not indulge in any lethal drugs or advocate abortion, shall never commit any other corrupt acts and shall maintain the anonymity of his patients, that is, he shall not share the problems of his patients with anyone outside his practice. That's like all the medical oaths of the world put into one!

271 Robotic Surgery

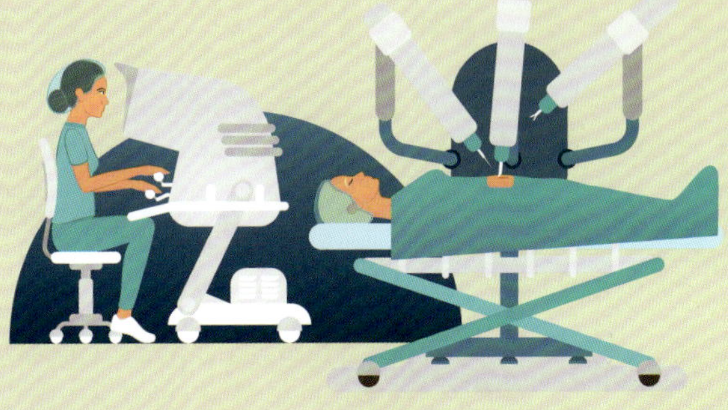

At one point of time, imagining a robot operating on you would have been a far-fetched and rather scary thought. But today, technology has progressed by leaps and bounds, and this too has become a reality. Known as Robotic Surgery or robot-assisted surgery, it is a great tool when doctors have to perform many different kinds of complex procedures that require the utmost precision, flexibility and control.

In such situations a robot comes in far handier in comparison to conventional surgical techniques. Robots are used in cases of minimally invasive surgeries, i.e., procedures performed through tiny incisions. However, there are times when it is also used in certain traditional, open surgical procedures. Generally, robotic surgical systems include mechanical arms and a camera arm that have surgical instruments attached to them. The surgeon who heads the operation controls the arms while sitting at a computer near the operating table, with other surgeons assisting during the procedure. This is truly one of the best technological inventions in the field of medicine so far!

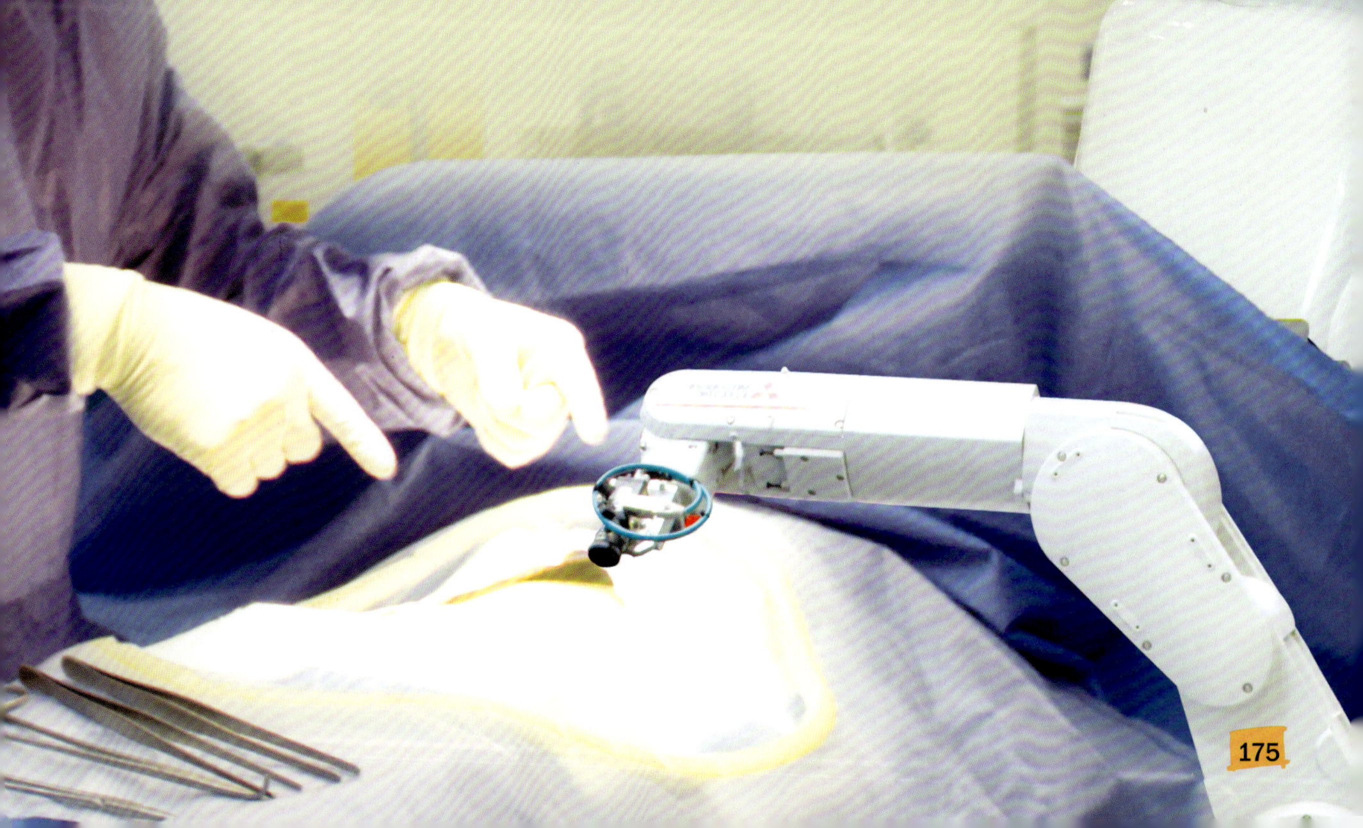

272 The Father of Ayurveda

Ayurveda is an ancient form of Indian medicine that uses herbs and minerals. It is nearly 5,000 years old. The two established Ayurveda books are the *Charaka-Samhita* named after Charaka and the *Sushruta-Samhita* whose author is Sushruta. Charaka, also known as the 'father of Indian medicine', describes the principles of maintaining health and the treatment of disease. He was the first physician to raise the concepts of digestion, metabolism and immunity. He stated that each body functions on the basis of three constitutions or *doshas*. These are movement (*vata*), transformation (*pitta*) and lubrication and stability (*kapha*). According to his theory, illness occurs when there is an imbalance among the three doshas, and that is when the body gets disturbed.

273 More about Charaka

Apart from the three *doshas* and their functioning, Charaka also had knowledge about the basic concepts of genetics. He studied the anatomy of the human body and the different organs. He stated that the total number of bones in the human body were 360, including the teeth.

Charaka believed that the heart had one cavity, but it actually has four chambers. He believed it to be a controlling centre of the body and how right he was! He claimed that the heart was connected to the entire body through 13 main channels. Apart from them, there were many other channels, which supplied nutrients to various tissues and organs. He also claimed that a block in one of the main channels would lead to a disease in the body.

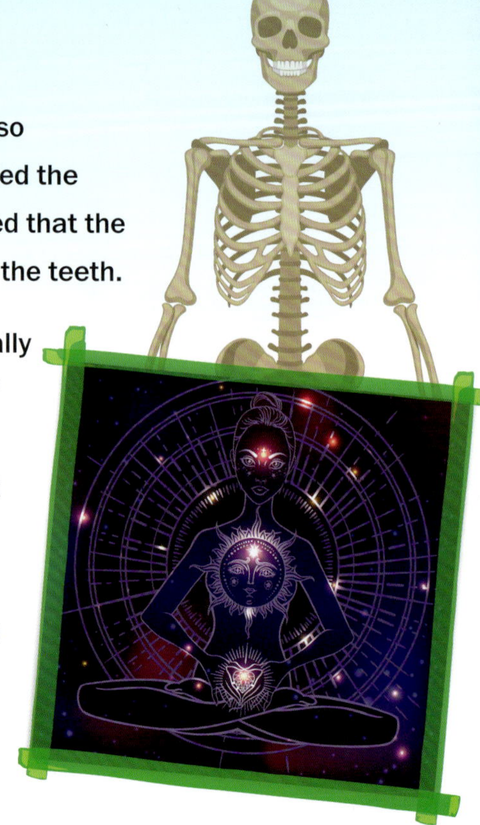

274 Rosy Periwinkle

Also known as 'Good Night', 'Shameless Maria', 'Cat's Vinca' and 'Sorcerer's Violet' in various cultures, the Rosy Periwinkle has innumerable medicinal properties.

It was used in Ayurveda to treat wasp stings, in traditional Chinese medicine to treat diabetes and malaria, and in Jamaican folk medicine to treat diabetes. Other folk uses of the plant include treatment for memory loss, circulatory disorders and toothache.

Found in Madagascar, this plant also has some potent anti-cancer properties. The plant contains about 70 alkaloids of immense medicinal value. Some of these include anti-cancer compounds like vinblastine that increase the chances of surviving childhood leukaemia from 10 per cent to 95 per cent, and vincristine that is effective in the treatment of Hodgkin's lymphoma, a fatal kind of cancer.

275 A Secret Scroll

The Ebers papyrus is one of the oldest medical documents recorded from ancient Egypt, and dates back to 1550 BCE. It was discovered in 1862, when Edwin Smith, an adventurer and dealer of antiques, purchased it from a market in Luxor, Egypt.

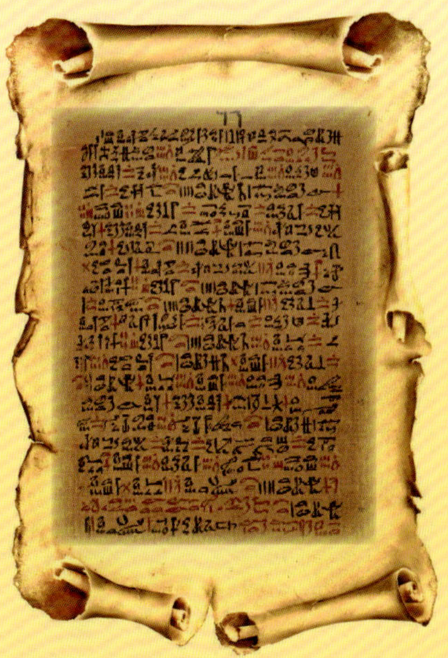

The Ebers Papyrus contains a large spectrum of medical texts and vast knowledge about Egyptian medicine. It speaks of a variety of ailments–from reptile bites, intestinal diseases, diabetes, arthritis, tumours, burns, fractures, to even dentistry. It also talks about mental disorders and the role of the heart and blood vessels in the circulatory system. It provides a wide range of cures and remedies, and some magical formulas as well. It states 700 magical remedies for ailments.

276 Gingko Biloba

Native to China and also known as the 'maiden-hair' tree, Gingko Biloba has fossils dating back to about 200 million years. And although it may seem like just a street tree with foul-smelling fruits, the Gingko Biloba is much more than that.

It is in fact a tree that is highly priced for its medicinal value. Apart from it being an energy booster, the plant is also used in a number of medicines used as memory boosters. Not just this, Gingko is also used as a blood thinner, thus preventing blood clots. It also acts as an anti-vertigo agent, and it helps protect against oxidative cell damage that is brought about by free radicals in the body. The saying, 'Never judge a book by its cover', is true in the case of Gingko Biloba!

277 Pan-Tsao

The Chinese *materia medica* book called 'Pan-Tsao', was written in 2735 BC by Li Schizen.

Materia medica is a Latin medical term about the knowledge of healing and the curing properties of medicines. It speaks of the therapeutic or beneficial effects of a drug. The book contains many plant and metallic preparations. It also mentions some animal by-products. More precisely, the book has a total of 53 volumes. Volume one to four is an 'index', and it contains a complete and concise list of herbs to treat the most common sickness. The core matter of the text is present in Volume 5 to 53, which has 1,892 distinct herbs, of which 374 were added by Li himself.

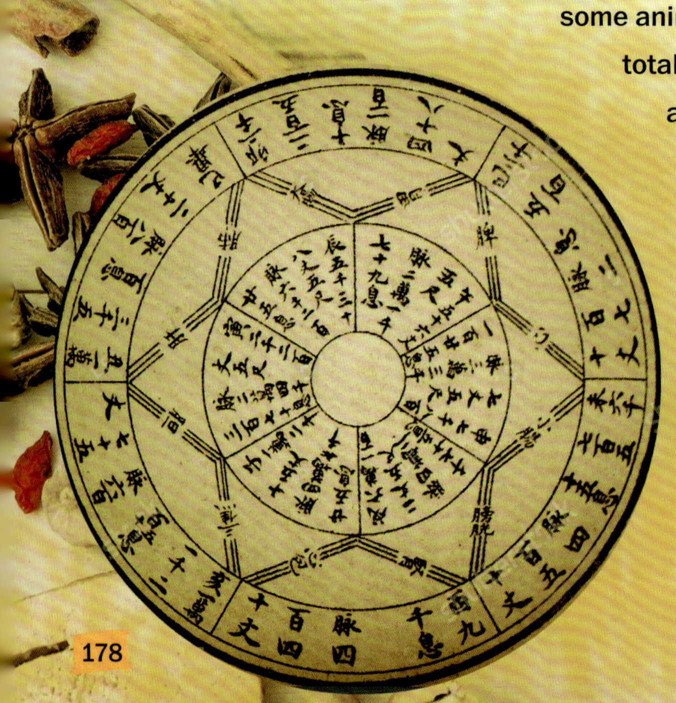

278 A Sweet Medicine

Honey, apart from its nutritional value, has been of utmost importance in the field of medicine as a treatment for several diseases and conditions. Honey has been known for its antimicrobial property against several species of harmful disease-causing bacteria. This is because natural honey is hygroscopic, which means it can absorb or remove moisture of the environment and thus dehydrate bacteria. In addition to this, pH levels of honey are low, which do not favour the growth of micro-organisms.

Fun Fact
Honey bees from a typical hive visit approximately 225,000 flowers per day.

Honey is also used in the treatment of ulcers and skin infections resulting from burns and wounds. Different varieties of honey are found across the globe. Reports show that Tualang, which is a Malaysian multi floral jungle honey, has a wide range of effects on different kinds of wound and gut or enteric bacteria. Then there is the Manuka honey that originates from New Zealand, and is supposed to have fantastic effects on the skin as well as the gut.

279 Probiotics

Probiotics are beneficial live microorganisms (often yeast and bacteria) that can prevent and treat illnesses by improving the health of the digestive tract. They are found in food or taken as supplements. Probiotics are naturally found in fermented foods like yogurt, curd, buttermilk, fermented pickles, cheese, etc. Probiotics resemble the naturally occurring good bacteria found in the intestines or gut of human beings.

Lactobacillus and Bifidobacterium are examples of good bacteria.

It is believed probiotics work by improving the balance of good and bad bacteria in the intestinal tract. It was Nobel Prize winner Eli Metchnikoff who first suggested in the early 1900s that Bulgarian villagers lived long, healthy lives despite poverty because they regularly consumed yogurt. Probiotics can potentially treat diarrhoea, irritable bowel syndrome, gastroenteritis, and inflammatory bowel disease.

280 Healing Herbs

Our Earth is home to innumerable herbs that have immeasurable benefits to mankind. Let us take a look at a few of these herbs and their benefits.

Methi, or fenugreek seeds, have certain medicinal properties, as they help to reduce blood cholesterol levels, as well as to treat inflammation and ulcers of the stomach and intestines. Sage, another medicinal plant, is used for conditions such as indigestion; skin, throat, mouth and gum infections.

Cardoon leaves aid in the treatment of liver and gall bladder diseases as well as help in lowering blood cholesterol levels. *Ashwagandha*, a well-known Ayurvedic herb, is beneficial for boosting the immune system, relieving pain, reducing cholesterol levels and regulating blood sugar levels. It also helps combat depression, anxiety, stress and helps maintain heart health.

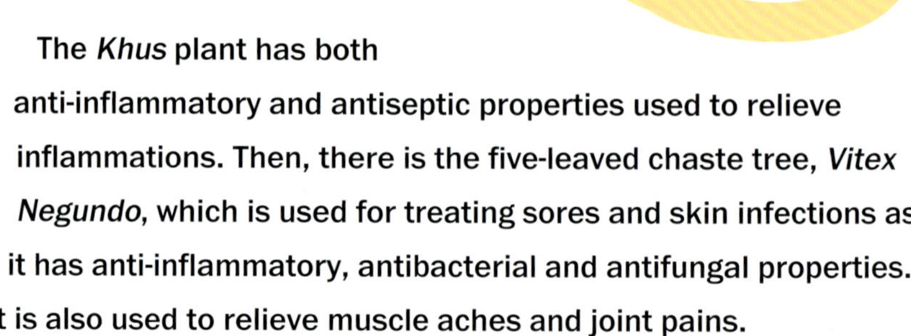

The *Khus* plant has both anti-inflammatory and antiseptic properties used to relieve inflammations. Then, there is the five-leaved chaste tree, *Vitex Negundo*, which is used for treating sores and skin infections as it has anti-inflammatory, antibacterial and antifungal properties. It is also used to relieve muscle aches and joint pains.

281 Gifts of Nature

The medicinal value of spices is immeasurable. Let's take a look at how these little gifts of nature can help us stay healthy.

Black pepper reduces blood pressure and contains a good amount of iron that is beneficial for the body. It is anti-bacterial in nature and can also aid in digestion. Nutmeg is also anti-bacterial, and small amounts of it act as an excellent sleep aid. It helps in combatting Alzheimer's and is also shown to improve memory.

Fun Fact

Black pepper is considered to be the king of spices.

Saffron is capable of treating depression. It can also prevent loss of vision and keeps the skin youthful. A lot of modern day beauty products use saffron as an active ingredient. In medicine, saffron is used to treat fevers, and the enlargement of the liver and spleen. In Ayurveda, saffron is used to heal arthritis.

Black cardamom has anti-inflammatory properties, and is used to relieve muscle spasms. It is also used for respiratory problems such as asthma.

Cinnamon is widely used for the treatment of diabetes, as it can help maintain and control the levels of blood sugar.

Ginger is another spice that is extremely useful in helping with digestive problems. It also helps in reliving a dry cough. Ingestion of ginger is also known to have a positive effect on our skin.

With an array of spices at our disposal, it wouldn't be wrong to say that nature is the best healer.

282 Vitamin E-ssential

One of the most essential vitamins needed for optimal functioning of our bodies is vitamin E. It is also important in the formation of red blood cells and acts as an antioxidant that protects our body tissues from free radical damage. Although its deficiency is not commonly seen in people, it is used in the treatment of certain medical conditions. A movement disorder called ataxia leads to serious deficiency of vitamin E. It is a genetic disorder, and vitamin E supplements are given as part of the treatment schedule. Vitamin E is also very effective in reducing memory loss in patients with moderate Alzheimer's disease. Research shows that vitamin E is also effective in cases of anaemia. Applying vitamin E to the skin may also treat skin sores called granuloma annulare (bumpy sores on the skin). Consumption of vitamin E daily, improves the symptoms of certain liver diseases. It is also effective in certain eye disorders in new borns, infants and adults.

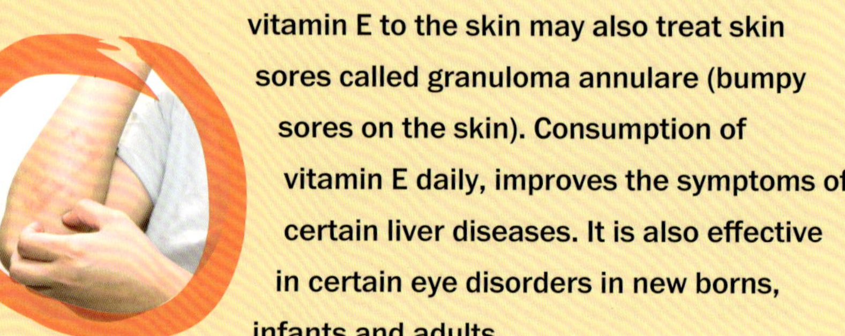

283 Pass the Flax

Flaxseeds are the products of the *Linaceae* plant. The seed and its oil, are both used as medicine, especially among diabetics.

In fact, consuming flaxseed powder for one month can decrease fasting blood glucose levels in people having type 2 diabetes. It can also decrease the blood sugar levels in people with glucose-intolerance, when taken over a certain period of time. Certain flaxseed preparations also help with reducing the levels of low-density lipoprotein (LDL) cholesterol, which is considered to be 'bad cholesterol'.

284 Hippocrates the Great

Known as the 'Father of Medicine', Hippocrates was also the founder of clinical medicine. He proved that a disease was a natural process, not caused by superstitions or the supernatural forces, but by natural reactions caused by the body to certain conditions. As he performed experiments and gathered information about diseases, he concluded that, the clinical signs and symptoms seen when we get a disease is not based on magical beliefs, but on rational science.

Hippocrates believed that the body functioned as a whole or a complete unit. In case of a disease, the body must be treated at a holistic level. As he formulated his theory about the body and how it functions during disease, he bridged the concept of the four humors or the four fluids present in the body. These were black bile, yellow bile, phlegm and blood. These elements, made up the nature of the body, and are responsible for pain and health, he believed. Furthermore, he proposed that people are healthy when there is a right balance between these four humors. Disease on the other hand, is caused when there is imbalance between the four humors. He believed that a physician must restore a healthy state of the body by correcting the metabolic imbalance as well as the disharmony between the four humors in the diseased state.

285 Laugh Your Guts Out

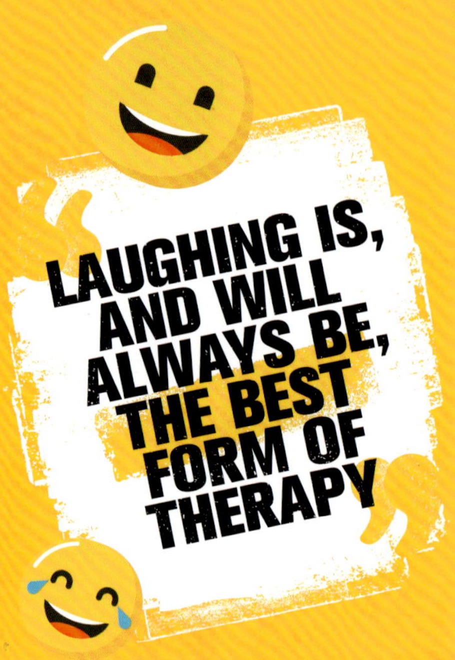

The age-old adage of laughter being the best medicine is now being recognised and acknowledged in the medical world. Today, laughter as a therapy is gaining momentum in a number of psychiatric institutions as well as medical institutions around the globe.

This is a type of therapy that makes use of humour in order to help relieve stress and pain and improve a person's overall sense of well-being. So how does laughing help? Laughter releases endorphins (feel-good hormones), decreases blood pressure and increases the supply of oxygen to the blood, all of which are vital for the healthy functioning of the body.

Laughter therapy includes laughter exercises, comedy movies, books, clowns, puzzles and games. Some hospitals even have humour carts that provide funny materials for people of any age. The best part of laughter therapy is that it has absolutely zero negative side effects and leaves you with only smiles!

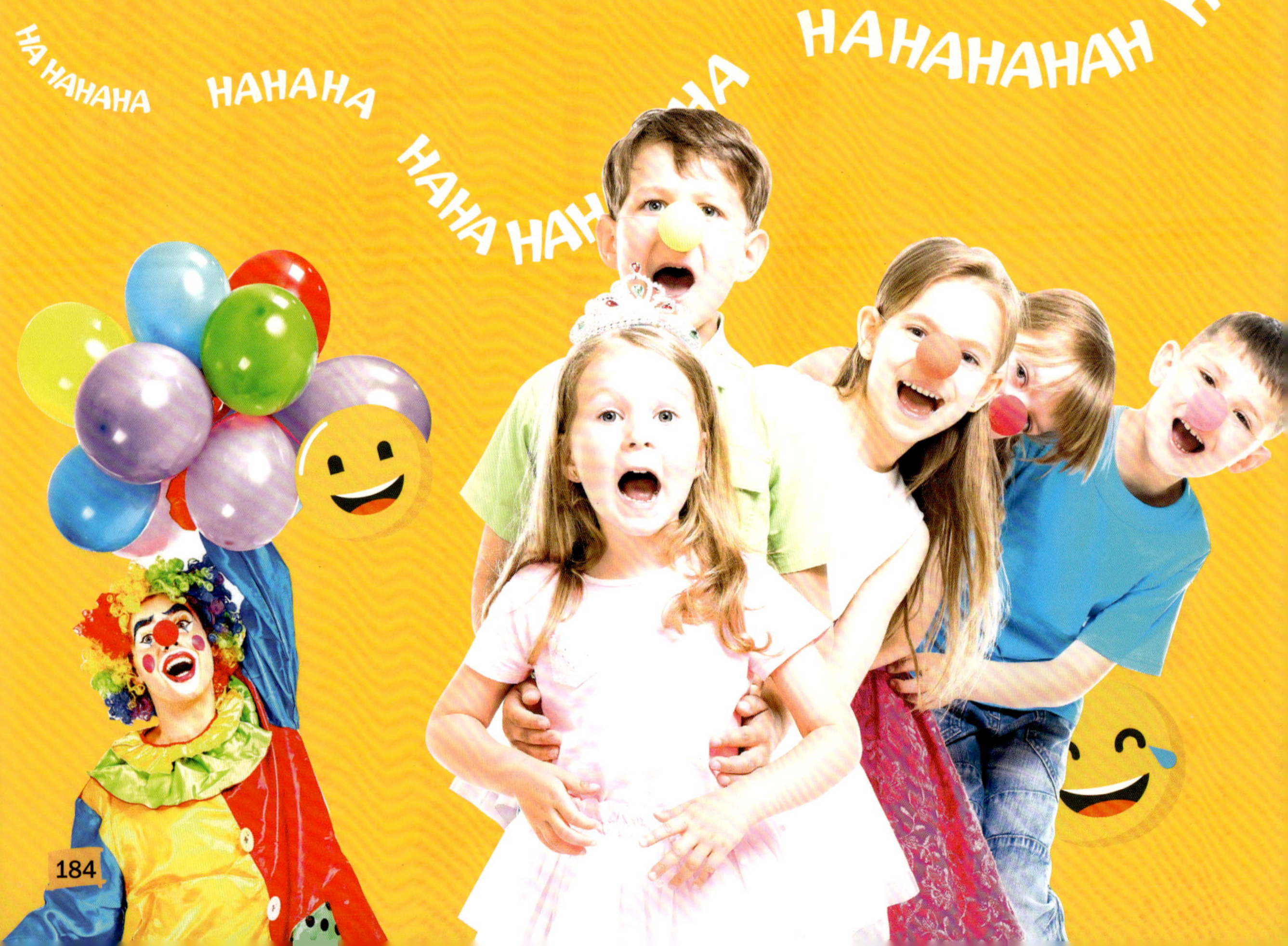

HAHAHAHA HAHAHA HAHA HAHAHAHAH HAHA

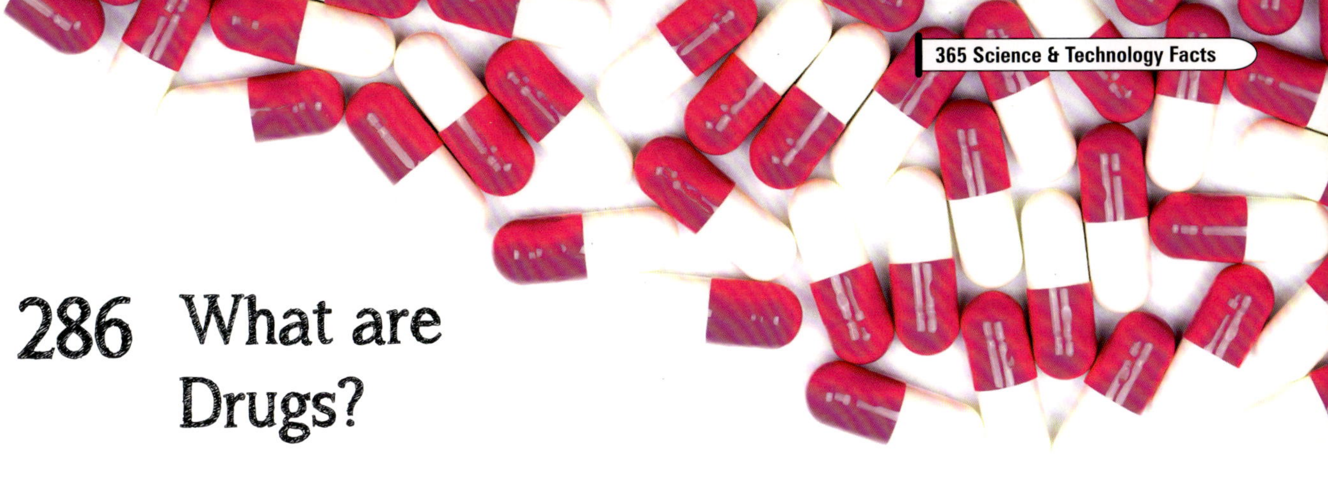

286 What are Drugs?

'Drug' is a word we hear often – from our parents, the doctor and even the guy over the pharmacy counter. So, what is a drug really?

Drug is a term used for medicines. It is named after the French word, *drogue*, which is a dry herb. It is a substance which is used for the prevention, relief or cure of a disease. Therapeutics is a branch of medicine that studies the prevention and cure of diseases through drugs, as well as relief of the symptoms of the diseases. For example, chemotherapeutic drugs are medicines used for the treatment of different kinds of cancer. The opposite to therapeutic drugs are toxic drugs, and while most drugs can do the body good, there are some that can also have a toxic effect on us.

287 For the Young and Old

The bodies of children and adults differ, which is why they both react to drugs in a different manner. Drugs are primarily metabolised in the liver. However, the ability of the liver to metabolise drugs is lower in children since their organs are not completely developed and functional. Also, the kidney function in children is low. Certain drugs may also show different effects in children as compared to adults. Some drugs could cause harmful effects on the growth and development of children. The more active the drug, the more toxic it is to the infant. The dose administered to a child is generally given with respect to their body weight.

288 Happy 120 Years

What if we told you, that it was possible for you to live for 120 years? Exciting? Scary? Unbelievable? Yes, that's what it feels like – unbelievable! But the truth is that today, science has discovered a drug that could help you live that long. We are referring to a diabetes drug, 'metformin'.

Researchers believe that this drug could stall aging. Scientists believe that Metformin could increase the number of oxygen molecules that are released into a cell, thus boosting robustness and longevity. A number of experiments conducted on round worms and mice have confirmed this as well.

289 Source It

From where do we get drugs? A large number of sources are used for the manufacture of drugs. These include minerals, plant products, certain bacterial and fungal micro-organisms, and synthetic sources as well. Drugs derived from animal sources are used in the manufacture of insulin, which is used in the treatment of diabetes.

Biological agents such as complex proteins are also used as sources. With the development of science and technology, nanomedicines are being made with the help of nanotechnology. This branch deals with materials whose size and shape are in the nanoscale range, that is, 1-100 nanometer (similar to the size of biological molecules present in our body).

290 Artificial Retina

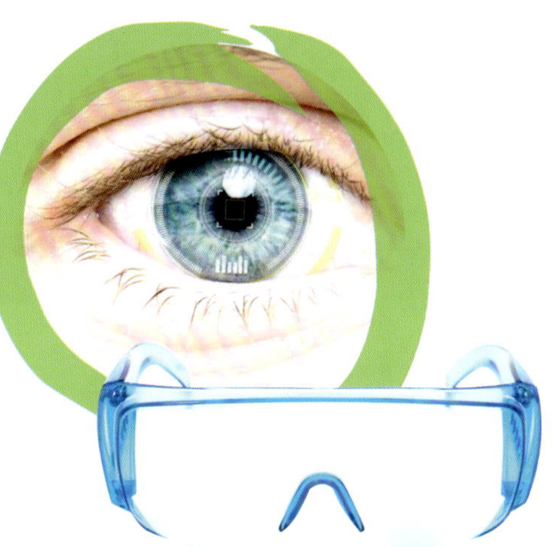

Human beings are truly one of the most wonderful creations that walk this Earth. But like most things that wear out, so do our bodies. This process is also known as degeneration. As we get older, our bodies tend to degenerate, and for some of us, it begins with our eyes. Cataract is one of the most widespread degenerative visual diseases. However, thanks to technology, this is something that can be rectified. An 'artificial retina' can help restore lost eyesight. This miniature device does the job of the damaged photoreceptor cells, while causing electrical stimulation. This electric stimulation is needed to activate the remaining healthy cells in the retina. This device is made up of two parts; a tiny implantable chip and a pair of eyeglasses that the patient wears.

291 The Oral Route

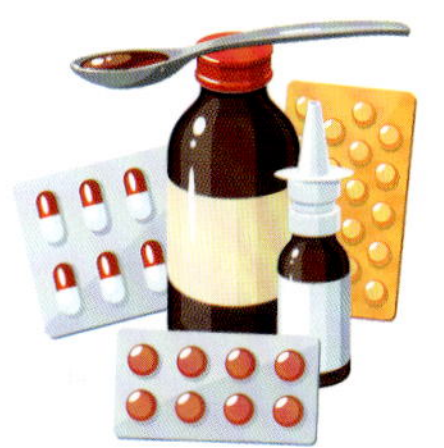

Most of the medicines we take are through the mouth or oral cavity. This is called the oral route. Although this route has its advantages it also has some disadvantages. The advantages are that it is generally safe and convenient. However, tablets cannot be consumed in cases where the patient is vomiting. Also, the oral route cannot be used in unconscious patients. Most importantly, drugs which can be destroyed by the effects of the acidic juices present in the digestive tract, cannot be consumed by the oral route. Tablets are now covered with a layer of chemicals, such as, waxes, gums and colouring agents. These substances fight the effects of the acidic juice of the stomach and prevent irritation in the gastrointestinal tract.

292 Your Body – The Healer

It indeed is a blessing and one of nature's marvels as to how our own bodies can produce their own medicine. Like the case of certain orthopaedic (bone and joint) conditions that can be treated with stem cells. This therapy is also able to curtail the progress of neurodegenerative diseases of the central nervous system, such as multiple sclerosis, Alzheimer's (memory loss) and Parkinsons disease (loss of muscular movement and balance).

Diseases of the autoimmune system, cerebral palsy (a type of brain malfunction), autism, heart failure and spinal cord injury, hair loss, serious kidney failure, diabetes, liver cirrhosis, thalassemia and even a stroke, etc., can all be treated and corrected with the use of stem cell therapy. It is also used to restore the health of the blood system after cancer treatment. The stem cells of a donor are called graft. The patient to be treated is the host.

A classic example of stem cell therapy is 'stem cord banking', that many of the gen-next parents are opting for. The umbilical cord that connects the mother and the baby is filled with the most nourishing form of blood. This blood contains stem cells and is preserved for years together in cryobanks (banks that specialise in stem cell preservation). This process is known as, 'cryopreservation'. In dire situations, like leukaemia, new cells are needed from the bone marrow of a donor. During times like these, the patient's own cells come to his or her rescue, i.e., if their stem cells are preserved at birth. Stem Cell Therapy has taken new strides in improving the quality of life!

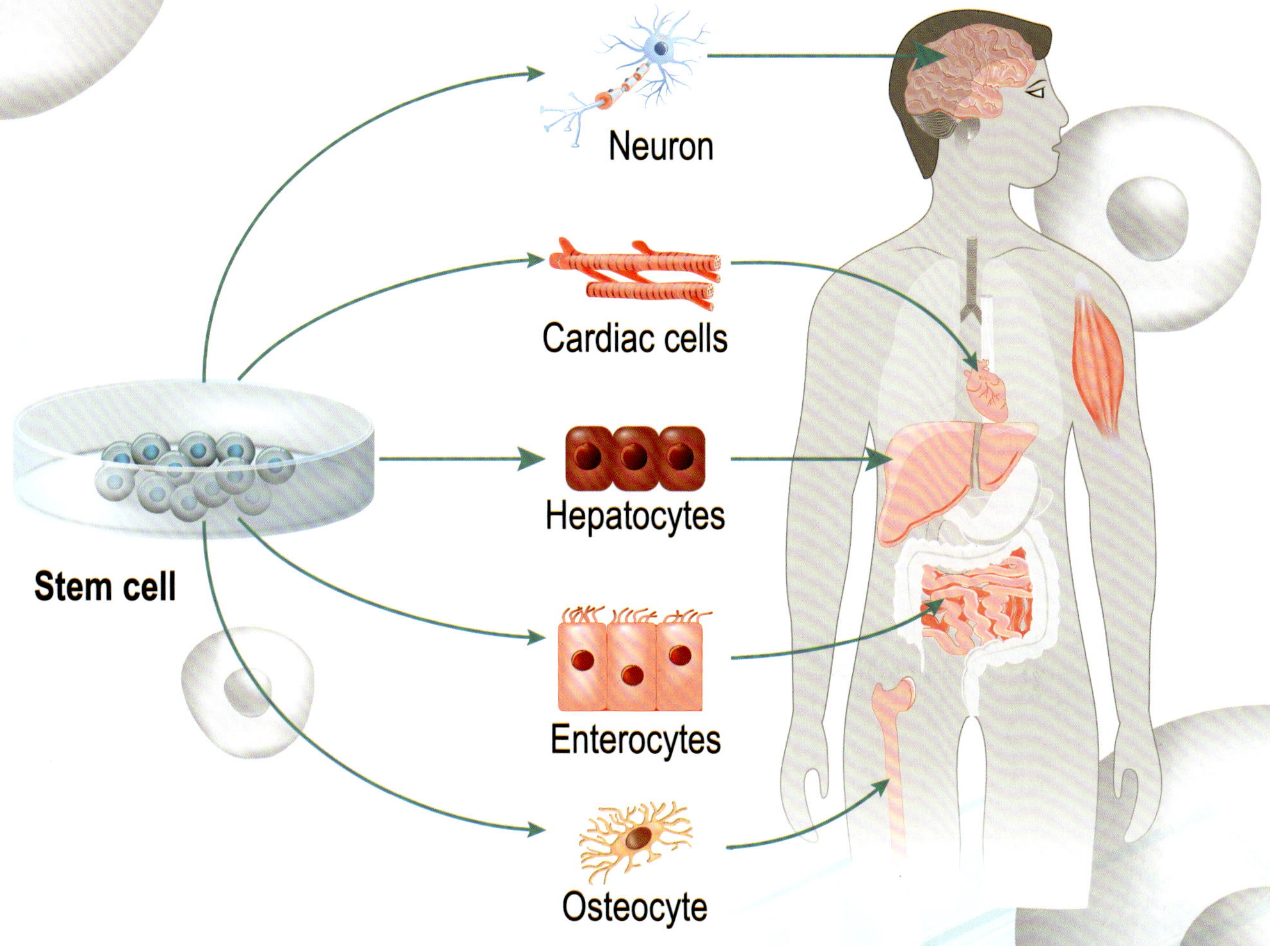

293 Autoimmune Diseases

Our immune system is our natural defence system and protects us from disease and infection. But in an autoimmune disease, our immune system is unable to differentiate between the body's own cells and foreign cells and by mistake starts attacking the body's healthy cells. Responding to an unidentified stimulus, the immune system starts making antibodies which instead of fighting diseases, attack the body's tissues.

A common symptom of autoimmune diseases is inflammation which causes swelling, redness and pain. Other symptoms include recurring fever, pain in joints, fatigue, etc. Treatment involves medicines that reduce the immune response. An autoimmune disease can also go into remission i.e. the symptoms cease to exist.

More than 80 types of autoimmune diseases exist. Some of them are rheumatoid arthritis (a type of arthritis that affects the joints), lupus (a disease that harms various body parts that include skin, joints and organs), psoriasis (a condition in which thick, scaly patches appear on the skin), multiple sclerosis (a disease where the immune system attacks the nerve cells), etc.

294 Polio – The Killer

While you may have been too young to realise it, as a baby, you have been immunised. We all have, against a deadly disease called Polio. So what is Polio really?

Polio is caused by a virus called the poliovirus. It is a dangerous and rather deadly condition that can cause lifetime paralysis. This means not being able to move the parts of your body. Polio is a highly contagious disease. It can easily spread through contact with the stool of an infected person and droplets from a sneeze or cough. It is estimated that about five children out of 100 who suffer from polio and paralysis, die. This is because the virus also affects the muscles that help you breathe.

295 Germ Killer

As kids we have all fallen and may have cut and injured our hands or legs. This cut, or scratch is an open wound. It allows tiny micro-sized germs to enter the skin. The result is an infection. These wounds serve as a haven for germs to thrive in. They have easy access through the skin and can penetrate the tissues, should the wound not be treated quickly.

Wounds are generally treated with an antiseptic liquid, which is a chemical agent that can destroy or curb the growth of bacteria in the injured area. Antiseptics are substances that can prevent the growth of germs on the external surfaces of the body.

296 Prosthetics

Prosthetics are artificial limbs. They help you perform daily tasks like eating, walking and even running, like you would with a real limb. Success rates in the case of prosthetics are very high, when an expert team of medical specialists that include doctors, prosthetists (an expert who designs, builds, and adjusts prostheses and advises how to use them), physical therapists, rehabilitation counsellors, work with the patient to determine the best possible fit. Some amputees with prosthetic limbs even participate in the Olympics!

297 Thiamine for Medicine

For those of you who have B complex deficiencies, B complex supplements are here to prevent it from getting worse. One of the important vitamins from the B complex group, is thiamine or vitamin B1. Not only does it regulate appetite, but it also maintains the health of the nervous and heart systems. Thiamine provides nutrients to maintain the proper structure and function of the nerve cells as well as the red blood cells. Vitamin B1 is also needed for the metabolism and consequent release of energy from carbohydrate rich foods.

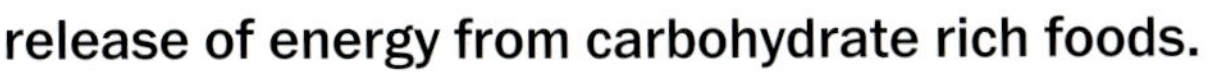

298 Good for Your Gut

Probiotics are being marketed under fancy brand names but they are nothing but live bacteria and yeasts (microorganisms), which are believed to have positive effects on the digestive system. The most common bacteria found in probiotics are lactic acid bacteria, which helps in maintaining optimal microbial health and balance.

While traditionally probiotics like curd, buttermilk, etc., were homemade, today readymade probiotics are available in stores. Probiotics are useful in treating disorders associated with the gastrointestinal tract. Disorders that can be treated with the use of probiotics include different forms of diarrhoea, gastroenteritis (inflammation of the membrane of the stomach and intestines), irritable bowel syndrome, liver diseases as well as urinary tract infections.

299 Regenerative Medicine

It is a branch of medicine that replaces tissues and organs which are otherwise damaged by disease, injury or congenital defects. The process is carried out through tissue engineering, cellular therapies, medical devices and artificial organs. This field of medicine uses the expertise of biology, chemistry, genetics, core medicine, computer science, biotechnology, cell and molecular sciences and many other fields.

Regenerative medicine has been used in children who have a spinal defect known as spina bifida, due to which they are unable to control their bladder. These patients need a new bladder grown from their own cells. Similarly, when heart valves are affected in heart diseases, a mould of the heart valve is created using biomaterial, and the cells are so engineered that they grow in the form of a heart valve.

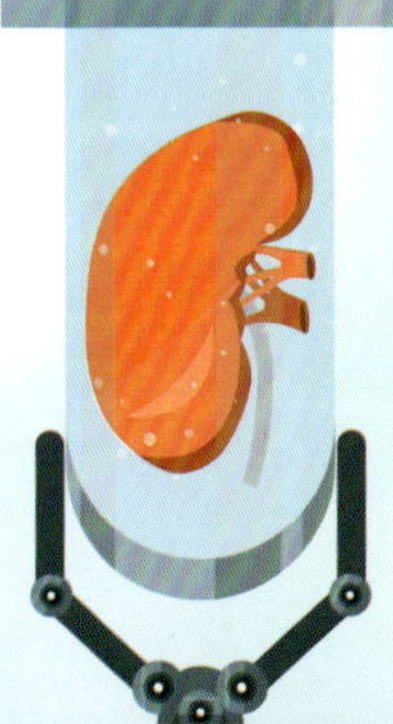

300 Rooting It Out

Unlike the conventional medicines that we consume, like a Crocin for a fever or an antibiotic for an infection, homeopathic medicines are used to treat a disease with a different approach or aim. Homeopathy is a branch of medicine that treats the person on a more natural and holistic level. It seeks to find the root of an ailment and heal it from the root, so that the ailment does not occur again. This is one of the reasons why homeopathy as a healing process can take a longer time as compared to conventional medicine.

The word Homeopathy is derived from the Greek word which means 'like disease'. Homeopathic medicines are produced from natural sources, such as mineral, vegetable or animal sources. Homeopathy does not focus on the diseased part, but does so, on a holistic level, that is, at a complete level.

301 Shots of Insulin

A commonly heard disorder is the classic, 'diabetes'. This lifestyle disease has affected a large proportion of the human population over the years. But what really is diabetes? Diabetes is caused because of the consumption of too much sugar. In this condition, the level of glucose in the blood is very high, that is, beyond normal. Insulin is a hormone which is secreted by the cells of the pancreas. But because of destruction of these specific beta cells of the pancreas, diabetes is marked by what is called insulin deficiency. This also results in insufficient insulin secretion. Hence, in patients who have diabetes, insulin shots are administered over time, via injections, to treat the condition. These injections help in moving sugar from the blood into other body tissues where it is used for energy. It also stops the liver from producing more sugar.

Fun Fact

A healthy diet and 30 minutes of moderate physical activity every day can reduce the risk of developing Type 2 diabetes.

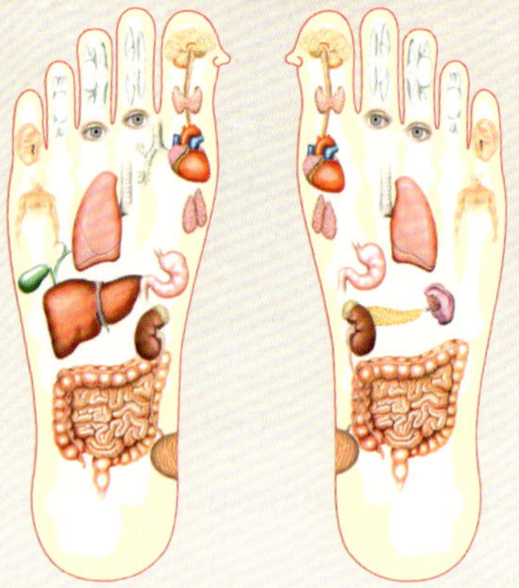

302 A - Puncture

Most of us think that when a needle is poked into our body, all you hear is an ooh, aah, ouch! But in acupuncture, along with the ooh, aah, ouch, also comes a lot of healing.

With its roots in traditional Chinese medicine, acupuncture is a therapy in which extremely fine needles are inserted into the skin. By doing so, specific points on the body are stimulated. Each point in our body is related to certain bodily functions and imbalances.

For example, the inner part of the foot is related to the stomach, while the centre of the foot is related to the kidney. Similarly, there are hundreds of points in the body that are related to different parts of the body. By stimulating these corresponding points with needles, the *chi* or *prana* (the life force energy of a human being) that is stuck at that particular point is released and flows freely once again, thus healing the part of the body it is related to.

303 Cup It Out

While new age medicine has taken over the market, there still exist a number of alternative healing therapies. One of them being the 'cupping therapy'.

This ancient therapy dates back to the Egyptian, Chinese and Middle Eastern cultures, and makes use of cups made of bamboo, glass, earthenware or silicon. In this form of therapy, the therapist puts a flammable substance - either alcohol, herbs, or paper in a cup. This is then set on fire and as the fire goes out, the cup is placed upside down on your skin. The air inside the cup then cools down, creating a vacuum between the cup and your skin, thus causing your skin to rise and your blood vessels to expand. The cup is typically left on your skin for up to three minutes. And while this form of therapy could be a bit painful, the benefits of it are immense!

304 Balneotherapy

Medicine made using science does wonders, but there are people who swear by natural healing methods. Balneotherapy for example is becoming a worldwide rage. This therapy has existed for eons and the remains of ancient baths found in the Indus Valley and parts of Europe are proof of this.

Patients sit in baths that contain thermal mineral waters sourced from natural springs and are at a temperature of 20 – 34°C. As per this therapy, there also needs to be a mineral content of at least 1 gram per litre of water used. Balneotherapy has been used to treat rheumatoid arthritis, sinusitis, as well as vascular disorders.

305 Water to the Rescue

The advancement of technology has seen many kinds of therapies emerge in the field of health and medicine, hydrotherapy being one of them.

Vincenz Priessnitz brought to the world his much tried and tested healing method of hydrotherapy. What happens during a session of hydrotherapy is that patients perform certain exercises in a warm, temperature-controlled pool (with the temperature ranging from 33–36°C). This therapy is especially useful for patients suffering from arthritis or rheumatoid arthritis.

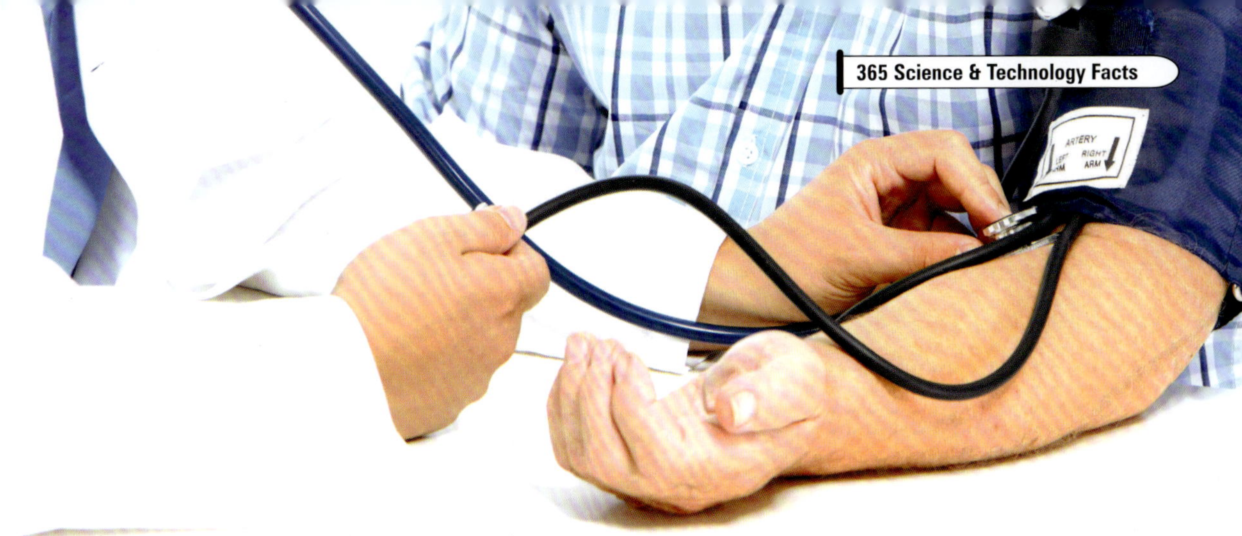

306 Keeping It Low

Although lifestyle changes can help prevent high blood pressure, medicines are given in severe cases. They lower blood pressure. A wide range of medicines is available for hypertension. Diuretics (water pills) remove the excess sodium from your body, which helps in reducing blood pressure. Calcium Channel Blockers prevent excess calcium from making its way into the blood vessels and the muscle cells of your heart. This allows for relaxation of the vessels, which in turn keeps blood pressure at bay. Medicines called Alpha Blockers cause the blood to flow more freely, reducing high blood pressure levels. Alpha-Beta Blockers allow the heart to beat at a slower rate, maintaining normal levels of blood pressure. Vasodilators cause relaxation of the muscles in the walls of the blood vessels, and lowers the blood pressure.

307 Lasik and Laser Eye Surgery

Gone are the days of wearing eye glasses, to correct near sightedness and far sightedness. Medical procedures like Lasik or laser surgery are very popular today. It does not require even a night's stay at the hospital.

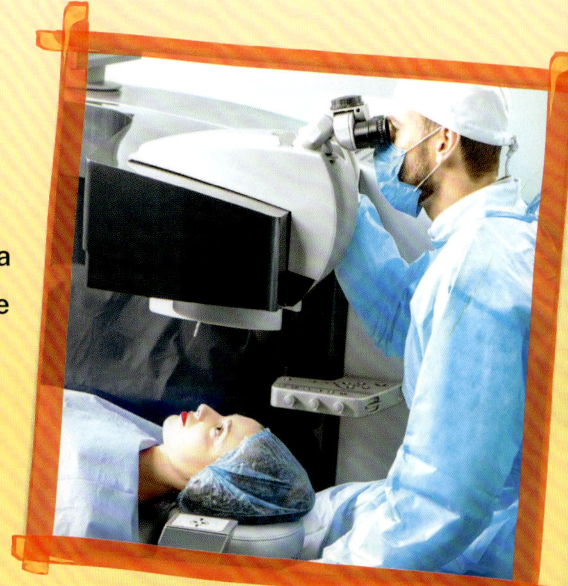

The person undergoing this surgery is asked to look at a target source of light. Light waves are sent through the eye to determine what affects the patient's vision. The Lasik surgeon watches the patient's eye through a microscope. The laser reshapes the cornea and the condition is corrected with negligible use of medicines. There is no pain during the procedure.

308 Pharmacokinetics

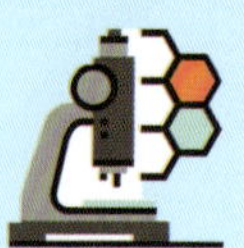

What happens to medicine after we consume it? Does it go into the bloodstream or the tissues or does it directly reach the organ that needs it? Will the drug stay in us, or will it be removed by the body? This list of questions makes us think about how our biological system works in this area.

A branch of pharmacology called Pharmacokinetics, is the science which studies four major factors. Firstly, where and how is the drug absorbed by the body? Secondly, once absorbed, to which parts of the body does it get distributed? The third factor is the metabolism of the drug. Finally, how and where is drug excreted from the body? Another branch called Pharmacodynamics deals with what the body does to the drug. More precisely it studies the biological and therapeutic effects of the medicine. It helps in identifying the mechanism of drug action. All these aspects help us identify how the body reacts to the medicine and the other way round too.

309 Aminoglycosides

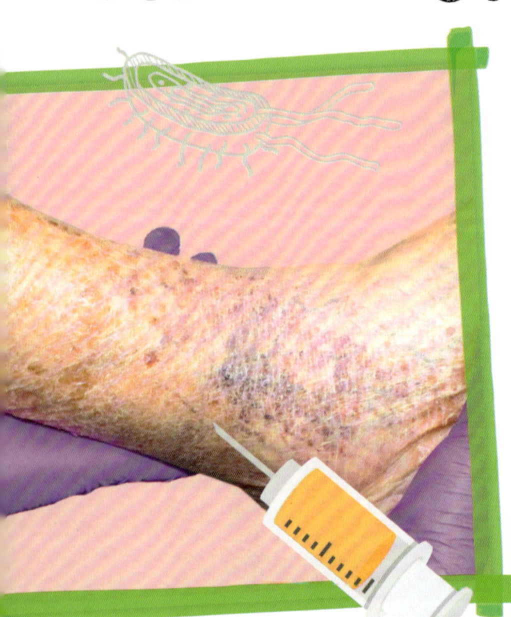

Aminoglycosides are a group of antibiotics that are used to fight common bacterial infections. They stop protein synthesis in bacteria, inhibit their action and their adverse effects on the host cells. They are generally administered through the intravenous route (via the injection route), as they are not well absorbed when consumed orally.

A few classic examples of aminoglycosides are gentamycin, neomycin, amikacin, streptomycin and erythromycin. They are used to treat infections such as complicated skin, bone or soft tissue infections, serious, life-threatening gram-negative infections and other severe abdominal diseases. Certain eye and ear infections can also be cured with the use of these drugs. However, as useful as aminoglycosides are, they can also cause certain side effects like skin rash or itchiness, unusual drowsiness, dizziness and weakness.

310 Scare-jections

Will a needle actually pierce my skin? What's in it? Our mind ponders over these questions whenever we have to take an injection.

A variety of injections are now used for the treatment of different disorders. The types of injections depend on their route and site/passage of entry. Intradermal injections are given into the layers of the skin. For example, vaccines are commonly given by this route. Intramuscular injections are given in the muscles.

Drugs given via this route could have some side effects like local pain, damage to the nerve and damage to the cells. Intravenous injections are given directly into the vein. In this route, the drug solution can be administered in rather large volumes i.e., 100 ml or larger. The drug can also be mixed with 10-20 ml of saline and administered for 5-10 minutes. These are called infusions. Like the intramuscular route, it also has its disadvantages. It could cause certain discomfort and irritation in the patient.

311 Plasticky

We must have all heard of the term, 'plastic surgery'. No, this surgery doesn't make use of plastic. It is a kind of corrective surgery that is divided into 'cosmetic surgery' and 'reconstructive plastic surgery'. The goal of cosmetic surgery is to improve the look of a person. It includes face uplifts, neck tightening surgeries, lip enhancing surgeries, nose shaping surgeries, etc. On the other hand, the primary goal of reconstructive plastic surgery is to improve the overall functioning of a person's body. It includes surgery on burn scars, hand repair surgery, etc. Reconstructive plastic surgery is often also referred to as reconstructive surgery.

312 The Flu

Influenza, commonly known as the 'flu', is a disease of the respiratory tract generally caused by the influenza virus. It is highly contagious, and infects the nose, throat and lungs. Most of the general symptoms include fever, cough, a sore throat, runny or stuffy nose. Others include body pain, headaches, weakness and feeling of extreme tiredness or fatigue. The flu spreads through droplets released by coughing, sneezing and talking. These droplets of saliva have the influenza virus and are emitted into the mouths or noses of people nearby. Complications of the flu could include bacterial lung infection called pneumonia, ear infections and sinus infections. One way to prevent influenza is to get the flu vaccine. It is believed to be a safe vaccine, with negligible side effects.

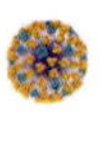

313 A Blood Thinner

Thought it might sound like something used in war, Warfarin is a medicine that is used to prevent blood from clotting. In medical terms, Warfarin is a blood thinner. Hence, it is even known as an anticoagulant.

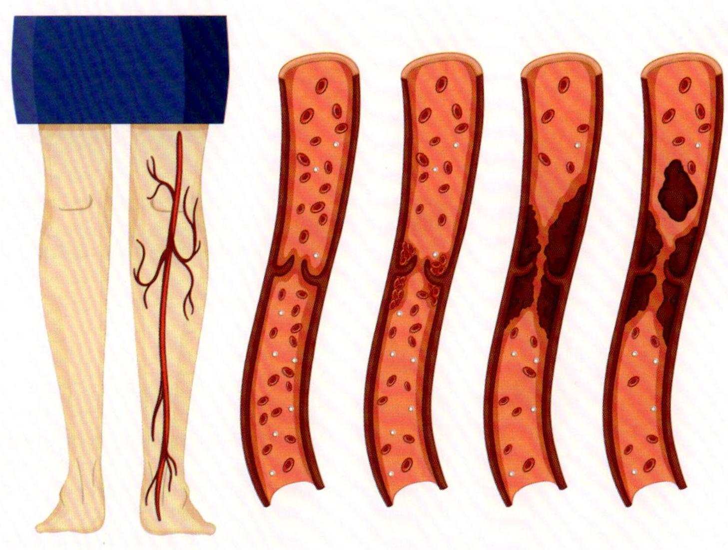

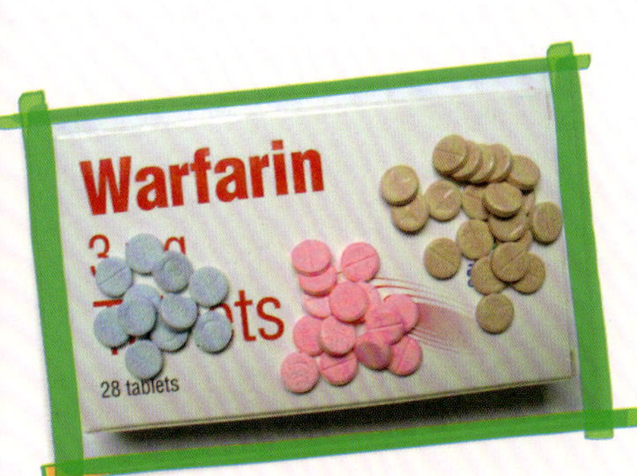

The process of blood clotting or coagulation occurs as there is thickening of blood beyond normal levels. As the blood thickens, it forms a solid mass or complex mass of blood fibres that bind together. Blood clots are dangerous to the body as they cause heart attacks, strokes and other serious cardiac disorders. Chemicals called clotting factors present in the body are responsible for blood clots. However, Warfarin must be taken in the amounts prescribed by the doctor as it has some side effects. It could lead to bleeding in the gastrointestinal tract, gums, nose, and other parts of the body. In certain cases it could also lead to the patient throwing up blood. Therefore utmost care must be taken while consuming Warfarin.

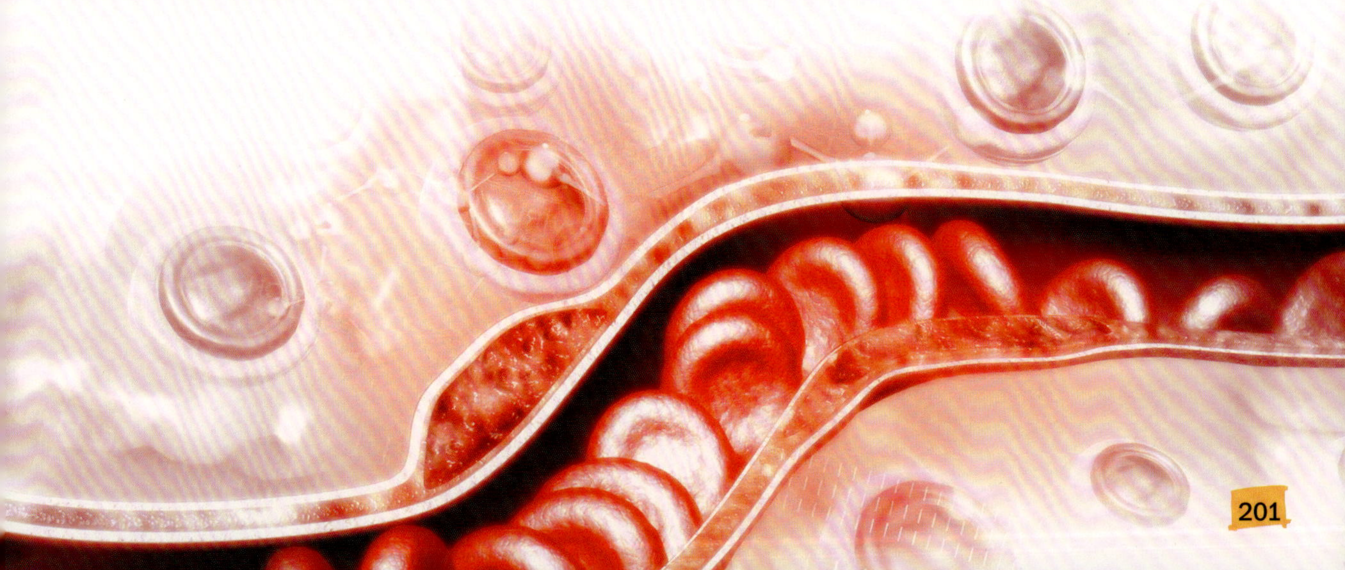

314 Grow New Teeth!

You no longer have to be a child to have your teeth growing back. And yes, we are not talking about milk teeth here.

Researchers from Georgia who did an in depth study on Cichlids, a fish that is found in Africa's Lake Malawi, have come to believe that these fish are the answer to teeth regeneration. Cichlids are known to regenerate their teeth once every 50 days. They believe that teeth and taste buds start out as the same tissue and then move on to perform different functions.

Studies on this are currently still under process, and once these studies are successfully completed, and there is clarity on how taste buds (which can regrow) and teeth are connected, dental healthcare could see a break through like never before!

TECHNOLOGY

The world today is a world of technology. Any tool, machine or process created to make performing tasks simpler, quicker and interesting are some aspects of technology. High rises, mechanised vehicles, different forms of communications, smart phones, machinery, computers and many more things are the result of technology. As a matter of fact, what you're reading right now is also a result of technology – the book, the print and the colours.

315 Fax-It

Fax is short for 'facsimile'. It is also called tele copying or telefax. Scanned, printed text and images are sent to recipients via telephonic transmission. It is a form of communication that sends or receives texts and images. Fax machines are of 2 types – a standalone unit, and a unit that has a scanner, a copier, a printer and a fax machine. Documents sent via e-mails bear electronic signatures, which are not acceptable everywhere, but a fax machine besides sending the physical documents of a text or image also has the signatures. With advances in technology, there is no longer the need to install a fax machine. Instead, with the use of software, faxes can be sent and received by personal computers.

316 Robotics

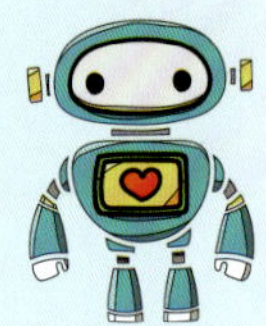

Robots are a marvel of science and engineering technology. They carry out repetitive work very precisely. All robots have a form or shape that is designed to carry out a particular task. A robot whose body resembles that of a human being and that can walk and talk is called a humanoid robot. It has a head, a torso, arms and legs. Although these robots resemble human beings, they lack human emotion. On the other hand, they do have intelligence with the help of which they react to different situations.

A humanoid robot can assist the ill and the elderly; and can also perform dangerous tasks. Today, robots are used in bomb detection and deactivation, finding survivors in ruins, and exploring mines and shipwrecks. These robots are programmed to work in areas of manufacturing, packaging, surgery, earth & space exploration and laboratory research.

Robots also work as couriers in hospitals and waiters in hi-tech homes. There are military robots, industrial robots as well as agricultural robots. They can even clean up toxic waste. There are sensors which enable a robot to perform its tasks or warn it about safety and malfunction. Robots are not restricted by fatigue and health risks. Electrical components are embedded into them for power and control. All that robots require is to be programmed perfectly because if they are not, their performance will be affected.

Fun Fact

Electro was the first humanoid robot which was exhibited in 1939.

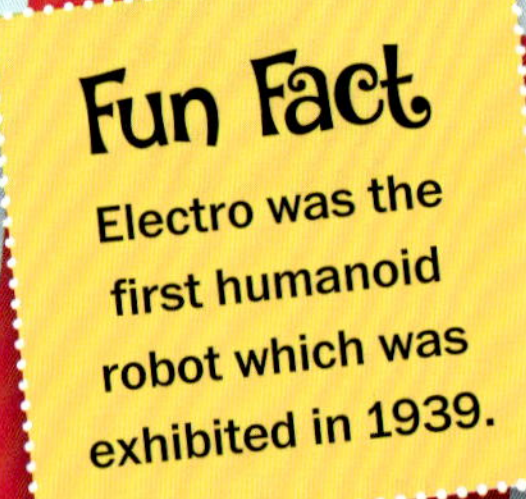

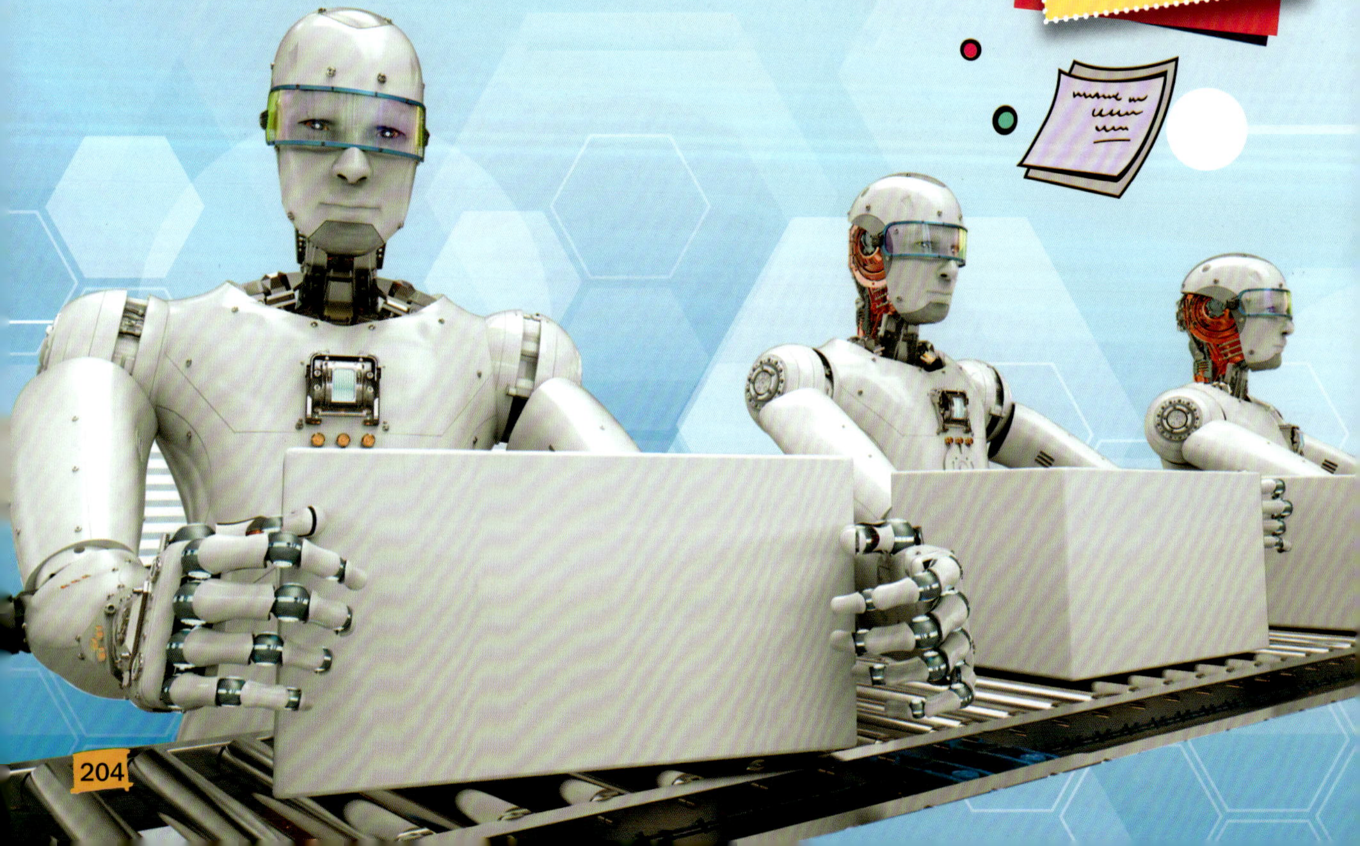

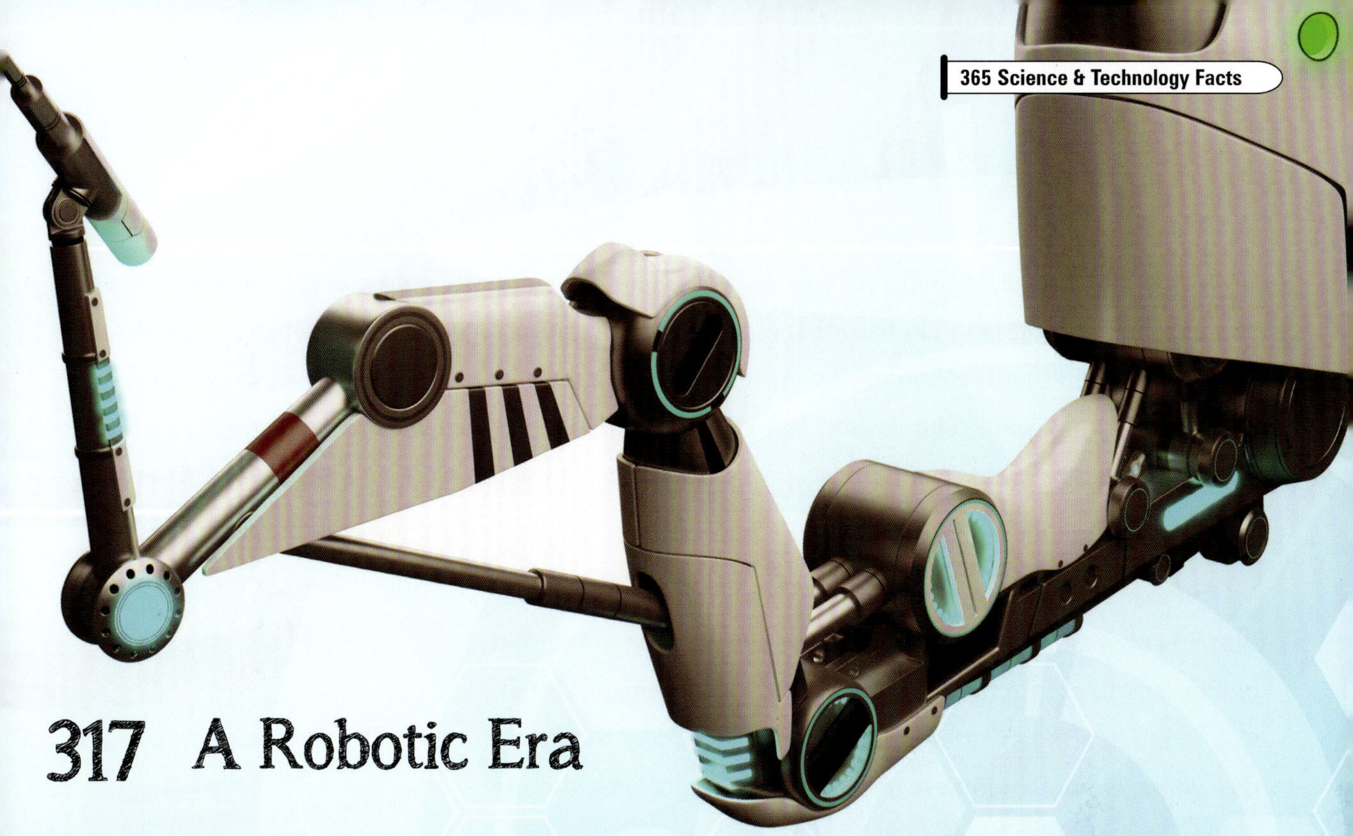

317 A Robotic Era

There are different kinds of robots. Let us have a look at a few of them. In industries, robots carry out tasks like installation, painting, welding of products that the factory is manufacturing.

Military robots examine suspicious matter and deactivate explosive devices and mines. They are used to trace enemy whereabouts and find concealed explosives.

In space exploration, remotely operated vehicles capture data and visual images in space for scientists and researchers to study on Earth.

They are also used in minimally invasive surgery. Robot-assisted surgeries are characterised by finer cuts, lesser pain and decreased loss of blood. They are also used in gynaecology, angioplasty and bypass, besides brain and eye surgery.

Underwater exploration is undertaken by robots that can dive longer and deeper than human beings. They collect data and images of marine life. Robots , especially the heavy duty ones, shoot a cannon of water to detain a criminal, thereby protecting people in danger. Robots also investigate hazardous environments, and can even enter active volcanoes to collect data.

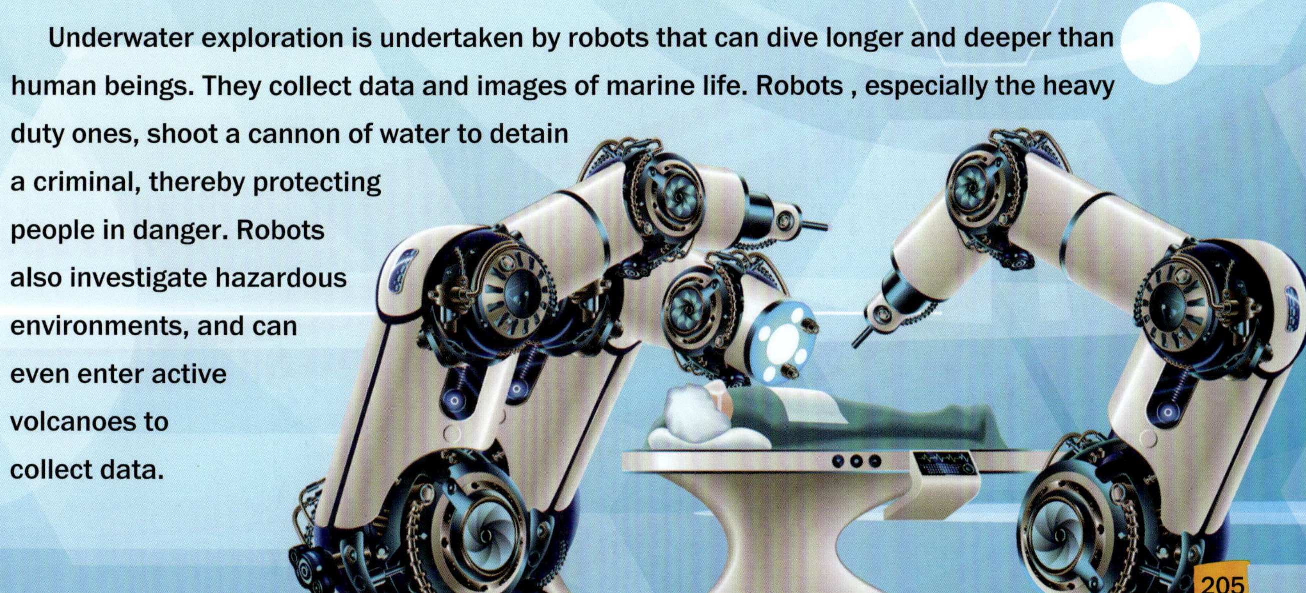

318 Virtual Reality

You are sitting in a classroom, yet you are convinced that you are in space. Is that even possible? The answer is yes. It is the outcome of something called reality technology, which convinces the human mind that it is in a particular place, while in reality, it isn't. This process is also known as 'virtual reality simulation'. With the help of specific hardware and software, artificial environments are created and are so presented that the user's mind accepts them as real environments.

The experience is so real that we interact with it forgetting that it is an artificial environment. These are used to stimulate our senses to create the illusion of reality. Our sense of touch, vision and hearing are stimulated, making our mind believe in that which is not. The 3D environment is thought to be the real world. It is said that the human mind remembers 90 per cent of what it does or simulates. Hence, virtual reality is a highly effective way of learning.

Fun Fact

One can even experience the sinking of the Titanic, the first moon landing by Apollo 11, all through visual reality technology.

319 Biometrics

Biometrics is the study and automated analysis of body identifiers like DNA, fingerprints, facial features; as well as human behaviour traits like voice, walking, gestures, vein scanning, etc. The idea of this technology is to identify people using their physical or behavioural characteristics.

Instead of opening the door of your house with a key, you just put your thumb on a machine and voila, your door is open! With a biometric locking system one wouldn't even need a key! Smart phones today use the same technology to unlock phones. And since no two persons can have the same fingerprint, DNA or retina structure; this identification system is fool-proof.

320 Where's the TV?

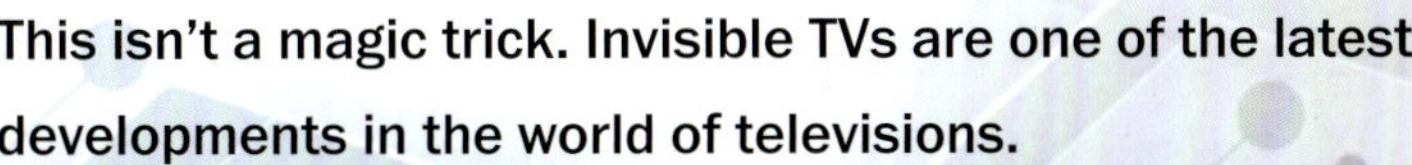

This isn't a magic trick. Invisible TVs are one of the latest developments in the world of televisions.

With looks as ordinary as a sheet of glass, this invisible TV could easily give a magician a run for his money. The previously used LED screens are now replaced by OLED (organic light-emitting diode) screens made from an extremely fine mesh and are embedded into the glass of the TV. When the back-light of the TV is on, the image on the TV is easily visible. However, it is when the television screen is dimmed, and not in use, that the screen turns transparent leaving it completely undetectable. Truly the TV of the future this one!

321 Drones

Drones are unmanned aerial vehicles made of light materials to make them lightweight and easy to manoeuvre. In short, a drone is a type of flying robot. The circuit boards, chip-set and software are its brains. They are used, by the military and police for surveillance. They carry out aerial inspection of aircraft, and in some western countries they are also used for home delivery of goods. They are also used in scientific and agricultural applications. Sometimes, drones are also flown as a hobby or a recreational activity. However, drones are banned in certain countries because it is believed, through past experience, that by using drones terrorists can easily plan their attacks.

322 Satellite Radio

The first image that comes to mind when we hear the word 'satellite' is a huge machine-like device that circles around planets. However, satellites do more than just that. They perform many tasks like broadcasting radio programs and bringing live cricket matches to your living room.

Radio services use a satellite that orbits the Earth to broadcast its program and is called satellite radio. The broadcast has lots of music, news, sports, and other programmes all broadcasted from as far as 35,000 kms from the Earth. The equipment is highly specialised. It is better than terrestrial radio, because it can reach the entire planet whereas terrestrial radio covers a limited area. Satellite radio is truly a gift of technology!

323 A Blue Tooth?

No, we are not speaking of a blue coloured tooth here. The Bluetooth we are referring to is actually a device which connects to a phone or a computer using radio waves. It has the ability to transfer data over short distances wirelessly.

A Bluetooth device has an in built computer chip with a Bluetooth radio and software to get connected. Bluetooth is commonly used in headsets and wireless speakers, besides hundreds and thousands of other devices. Bluetooth technology has crept into mobiles and medical equipment too. You can manage your lighting, household appliances, door and window locks and security system with the help of Bluetooth. Bluetooth technology in products assures consumers of quality, safety and easy use.

324 On the Dot

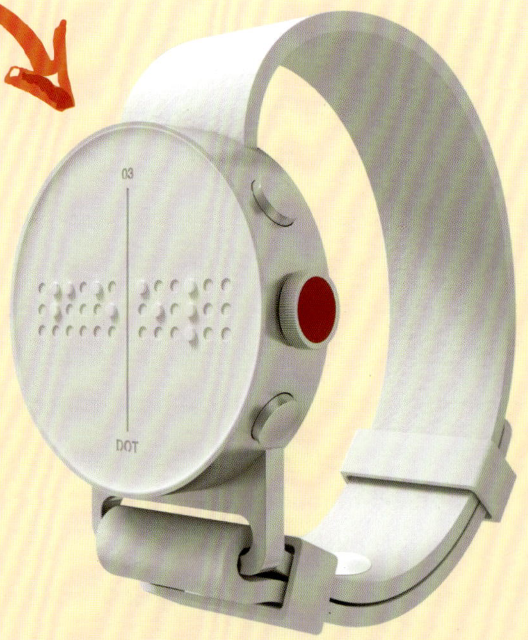

While most of us always look at what the time is, technology has now made it possible to 'feel' what the time is. We're talking about 'Dot', the newly launched braille watch for the visually impaired.

And while most assistive smart-watches for the blind are based on audio, the Dot displays the time with the help of four braille characters on its screen. The product hails from South Korea, and it has been tried and tested ever since 2014. It is now finally ready to hit the shelves and Stevie Wonder, one of the greatest, visually impaired musicians, has already placed his order for the Dot, among 140,000 other customers.

325 Bionic Eye

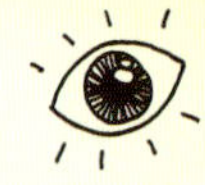

Also known as an eye prosthesis, this technology restores partial vision in the blind, thereby helping them see, and is known as 'bionic eye or bioelectric eye'. The vision in a bionic eye is different from natural vision.

It is a retinal implant, and in this process a tiny implant with microchips and a set of electrodes is placed in the back of the eye surgically. The microchips receive radio signals from the camera which are attached to the glasses. These signals are converted to electrical impulses. These impulses are passed on to the vision processing centre in the brain, via the optic nerve, where they are interpreted as an image.

After a week or so of the surgery, the patient is given glasses to which is attached a digital camera, and with its help the patient implanted with the bionic eye can see shapes, outlines, and partial images within a few weeks of the surgery. This technology has helped repair malfunctioning human eyes to a great extent. A bionic eye sure puts a spark into vision less life!

326 Bioinformatics

This is a branch of information technology also known as computational biology. Bioinformatics uses operations in mathematics and statistics along with computer-related methods to assess biological information. It is a highly developing field today. Bioinformatics is a field of science and technology which processes biological data and organises this information into databases. It then extracts more information from these databases, combines the data from different sources, and relates it with one another. Bioinformatics is applied to four different areas, namely acquiring or obtaining data, developing databases, collecting and combining data, and finally assessing this data.

327 Healing Your Genes

Once information about the sequences of normal and abnormal genes has been studied by technology of genomics and bioinformatics, something known as gene therapy comes into the picture. It is a technique in which abnormal genes are replaced by normal genes, thereby correcting genetic diseases. Medical professionals are hopeful of treating cancer, HIV/AIDS, and other chronic diseases with this therapy. In this therapy, the mutated disease-causing gene, is replaced by a healthy gene. The therapy is still in the infant stage. Studies are underway to see if it is an effective option. This mode of treatment was developed in 1972, but its success has been limited.

328 Cloning

Genomics is the study of the complete genome of the organism. But what is a genome? Genome is the complete set of genes that builds us into who we are. DNA contains all the genetic or hereditary information that makes up an individual. This information is passed from the parents to the child. This inherited information of the DNA sequence is coded in genes. Therefore, it is said that genomics is the study of the information present in the DNA or genes. A very interesting application of genomics is cloning. Clones are identical genetic copies of an organism that are created in a laboratory. Dolly, the sheep, was the first mammal to be cloned.

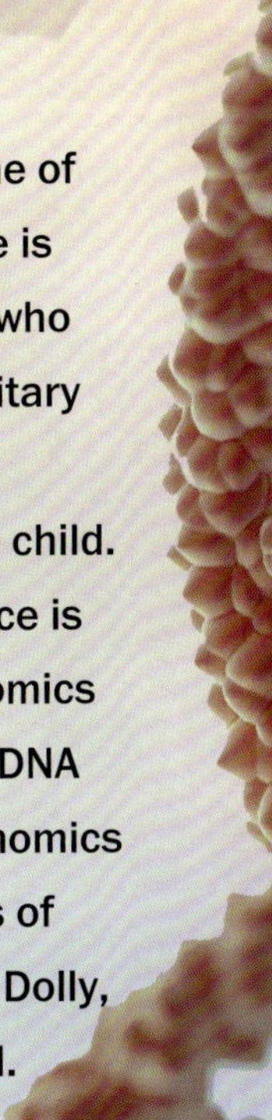

329 Paperless Technology

The whole world has gone digital. Converting written or printed material into digital form, thereby curtailing and reducing the use of paper, is called paperless technology. It is claimed that besides saving money, paper and the space needed to store numerous files, it makes the process of documentation much easier, and information can be stored safely and securely. It is environment-friendly, because the cutting of trees for paper production leads to deforestation and climate change. Apart from that, the process of paper manufacturing gives out polluting gases. Even printing ink is made with heavy metals and organic compounds that damage the environment. Here technology aids in eliminating the use of paper. If the information and documents are automated on computers and laptops in the digital form, the use of paper is reduced. Sending e-mails in place of letters and faxes, surfing the Internet for reference purposes instead of referring to books, filling of e-forms for applications rather than hand-written applications are the major ways in which digitisation of information can be done. Even ATMs today, give you an option of receiving your transaction details via SMS rather than through printed statements.

Fun Fact

Nearly four billion trees are cut down each year in order to make paper.

SAVE TREES

330 Feeling Hot! Hot! Hot!

With the increase in global temperature, an air conditioner commonly known as an A/C, is the perfect answer to our heat woes. Invented by Willis Carrier of New York Air Conditioners, A/Cs help regulate and maintain a cool indoor temperature. Today we find ACs almost everywhere – in homes, offices, shops, malls, hospitals, rail cars, luxury buses and cars. The way an air conditioner works is that the refrigerant fluid (gas) when compressed condenses and releases heat outside, cooling the air inside, and the cool air is blown into the room. However, like most things, A/Cs can act as double-edged swords, releasing chlorofluorocarbons that contribute to global warming.

331 A Warning System

An earthquake is a natural calamity. An earthquake under the sea can bring huge amounts of devastation owing to the tidal waves it causes. These waves can wipe out life and cause unimaginable destruction. To minimise the damage caused by tsunamis, countries use a Tsunami Warning System (TWS). A TWS predicts tsunamis beforehand, and issues warnings so that damage to life and property can be minimised.

A TWS is made up of a network of seismic monitoring stations that detect earthquakes or changes in the sea level. Within minutes of detection, the TWS sends out an alert.

332 Cybercrime

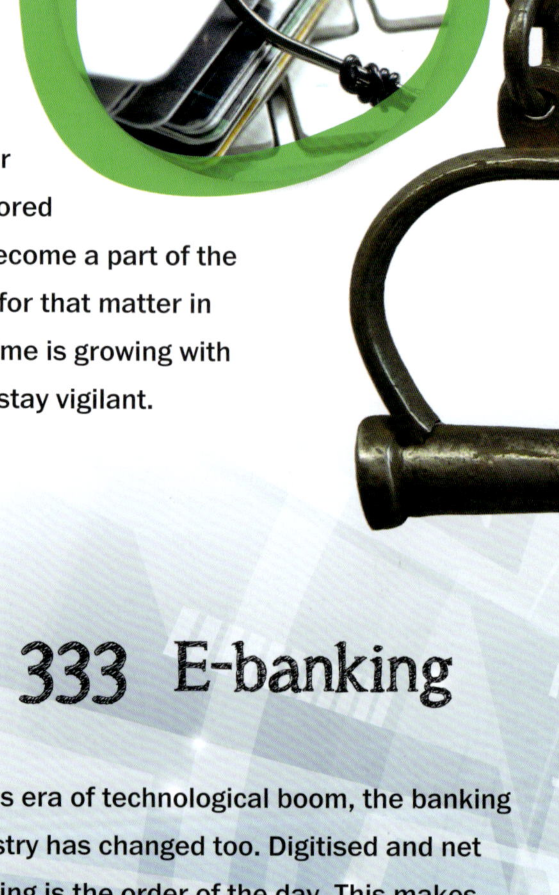

It is indisputable that advancements in technology have made life simple, easy and fast-paced. Yet there are some who face a dilemma created from the misuse of technology. Yes, we are talking about 'cybercrime' – crimes that are committed electronically using computer network or devices. Cybercrimes are committed to steal credit card details or personal information, to harm a person or organisation's reputation, to alter or delete data stored in a computer and for extortion. Computers have become a part of the system in business, entertainment, government or for that matter in any other field. Owing to this dependency, cyber crime is growing with each passing day. The key here is to be aware and stay vigilant.

333 E-banking

In this era of technological boom, the banking industry has changed too. Digitised and net banking is the order of the day. This makes banking services more convenient. Transfer of money from one account to another can be done electronically, rather than by cash or cheque. Salaries and tax returns can be directly deposited in the concerned account. Customers can make inquiries online regarding their banking transactions. ATMs dispense cash even in the middle of the night. From within the comfort of their homes, with just a click of a button, without waiting in queues, customers can now avail most banking services.

334 Ethical Hacking

Hacking is technically defined as, 'unauthorised intrusion into a computer or a network', and is a wrong practice! However, there is also 'ethical hacking', a sort of hacking, which is legal. Let us take a look at what ethical hacking is.

Also known as intrusion testing, ethical hacking is a sort of a defence system against malicious hacking. There are certificate courses in ethical hacking, and the person doing this type of hacking is called a white hat hacker. His job is to check the vulnerability of the network from outside attack. He is the security man of information technology. He can break into a system legally. Huge business houses employ white hackers to learn potential threats on their systems. The role of a white hacker is to penetrate a computer system or network to search for vulnerabilities which can be used by a malicious hacker. This, of course, must be done with the permission of its owner. Thus, white hacking is not illegal because the hacking is done with the purpose of safety. Ethical hacking uses the same techniques as a malicious hacker but with the purpose of redeeming the weak points in the system, and at the same time not stealing information or damaging the system.

335 Barcode Scanner

Have you ever felt like a part of Star Wars while walking out of a supermarket, and your purchases are scanned under a little gun-like device that emits a red light? What we are referring to is a barcode scanner.

A barcode scanner is an electronic device consisting of a lens, light sensor and a light source. They are mostly used in malls and department stores, and the barcode is passed under them. Barcodes are provided on products which are manufactured and sold in markets like food items, cosmetics, clothes, DVDs and books. Data on codes, which are found on websites, can be transferred to an android device by using the camera of a phone.

A barcode scanner is made up of three main parts – the illuminator, the decoder, and the sensor/converter. To scan information, a red light (illuminator) from the scanner falls on the barcode. The sensor in the scanner detects the reflected light and sends the signal to the decoder, which then changes it into data and text. When light from the scanner falls on the barcode, the light energy is converted into electrical energy. This is converted into data and is forwarded to the computer in the form of text.

336 Scan It

In today's day and age, the security of every human being is of utmost concern. But how is it possible to keep places like airports, railways stations and malls that are flooded with thousands of people, safe? One way to do this is with the help of a full body scanner. Every person entering these areas is screened. Without removing clothes, this device detects objects on the person's body. It is possible to detect metal as well as non-metal objects. The scanners can also detect objects hidden in shoes. The detection of objects on a human body takes about 15 seconds.

337 Seeing Through You

While scanning, if a case appears suspicious and an object is detected through the scanner, a 'pat down' is done with one's clothes on. The technology used by the scanner is called, 'Millimeter Wave Imaging', which detects objects hidden under clothing. A software called 'Automated Target Recognition' is used in this technology, which scans the bare body, but a cartoon like picture appears on the screen. The person viewing the screen can only see the outline of the body of the person being scanned. Scanners are considered safe for children and pregnant women as well.

338 Mobile Apps

A phone without an app is like drinking coffee without sugar! In other words, today apps have become an integral part of our entire phone experience. But what exactly are all the apps that we download and frequently use on our mobile phones? Let us learn something interesting about them.

The first mobile phone app was the 'Snake' game played on the Nokia phone model 6110 in 1997. The Apple App Store, on the iPhone was later launched with iOS 2. In October 2008, Google launched Google Play Store and a Windows Store was also launched. Applications for a variety of purposes, subjects, topics are used by children and adults. Today there are apps for gaming, education, safety, communication, music, travel, business, entertainment, food, health and fitness, maps and navigation, shopping, weather and more. Thanks to apps, a phone has become more than just a phone!

339 Phablets

Innovations in technology have never failed to amaze its users.

Earlier, desktops made way for laptops, which in turn made way for tablets, a handheld version of a computer, which is smaller and can be carried anywhere. Then came smartphones, which were phones that served as computers. But now is the era of 'phablets', a combination of phones and tablets. They are the size of a smartphones and have all the functions of a tablet and a mobile phone merged together. While the desktops work on electricity, a phablet works on a rechargeable battery as well as electricity. This gives a person the freedom to work, study or play on their phablet while on the move. Oh, how we love phablets!

340 Smart Cards

Smart cards serve the purpose of identification and authentication. They are plastic cards the size of a credit card with a microchip embedded in them. There are two types of smart cards – simple and complex. Phone cards are examples of simple cards. They contain memory that can store and read data. Sim cards and bank cards are examples of complex cards. They store and process information, access to which is difficult. They cannot be tampered with. Smart cards are easy to use by adults and children, the most common use being sim cards and mobile phones. Schools in Kenya use the smart card technology to keep track of children and reduce parents worry regarding their safety.

341 3D Printing

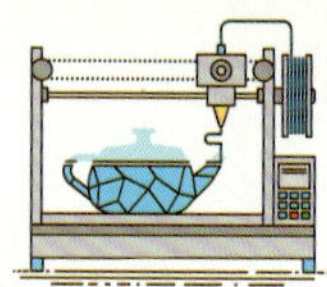

3D printing or additive manufacturing is the method of producing a three-dimensional object using a digital design or file. A special printer creates or prints the object by depositing raw materials such as plastic or metal, layer by layer. 3D printing is finding applications in various fields. For example, car and aeroplane manufacturers are creating complex parts using 3D printing. In the biomedical field 3D printed implants, tissues and organs are being created. A company in China even created an entirely 3D printed house! 3D printing is quicker than traditional manufacturing and saves costs in terms of machine operations, labour and raw material. But, at present, it cannot be used for mass manufacturing.

342 Going Digital

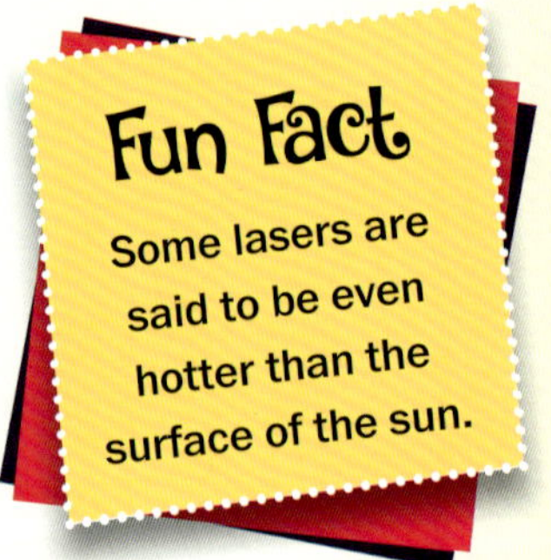

Fun Fact

Some lasers are said to be even hotter than the surface of the sun.

Today digital technology has taken over our homes. From surround sound to Dolby technology, most of our movie experiences have taken on a whole new meaning. So what exactly is digital technology?

Digital technology is the latest technology that is used to make and project movies. The basic idea behind this technology is the use of digital projectors instead of reels. As technology in this sphere advanced, most of the cinema houses across the globe have now become digital. Digital technology in cinemas offers a theatrical experience and is different from conventional cinema. Through this technology, movies can be distributed over the Internet, blue-ray disc and satellite links. Earlier, before digitisation, a number of reels had to be physically sent to cinema houses. Digital technology today offers users some of the best media experiences.

343 The Other Side of Technology

Yes, mobile phones and cellular communication form the core of information technology. But they have their ill effects too. A widespread concern is that cell phones pose a risk of cancer and other health hazards. But how and why?

Cell phones give out radio waves or electromagnetic radiations from the antennae, which are absorbed by the body tissues exposed to the antennae, thus heating up that part of the body. The number of mobile phone users, number of calls per day and the duration of each call has increased tremendously. It is established that radio frequency energy does not change DNA, but its tissue heating effect on body parts it is held close to, can be fatal. Hence, it is recommended that cell phone users use earphones, especially children. The radiation from cell phones can cause slightly raised blood pressure at the time of use and lead to mild fatigue after long use. Yet, there are some who strongly state that radiation from cell phones is harmful and can cause genetic damage, sleep disorders and brain tumours.

344 A Teacher Called Software

Like a teacher instructs her students on how to perform a particular task, in a similar way, software instructs a computer on how to perform different tasks that may be beneficial to the user.

Computer software is a set of instructions that the computer follows. Computer software includes applications and operating systems. You are aware that a set of hardware and software make up a computer. Software are those digital commands that impact the hardware of a computer. Each of these instructions, or commands, cause the computer to carry out an operation. So how does one feed software into the computer? While some software is already installed or fed into the computer, others are available on DVDs and also on the Internet. There are two main types of software; one is system software, which manages the computer itself, and application software, which helps in surfing, sending and receiving e-mails, playing games, word processing and other functions. A few examples of different kinds of software are antivirus, e-mail, games, internet browser, music player and word processor. And while most software is of the useful kind, you also have software that is malicious or in other words, harmful software. Just like biological viruses can infect a human body, computer viruses infect a computer. They can steal or delete data and even keep a check on your computer activities.

Fun Fact

Ada Lovelace, an English woman, born in 1815, was the first computer programmer.

345 Computers

Computers are an important part of today's life. They were first invented in the 1940s and were the size of a room. They consumed a lot of electricity, and were not anywhere close to the laptops and personal computers of today. The advent of modern, smaller computers was somewhere in the 1980s. There are two important aspects of a computer – the hardware and the software. The keyboard, mouse and monitor make up the computer hardware. Browsers, games, and word processors are computer software.

346 Computer Forensics

The process of investigating and analysing electronic data, like computers or digital storage media, is called computer forensics, digital forensics or cyber forensics. It is used to collect and secure evidence. It is widely used in the field of computer crime, and is also used in civil and criminal cases. Besides inferring digital data this branch of science and technology also helps in identifying suspects and determining the intent with which the crime was committed. The evidence thus collected is used to support or oppose the accused in the court of law.

347 Database

In today's age of communication and technology, information is everywhere. We compose a lot of information or data on the computer for a variety of different activities we undertake. What happens to this stored data?

The data we deal with daily is stored and organised in a system called a database. A database system is a computer programme that not only stores data, but stores information called 'metadata', which is special information about the data. Database systems can also modify the information as well as regain and manage large amounts of it.

348 Opticals

What is an optical disc? Let's find out. DVDs and Blu-ray discs, on which we can view hundreds of movies, documentaries and music, are what is known as optical discs. They can store large amounts of data digitally. In a DVD player the optical disc drive is where the DVDs are loaded. Hence it is called an optical drive. The word 'optical' means that it functions by using lenses. It also uses an extremely small laser. The optical drive has a tiny camera lens near the laser. It can read the microscopic codes which are written on the disc. The drive is connected to the computer. The

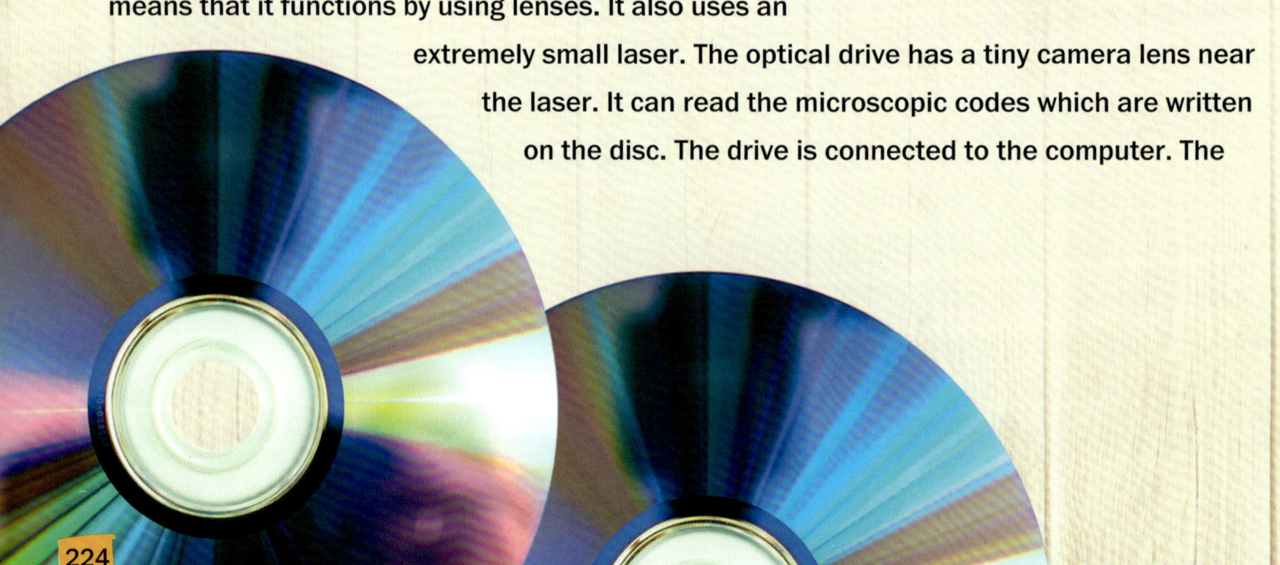

349 Store Your Stuff

Some memories are too precious to be lost, and being able to store them and revisit them time and again, just adds to the special experience. It could be a birth, a birthday, a wedding or even the first step of a little baby. So how can one store these precious and important memories?

In the past, everything from a photograph to a document of any sort had to be filed. Today things have changed. All we need is a device that records information and stores data for future reference. And the good news is that such devices, known as 'data storage devices', do exist. While cylinder phonographs and tape recorders were storage devices of the mid-1950's, today the computer is the most frequently used device. It can store, retrieve and transmit data with the click of a button. In earlier times, in electronic computers like Colossus, the data was recorded in the form of a series of holes on a long strip of paper. This technology has been taken over by CD-ROMs, DVDs and pen drives that store digital data magnetically. These are now replaced by the 'cloud' or in other words, the Internet. While information on CD-ROMs, DVDs and pen drives can get damaged, information once stored on the cloud remains for a lifetime. In other words, this system is damage proof. In the case of not having access to the cloud and large amounts of data, external hard drives, that are portable and have large storage capacity, come in really handy.

Fun Fact

James Russell, an ardent music lover invented the CD in the late 1960s.

350 Mark of the Beast

You know technology has reached its peak, when it can even be inserted into a living body. A biochip is a fascinating product of technological innovation. These are basically microchips that function inside the body of a living organism.

Biological or chemical molecules are used to form the components of biochips. They are like tiny labs that can perform many biochemical reactions. Through the information obtained, they help in diagnosing a disease within the host's body. Biochips are used in genetic findings and are used to study toxic substances as well as other forms of biological research. A biochip is barely as big as an uncooked grain of rice. They are expected to bring about a world of change in healthcare. Biochips could make possible early detection of diseases, correct diagnosis and administration of the right treatment. Scientists believe that there will be a day when these biochips will help even the blind to see. They are inserted under the skin. Biochips are also implanted in pets to trace them when lost. A software engineer from Minnesota had a biochip inserted in his finger to open his smart lock at home and control his smartphones.

Fun Fact

Biochips are implanted in homes to have access to computers using the password.

351 Read on the Go

Technological advancements do not cease to amaze us, do they? One of the latest and most amazing and convenient developments in technology are electronic books.

Invented by Michael Hart, electronic books, also known as e-books, are digital versions of printed books. Earlier, e-books were only available on special digital devices like the Kindle (a handheld reading device). However, today e-books are easily available on most devices like computers, smartphones and tablets. Just like a normal book, an e-book has a cover, text and even illustrations. Today an e-book is just a click away on the Internet.

352 Tracking Every Move

Tracking space objects, ballistic missiles, aircraft, weather formations or motor vehicles is now within man's reach. And all because of the invention of radar, which is an object detecting system that uses radio waves for the purpose. The radio waves powering the radar determine the distance, angle or speed of an object. RADAR stands for 'radio detection and ranging or radio direction and ranging'. Radar with large dish antennae, measures distances to planets, asteroids, artificial satellites, and the moon. Doplar radar detects wind systems, their speed and also storms such as hurricanes and tornadoes.

353 An Animated Timeline

In 2D animation, you create hundreds of drawings and animate them to be in movement. In 3D, animated images are created by using a particular software. This technology is used for making films and TV commercials. Children's cartoons and films use puppet animation. In this technique life-like puppets are used. Before the invention of computers, animators drew images on a flip book, each slightly different from the other, and when the book was flicked quickly, the series of images drawn on the book, seemed to be in movement.

354 Animated Delights

Cartoons are something that delight both children and the old alike. Telecasts of cartoons are eagerly awaited, and watching cartoons repeatedly is a pleasure.

Fredrick Avery, also lovingly called Tex Avery, is known as the pioneer of animation. During his tenure at Universal Studios, he directed 143 cartoons. As time went by, there was progress in the way cartoons were made. Animation has now become the fad. Animation is nothing but traditional puppetry brought to life with the help of digital technology. Animation then, is the process in which a drawing when viewed quickly creates the impression of motion.

355 Digi-learning

Isn't school always a lot of fun? But what if you are down with a bout of flu and are not able to sit in class? While earlier, this would sound nightmarish, considering the amount of learning you would have skipped, today, technology has a solution for that – digital learning!

Digital learning is backed by technology and gives students some element of control to learn at their own pace and place. It gives you access to reading material (PDFs, Power Points), online recorded lessons, that may be referred to at any time. You also have reference videos, quizzes, forums where topics of interest can be discussed, thus making the whole learning experience highly interactive. Apart from academics, today digital learning has also made its way into the corporate world, where conferences, seminars and trainings make use of technology in order to create a better and more conducive work environment.

356 Oculus Rift

Another fantastic piece of technology is the Oculus Rift. This is designed in the form of a 3D headset, which when worn, completely immerses the user into the world of virtual reality. The Oculus Rift is mainly designed for gaming. It makes you feel that you are actually living the game, where you can turn your head around and view your world in high definition.

A number of brands sell these headsets and they can be expensive. If virtual gaming excites you, the Oculus Rift would be a great something to gift yourself!

357 The Panono

Introduced into the markets a few years ago, the Panono is a green-rubber ball that makes for some fantastic 360-degree images.

Although it costs a whopping $1400, this imaging ball gives the best devices a run for their money. Apart from taking stunning outdoor pictures, the Panono can be thrown into the air for an effortless in-motion picture. The app on your phone also takes pictures exactly like the Panono ball, except that your phone cannot be thrown into the air.

358 I Spy with My Little Eye

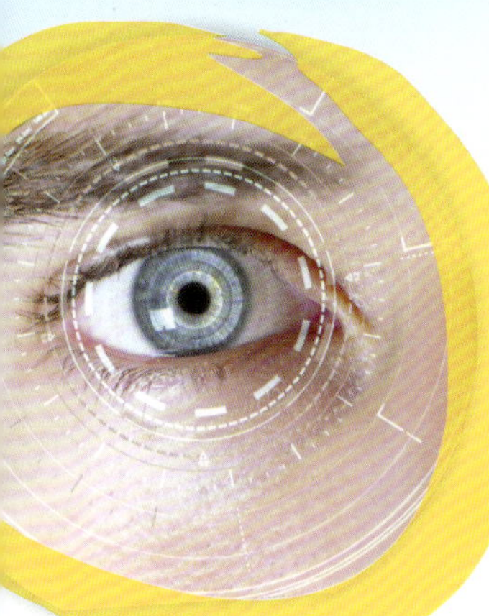

While technology has done a lot to blow our minds away, the Eye Tribe is something else altogether. While tech enthusiasts have long been discussing this kind of technology, this idea has finally come to life.

Eye Tribe is a fantastic software with which you are able to control your mobile phone applications with your eyes. As hard as this may sound to believe, this software allows for a hands free gaming and navigation experience. The Eye Tribe software was started by four PhD students at the University of Copenhagen.

359 Magnetic USB Cables

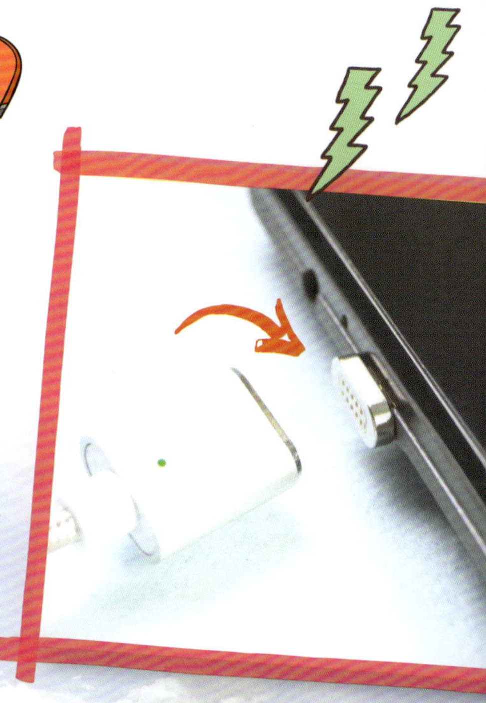

A Universal Series Bus, also commonly known as a USB, is something most of us use on almost a daily basis. USBs are generally cables used for connections, communication and power supply between computers and other electronic devices.

What if we told you that you can now get your hands on a magnetic USB? Hard to believe right? But it is true. Apple's new Bolt S is a magnetic charger for its MacBook laptops. The Bolt S helps charge MacBooks at lightning fast speed.

360 The Aflac Duck

The Aflac duck is a great initiative by Aflac to help children combatting cancer. This robotic duck has already bagged the Tech for a Better World Innovation Award at the CES 2018. Patients with the help of an augmented reality app can feed the duck, bathe it and care for it in other ways, virtually. This helps children fighting cancer get emotional relief from their disease, thus bringing out positive feelings within them. The best part of the Aflac duck is that it understands the child's moods and helps them through their tough time, by quacking, nuzzling against them and being a great companion when most needed.

361 A Pup Named Aibo

How many of us love dogs? We wouldn't be surprised if most of us do. And even for the ones that don't, Sony has launched a cute little robot pup called Aibo.

Aibo is little robotic pup that has the most adorable eyes, a roly-poly form that you would love to hold, squeeze and cuddle. Full of energy, Aibo is infused with enthusiasm and curiosity, and loves to learn from its environment and interact with people. With its almost realistic features like OLED eyes for enhanced expressions, voice control and motion-detection, Sony has done its best at bringing to life wonderful little Aibo who will make its way into your homes and your hearts.

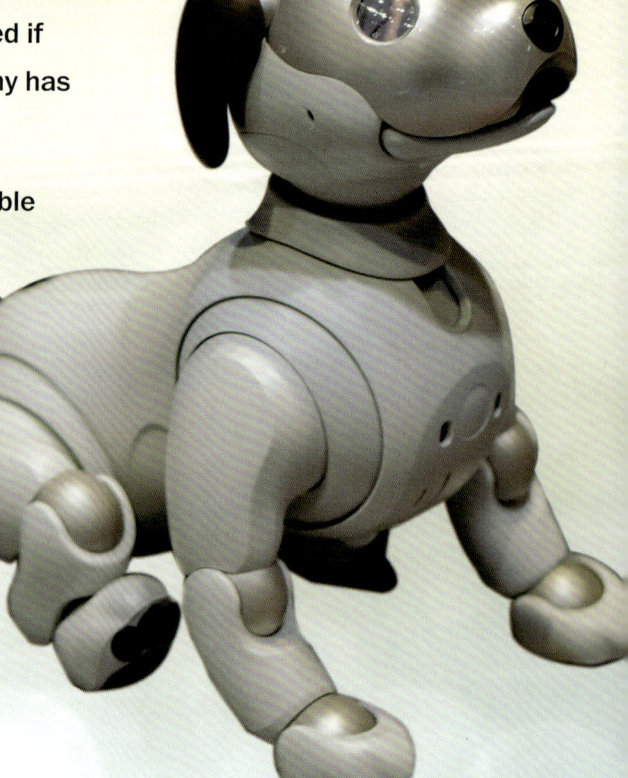

362 Smart Things

Imagine this – you need the temperature of your air conditioner a little lower or want to switch off your living room lights, but you do not have to move an inch from where you are. Wouldn't that be great? With 'Samsung's Smart Things' this is set to be a reality.

Smart Things is a router like device that uses cloud-based technology to connect everything you own like your car, refrigerator, washing machine, television and even smart phone under one single platform. For this, all you need to do is install a Smart Things hub, install the app and start syncing all your devices to it, including the tablet or smartphone with which you'd like to control your appliances.

363 Augmented Reality

What if we told you that you no longer need to look into your phone to read a text or watch a video?

Well then where do you look? Into your eye glasses! But not just any pair of glasses. Virtual glasses are an optical head-mounted display that are designed in the shape of glasses. These glasses are also referred to as 'wearable computing eyewear' and have a clear display and come with wifi and bluetooth. Google was the pioneer of these glasses and now other companies are offering these as well. But whoever thought that technology could scale such heights and bring to us augmented reality in such a cool way!

364 Self-driven Trucks

We've heard of driverless cars. And today the era of driverless trucks is just around the corner.

Tesla, the well-known American automobile company is soon to launch its own self-driven truck, that'll help manual truck drivers take a breather. The trucking market is a huge one, especially in the United States of America. However, sadly, each year the industry faces innumerable losses owing to accidents. In fact, owing to artificial intelligence, driverless trucks will be in motion on the road for much longer as compared to manually driven trucks, thus also increasing productivity. However, the only concern here is that as technology gets better by the day, more and more jobs will be lost. Apart from this, we don't see why anyone would have reason to complain about self-driven trucks.

365 Say Hi with Deepframe 

If you thought Facetime was cool, you haven't seen anything yet! Imagine being able to pop into someone's living room with the help of augmented reality. Imagine popping into your friend's bedroom to ask if he would like to join you for a game of football later on.

This is the power of Deepframe which is a life-sized augmented reality tool. This futuristic telepresence tool comes with a 64-inch glass window that is endowed with special opticals. These opticals reflect life-sized digital objects into a physical space. Deepframe was the brainchild of a Danish company known as RealFiction, and has some stunning real-life display quality. However, this technology has not yet reached the market, but is first looking to make its name among business spaces where this technology may be used for virtual meetings. So, hold on kids, for there is still some time before Deepframe makes its way into your homes.

OTHER TITLES IN THIS SERIES

ISBN: 978-93-52760-49-7

ISBN: 978-93-85031-29-8

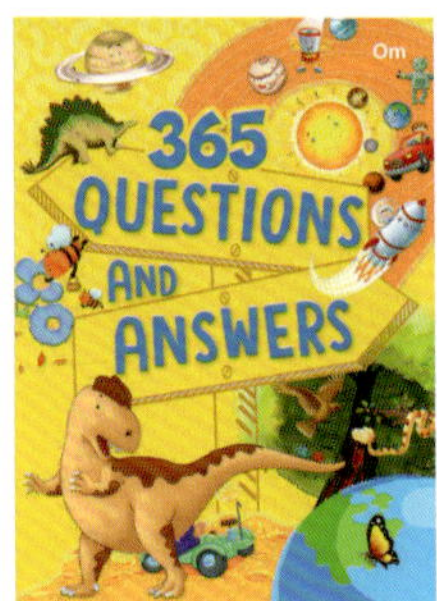

ISBN: 978-93-80070-79-7

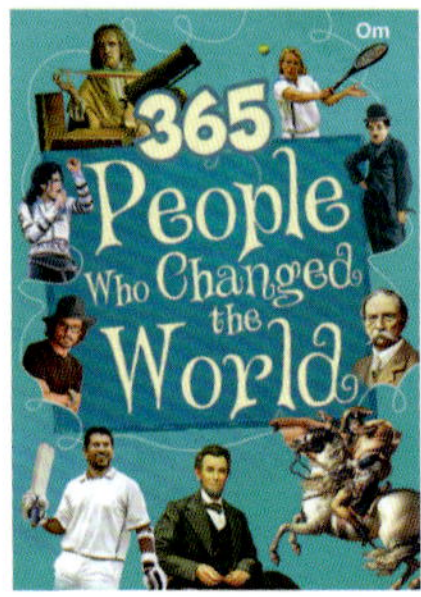

ISBN: 978-93-84225-34-6

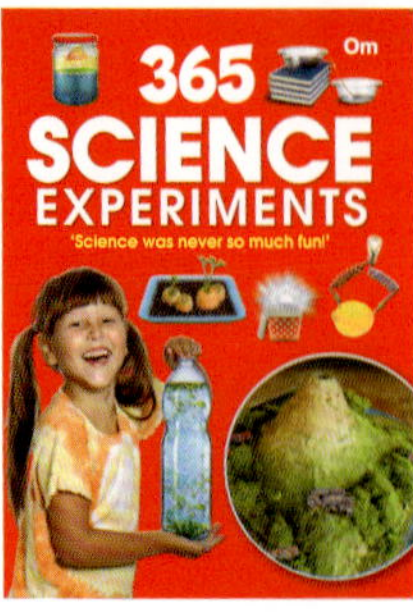

ISBN: 978-93-83202-81-2

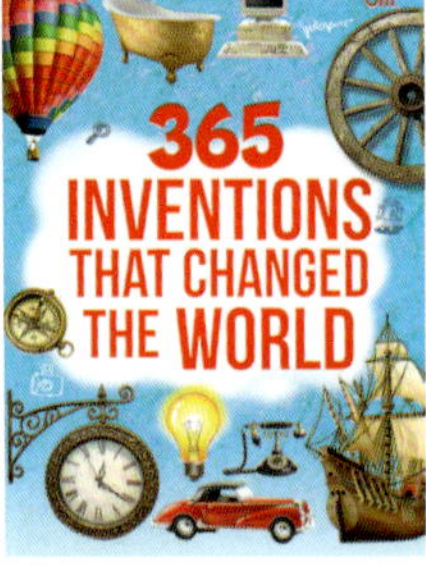

ISBN: 978-93-84625-92-4

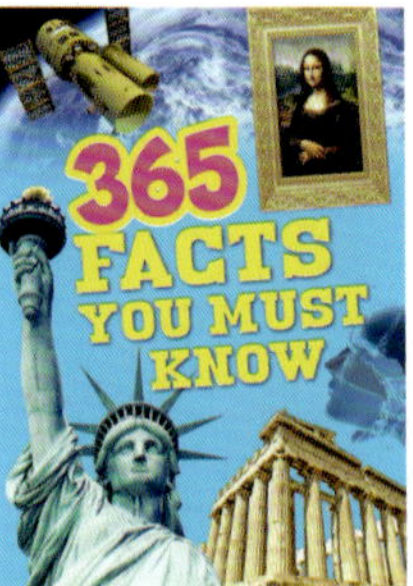

ISBN: 978-93-84225-33-9

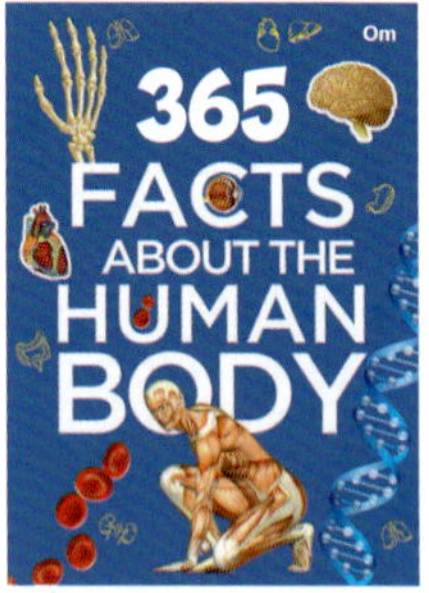

ISBN: 978-93-84625-93-1

ISBN: 978-93-52760-95-4

ISBN: 978-93-80069-35-7

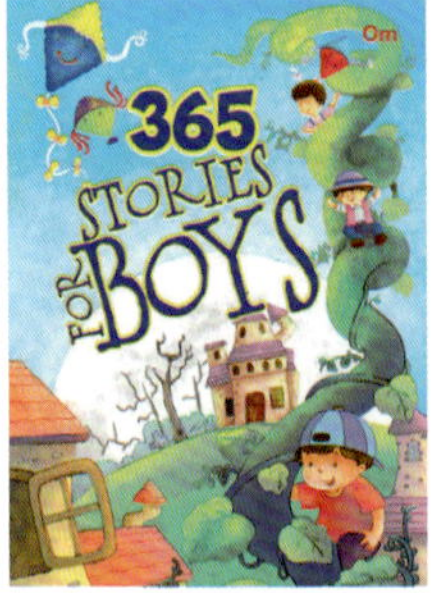

ISBN: 978-93-80070-83-4

ISBN: 978-93-80070-84-1

ISBN: 978-93-84225-31-5

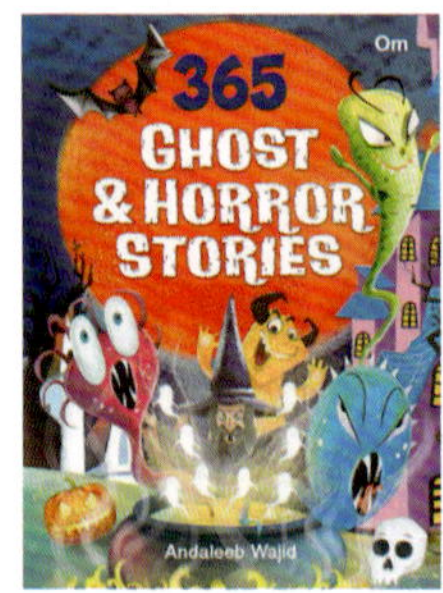

ISBN: 978-93-81607-57-2

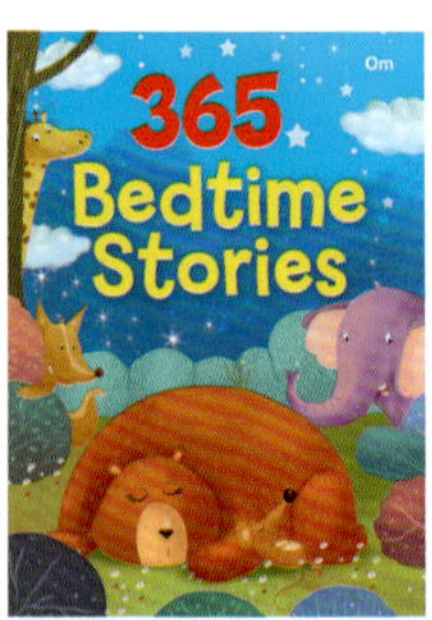

ISBN: 978-81-87107-53-8

ISBN: 978-93-81607-49-7

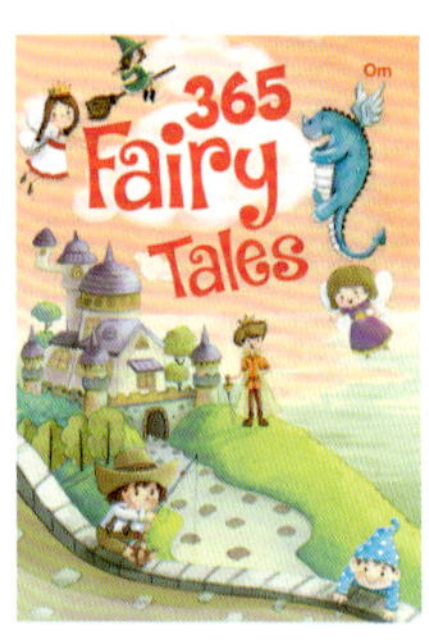

ISBN: 978-81-87107-55-2

ISBN: 978-81-87107-52-1

ISBN: 978-81-87107-57-6

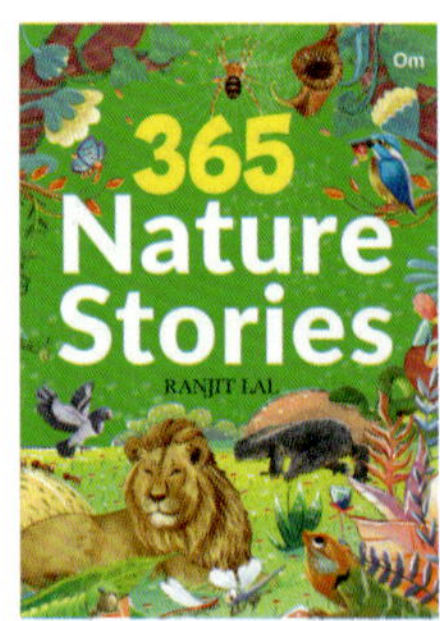

ISBN: 978-93-52764-06-8

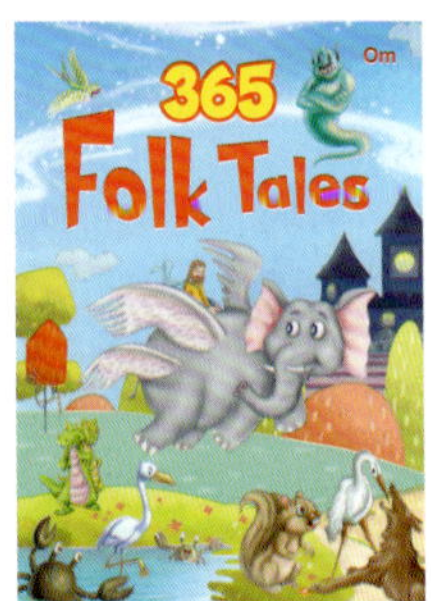

ISBN: 978-81-87107-56-9

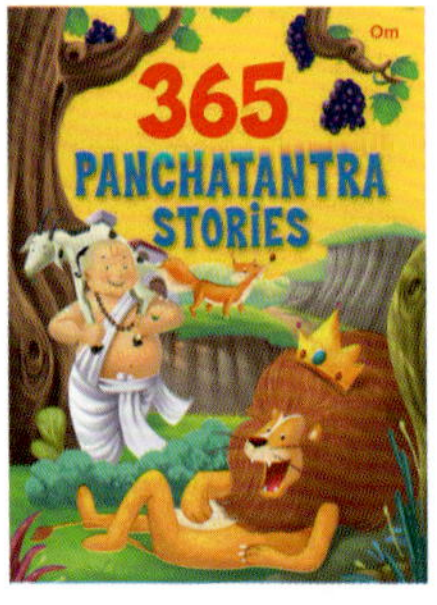

ISBN: 978-81-87107-58-3

ISBN: 978-81-87107-46-0

ISBN: 978-93-80069-36-4

ISBN: 978-93-52764-05-1